Working with MediaWiki

Yaron Koren

Working with MediaWiki

by Yaron Koren

Published by WikiWorks Press.

Chapter 17, "Semantic Forms", includes significant content from the Semantic Forms homepage (https://www.mediawiki.org/wiki/Extension:Semantic_Forms), available under the Creative Commons BY-SA 3.0 license.

Library of Congress Control Number: 2012952489
ISBN: 978-0615720302
First edition, second printing: 2014

Ordering information for this book can be found at:
http://workingwithmediawiki.com

All printing of this book is handled by CreateSpace (https://createspace.com), a subsidiary of Amazon.com.

Cover design by Grace Cheong (http://gracecheong.com).

Contents

Foreword

MediaWiki was born ten years ago to run Wikipedia, when it was still an obscure experiment rather than the household name it is today. I was lucky enough to get involved in its Open Source development early on, and have watched it grow up, serving both Wikipedia and many other sites, public and private, open and closed, humble and brave. Thanks to thousands of our users, administrators, and developers (both by choice and by necessity), MediaWiki has become become so much more than just one popular site's back-end software. From templates to gadgets to extensions to entire software suites, what has never ceased to amaze me in this last decade is the creativity and can-do spirit of MediaWiki's users.

Working with MediaWiki will introduce you to not just the core MediaWiki software, but a lot of useful extensions that have been created both for Wikipedia and for other sites. Some of MediaWiki's rough edges are called out, but so are the possibilities you gain from using a flexible, popular platform.

Of particular interest is the detailed introduction to the Semantic MediaWiki family of extensions, which can add a lot of power to what was originally conceived as a nearly-plain-text wiki engine. Even if you think you know MediaWiki well, if you're not familiar with Semantic MediaWiki you owe it to yourself to read these chapters to learn what you can build on top of a MediaWiki site.

Brion Vibber

Acknowledgments

I would like to thank the following people, who provided helpful advice and criticism during the writing of this book: Mike Cariaso, Jeroen De Dauw, Ike Hecht, Kristen Hunt, Max Klein, Markus Krötzsch, Niklas Laxström, Chris Mills and Jeremie Patonnier.

This is a book about MediaWiki, so it wouldn't exist without the software, and all of the people who have helped to develop it. In a sense, they created this book – I just had to write it all down. A big thanks to all the developers, designers and testers of MediaWiki and the extensions described here. It would be unwieldy to try to list everyone, but you know who you are.

This book consists of original content, except for the chapter on Semantic Forms, much of which was copied from the Semantic Forms documentation on mediawiki.org. That documentation was mostly written by me, though other people contributed to it as well (it's a wiki); so a specific thank you to everyone whose edits to those pages have shown up in this book.

I have run the MediaWiki consulting company WikiWorks since 2009, and my experience gained in that company has informed a lot of this book. I would like to thank all the WikiWorks consultants, past and present, who have done the challenging work of implementing all this software and seeing what works and what doesn't (often through a lot of trial-and-error), and figuring out the best ways to use all the technologies together. This book occasionally uses the terms "we" and "our" – that's not a literary conceit, but rather an indication that the views here represent, to some extent, the collective opinion of WikiWorks. I would also like to thank the clients of WikiWorks over the years, for constantly clarifying what's important and what's less important to the real users of MediaWiki; and of course, for keeping us in business.

I would like to thank two organizations in particular, one a nonprofit organization and one a wildly profitable company: the Wikimedia Foundation and Google.

They have both been instrumental in my involvement in, and continued benefit from, MediaWiki. It happens that, over the years, both have served all the following roles: reference source, software utility provider, sponsor of development, and client. These have been two tremendously valuable organizations, to me and to hundreds of millions of others, and I could never thank them enough for their contributions.

I would also like to thank the software development company 37signals, not for their software, but for the philosophy of development that they've popularized, which I would summarize as: *software should have an opinion, which is reflected as much in what's not included as in what is.* That philosophy has been helpful in my MediaWiki development process, and it has been a guide to some extent in the creation of this book as well.

I would like to thank the book's cover designer, Grace Cheong, for creating an excellent book cover.

Finally, I would like to thank my lovely wife Lee, for her invaluable edits and for providing support and encouragement for the book every step of the way.

Preface to the 2nd printing

Working with MediaWiki was first published in November 2012, and it's a testament to the hard work of the developers of MediaWiki and its extensions that so much of the content has needed updating by now, less than a year and a half later. There are new extensions, new settings, features that have been rendered obsolete, etc. Of special note is the VisualEditor extension, which, though it's still not ready for widespread use, has already been put to use across much of Wikipedia. The use of the Bootstrap framework, and the concept of responsive web design in in general, have also gained considerable interest since the book originally came out. For that reason, I decided to create a new "printing" for the book. Really it's a 2nd version, since this book is only printed – and sent out electronically – one copy at a time. (Perhaps one day the standard nomenclature for books, especially how-to books, will start to resemble that of software, with major and minor version numbers, but for now people still usually talk about printings.)

This printing contains significant changes and updates: around 25% of the pages have had at least one modification. That includes expanded sections on VisualEditor, Bootstrap and some other features, removal of obsolete content, new and updated images, and various corrections and wording improvements. And the extensions Semantic MediaWiki, Semantic Forms and Semantic Drilldown, among others, have undergone significant changes since the book first came out; this version reflects that.

Yaron Koren

April 2014

Introduction

"How to Succeed in Business Without Really Trying" was a 1961 Broadway musical, and a 1952 book (thanks, Wikipedia), that parodied corporate life. But the phrase could just as well serve as a description of MediaWiki's history. MediaWiki is best known as the software that powers Wikipedia; but it is also among the most popular, if not the most popular, application for internal, corporate wikis. And on public wikis, the wikis whose name often ends in "pedia" or starts or ends with "wiki", MediaWiki is unquestionably #1.

But the interesting thing is that all this happened without any real involvement from MediaWiki's creators. MediaWiki is managed by the Wikimedia Foundation, and developed by a large group of programmers around the world, many of whom work for the Wikimedia Foundation. And, as far as the development of MediaWiki is concerned, the main goal of the WMF, and most of the developers, is to create a stable platform that Wikipedia, and the WMF's other sites like Wiktionary and Wikiversity, can run on. MediaWiki's developers generally do take the idea of MediaWiki as a standalone application seriously, but at the same time, most (though not all) of MediaWiki's developers see that as a secondary issue, with the primary issue remaining improving Wikipedia. So, with MediaWiki, we have the rare situation where a software application becomes extremely successful despite being, at heart, a byproduct of another project. (Though it's not a unique situation – the bug-tracking software Bugzilla has a similar status, and there are probably others.)

There are some things that do make MediaWiki unique, and in my opinion the most important one is the extension called Semantic MediaWiki. Using Semantic MediaWiki, you can store the wiki's text as data, and then query that data elsewhere, both in the wiki and outside. But beyond that, it provides an entire framework for structuring data that makes MediaWiki not just a more powerful tool, but, in my opinion, helps to make it the most powerful, flexible knowledge-management tool on the market. This book covers SMW, and its related extensions, to a great extent.

I first got involved with MediaWiki in 2006, as a direct result of having discovered Semantic MediaWiki. Since then I've devoted my career to improving the workings of SMW and MediaWiki in general, and to helping companies, organizations and communities make use of the technology. Around 10 of the extensions covered here, out of over 60 mentioned in the book, were created by me, most notably the Semantic Forms extension, which gets its own chapter; so I could be accused of using this book to market my own technology. To that I would respond that this book represents my view of the best ways to use MediaWiki; I created those extensions because I thought they were features that were missing. Years of working with clients have helped to solidify my views on the most useful configurations. And, hey, it's my book – any author writing such a book is bound to favor the tools that have worked for them.

This book will be useful to some extent to average users of MediaWiki-based wikis – Wikipedia and many others – especially the early chapters on MediaWiki syntax and structure. However, the primary intended audience is for administrators: people who are running, or helping to run, or thinking about running, an instance of MediaWiki, and could benefit from a general reference guide.

The book is called "Working with MediaWiki", because it's meant for people who are trying to do real work with MediaWiki – whether it's for their company, for an organization, for a user community, or for themselves. Wherever possible, I try to offer a pragmatic approach, and straightforward answers to the common issues that people experience.

Chapter 1

About MediaWiki

MediaWiki is an open-source wiki engine originally developed for use on Wikipedia, and Wikipedia is still by far the best-known use of it. But MediaWiki is also in use on tens of thousands of wikis around the world – it's almost certainly the world's most popular wiki software. It's also most likely the world's most powerful wiki software, although that statement will require more justification – hopefully this book will provide suitable proof.

In this chapter, we'll start with some of the non-technical aspects of MediaWiki.

History of MediaWiki

The history of MediaWiki starts with Wikipedia, and the history of Wikipedia starts with wikis, so we'll begin there. In 1995 Ward Cunningham, a programmer who was already known for his work in defining software design patterns, created the first wiki, on his company's website, c2.com. It was a very simple website, with one bizarre-at-the-time feature: every page had an "edit" link, where random visitors to the website could modify its contents. The wiki was meant to hold information about design patterns, as part of a section on the website called the "Portland Pattern Repository". Cunningham was inspired by HyperCard, an Apple application from the 1980s that stored information on editable "cards" that could link to one another; he wanted to create something similar for the then-new World Wide Web. For the name of this concept, Cunningham originally thought of "QuickWeb", but then remembered the "Wiki Wiki Shuttle", an airport shuttle he had taken in Honolulu, Hawaii, and decided to call his new idea "WikiWikiWeb". "Wiki" or "wiki wiki" means "fast" or "hurry up" in Hawaiian; and in fact it apparently derives from the English word "quickly", so its new presence in English is somewhat of a return.

"WikiWikiWeb" for a while referred to four things: the website hosted on c2.com, the software used to run it (written in Perl), and later any user-editable website (what is now known as a wiki), and any application used to run such a site (now known as wiki software). There was no great distinction for the first five years or so between the code used to run a wiki and the content on it, partly because there was nearly a 1:1 correspondence between the two: many of the original wiki administrators were programmers, and they tended to create their own new, or modified, version of the software to run their own wikis.

In 2000, Jimmy Wales, an internet entrepreneur living in Florida, decided to create Nupedia, a free online encyclopedia that would compete with the various subscription-only encyclopedias like Encyclopedia Britannica. He hired Larry Sanger to edit it. Like traditional encyclopedias, each article was written by an expert on the subject matter. Nupedia was a failure, managing to get all of 12 fully-finished articles in its first year. While the two were thinking about how to increase contributions, Sanger heard from a friend of his about wikis, and suggested the idea to Wales for use as a way to supplement Nupedia's content. Wales, though skeptical at first, put up a wiki. Sanger suggested that it be called "Wikipedia", and Wales agreed, obtaining the domain names "wikipedia.com" and "wikipedia.org". On January 15, 2001, Wikipedia was launched at wikipedia.com. Though interest was low at the beginning, it started to increase exponentially, and Nupedia was soon forgotten. Several months later, the first subdomains for non-English languages were created; the first was "deutsche.wikipedia.com" in March 2001. In August 2002, the content was transferred to wikipedia.org, reflecting Wales' new view of Wikipedia as a non-profit public resource, instead of the side-project of a for-profit website.

Wales and Sanger later had a falling-out over philosophical differences, and now Sanger has become one of Wikipedia's most vocal critics. That fascinating turn of events is a subject for another book; but in any case, the path was in place for Wikipedia to achieve its meteoric rise in popularity. It soon fundamentally altered the course of wikis, and later it would fundamentally alter the world as well.

The software that Wales and Sanger originally ran Wikipedia on was UseModWiki, a Perl application written by Clifford Adams. UseModWiki, like most wiki software at the time, was the work of tinkerers: it was based on AtisWiki, which was based on

CvWiki, which in turn was based on WikiWikiWeb, Cunningham's original application. And again like most wiki software of the time, UseModWiki used flat text files to store all page revisions. That approach was slow, and, given Wikipedia's constant growth, was proving unworkable. Wikipedia also needed functionality that UseMod-Wiki didn't provide, so in late 2001 Wales hired Magnus Manske, a German programmer and active Nupedia contributor, to rewrite the software in PHP, now storing edits in a MySQL database. In January 2002, Wikipedia switched over to this new (unnamed) software. This new software had performance problems of its own, though. Programmer Lee Daniel Crocker started working on a newer version of the software, and in July 2002 Wikipedia switched to that software. Crocker's code was now known as "phase III", with UseModWiki and Manske's code retroactively referred to as "phase I" and "phase II", respectively.

A year later, in June 2003, Wales created the Wikimedia Foundation, also known as the WMF, to manage Wikipedia and its growing number of sister sites, like Wiktionary. The name "Wikimedia" was based on "Wikipedia", and had been suggested by Sheldon Rampton on a Wikipedia mailing list in March. The next month, Wikipedia enthusiast Daniel Mayer, writing on that same mailing list, suggested a name for Crocker's "phase III" software: "MediaWiki", a play on "Wikimedia". The name stuck, and was quickly made official.

MediaWiki has been used by all Wikimedia websites since 2004.

Almost since the beginning of MediaWiki's existence, it started getting heavily used on non-Wikimedia sites as well. Two of the non-Wikimedia sites that launched in 2003, that ran on MediaWiki software, remain among the largest wikis today: Wikitravel, a travel guide (though its growth has been curtailed by the WMF's own travel site, Wikivoyage), and Memory Alpha, the main Star Trek wiki. In the years since, there have been tens of thousands, if not hundreds of thousands, of wikis launched using MediaWiki software.

By now, most early wiki software, like WikiWikiWeb, UseModWiki etc., is no longer in widespread use, but there are certainly wiki applications other than MediaWiki that are still in regular use and under development. Interestingly, nearly all of the wiki applications in widespread use today were originally created between 2002 and 2006. They include, besides MediaWiki, the open-source applications PmWiki, Tiki and TWiki (an exception, since it was started in 1998), and the proprietary applications Confluence and Socialtext. There are also various content-management systems that include some limited wiki functionality; these include Jive and Microsoft SharePoint.

The first released version of MediaWiki was 1.1, and the current version, at the time of this writing, is 1.22. We won't get into the changes that happened in each version here, though suffice it to say that there have been a lot; virtually the entire codebase has been rewritten, in some cases several times. You can see the full version history for MediaWiki at:

> http://en.wikipedia.org/wiki/MediaWiki_version_history

During the over ten years that MediaWiki has existed, it has had contributions from hundreds of developers, translators and testers, along with a handful of usability experts, graphic designers, project managers, etc. It would be difficult to list here all of the people who have made significant contributions to MediaWiki, or even invaluable contributions. Two names stand out, though, for the scope of their involvement. The first is Brion Vibber, who is currently the Lead Software Architect for the Wikimedia Foundation, and who has essentially had that role in MediaWiki since nearly the beginning, adding enormous amounts of code and serving as the final word on what gets into the software and onto Wikimedia sites.

The second name is Tim Starling, who serves as the WMF's Lead Platform Architect, and who like Brion has been involved in development since nearly the beginning, has contributed a huge amount of code, and has had significant influence on the current state of the software.

Community and support

There's a strong community of users and developers around MediaWiki, who can provide support. The best ways to get support are the mailing list, the IRC channel, and on the MediaWiki website at mediawiki.org.

There are a large number of mailing lists for MediaWiki (15, at last count). Only two are important, though, for average MediaWiki users:

- mediawiki-l – the main mailing list for questions about MediaWiki and most of its extensions.

- wikitech-l – discussions about the use of MediaWiki on Wikimedia sites, as well as topics related to MediaWiki development.

You can see information on these two mailing lists (like how to subscribe), as well as on the other mailing lists, here

> https://www.mediawiki.org/wiki/Mailing_lists

Support is also always available at the MediaWiki IRC channel, #mediawiki, via freenode.net. There are other IRC channels, though they're not nearly as useful. You can see a full listing here:

> https://www.mediawiki.org/wiki/IRC

You can also get support at mediawiki.org. To ask questions about core MediaWiki, you can go here:

> https://www.mediawiki.org/wiki/Support

And for any specific extension, you can use its talk page on mediawiki.org to get support.

Many open source software applications also have their own user and developer conferences. MediaWiki doesn't exactly have such a thing, but there are various MediaWiki-focused "hackathons" each year, and there is also Wikimania, an annual conference on everything Wikimedia-related. In practice, Wikimania is mostly focused on Wikipedia, but MediaWiki does get significant attention. And Wikimania is a great way to meet the people behind the software.

The mediawiki.org "Events" page shows a constantly-updated list of MediaWiki-related events and hackathons around the world:

> https://www.mediawiki.org/wiki/Events

If you think you've found a bug in MediaWiki or one of its extensions, or you've created a software patch and want to submit it, the best way to do that is at the MediaWiki bug tracker (which uses the software Bugzilla), here:

> https://bugzilla.wikimedia.org

Often, using Bugzilla is the best way to make feature requests as well.

Finally, there are various ways to get paid support, either from individuals or from consulting companies. The most definitive list of both individuals and companies doing MediaWiki consulting is here:

> https://www.mediawiki.org/wiki/Professional_development_and_
> consulting

It would be odd not to mention my own company here – WikiWorks (http://wikiworks.com). We may be the most explicitly MediaWiki-focused consulting company at this point, though we're far from the only that provides such services.

Available hosts

Instead of setting up a new wiki on your own domain, from scratch, you may want to have your wiki hosted on an existing website dedicated to wiki hosting – such sites are usually referred to as "wiki farms", or, as Wikipedia prefers to call them, "wiki hosting services". The advantage of such a setup is that it's much easier to get started – you can often set up a wiki on a wiki farm, and start editing it, in minutes. Also, for the most part, you don't have to worry about the software – you don't have to set up MediaWiki or any extensions, and you don't have to update it as new versions come out, because the wiki farm presumably takes care of that.

On the other hand, there are disadvantages to using a wiki farm, as there are any time that one's data is put in "the cloud" – to use the current buzzword for online data. There's no guarantee that the wiki's contents won't be lost, if the website in question stops operating, or there's some technical glitch, or it gets hacked. And if your wiki is meant to be private, there's the risk that its contents will get revealed due to some security leak. Of course, all the same risks exist on any computer network that your wiki might run on – but on third-party websites, the perception, at least, is that the risk is greater.

Let's say that you do want to use a wiki farm, though, and (since you're reading this book) that you want the software it runs on to be MediaWiki. Thankfully, MediaWiki is a popular wiki engine for wiki farms – in fact, it appears to be easily the most popular, with at least five serious wiki farms that use it. By comparison, most other wiki engines power no more than one.

The biggest MediaWiki-based wiki farm, by far, is Wikia, at wikia.com. In fact, it's the most popular wiki farm of any kind; according to the Alexa traffic-monitoring service, it's currently among the top 200 most popular websites in the world, and among the top 100 in the United States. And that may be even understating its popularity, since some of its most popular wikis, like Memory Alpha (for Star Trek) and WoWWiki (for the video game World of Warcraft) have their own domains, which means that Alexa isn't counting them as part of Wikia's traffic.

Wikia was founded in 2004 by Jimmy Wales – the co-founder of Wikipedia – as well as Angela Beesley (now Angela Beesley Starling), who was a Wikimedia Foundation board member at the time. For that reason, some people think Wikia is affiliated with Wikimedia or Wikipedia, but in fact there's no official connection.

Wikia differs from most other wiki farms in that they have to approve every new wiki that is proposed, with the main criterion being whether this new wiki will get sufficient traffic (Wikia currently gets all their revenue from the ads they run on the pages). So a wiki meant for use only by a specific group or organization wouldn't be accepted, and a private wiki wouldn't even be possible – all Wikia wikis are public. In practice, most wikis on Wikia – and certainly most of the popular ones – are on pop-culture topics: TV shows, movies, video games and books, with a special focus on anything related to science fiction or fantasy. If the wiki you're considering creating is anything along these lines, Wikia is a very reasonable choice.

Other wiki farms tend to allow anyone to create a wiki, with each wiki getting either a subdomain of the wiki farm's main domain, or a directory. In some cases, wiki farms make their money from ads, while in others, they get money from customers who pay for extra service.

The MediaWiki-based wiki farm closest to my heart is Referata, at referata.com – that's because I created it and still run it, via WikiWorks. Referata has been around since 2008; it exists in order to provide hosting of a specific set of MediaWiki extensions based around Semantic MediaWiki – which you'll be hearing much more about later in the book. (To be fair, a few other wiki farms provide support for SMW as well.) Referata offers a standard usage of MediaWiki for free, with some options – like making one's wiki private – requiring a monthly payment.

Wikki (wikkii.com and wikkii.net) is another interesting host – wikkii.com offers standard hosting, while wikkii.net allows administrators to install any custom extensions and skins that they want. Both are free.

Other long-running MediaWiki-based wiki farms are EditThis.info (editthis.info) and Wiki Site (www.wiki-site.com).

How to choose one of these? For simple wikis, it shouldn't really matter. But if you have the need for special features, you can try looking at the site's "Special:Version" page, to see what version of MediaWiki it's running, and what extensions it has installed. You can also look at any of the wikis already hosted on that farm (usually there are a few linked from the homepage), to see what they look like, whether they're inundated with spam (you can check Special:RecentChanges for that), how quickly they load, whether they have a distracting amount of ads, etc.

Chapter 2

Setting up MediaWiki

The MediaWiki environment

MediaWiki is a program written in PHP, a very popular language for web applications. It can run on any operating system that PHP can run on, which is all the major ones. Similarly, it can run on any major web server. MediaWiki requires a database, which can be almost any of the major database systems: MySQL, PostgreSQL, SQLServer, Oracle and SQLite (Sybase is one major database system that is not supported). In practice, though, there are sometimes issues with running MediaWiki with database systems other than MySQL, since they get significantly less usage and attention. (Core MediaWiki, at least, seems to work fine with PostgreSQL as well.)

By far the most popular setup for MediaWiki is what's known as the "LAMP stack": Linux, Apache, MySQL and PHP. Only the last of these is required, but the other three are strongly encouraged.

You can see the following page to see what versions of PHP, and of the different database systems, each version of MediaWiki is compatible with:

> https://www.mediawiki.org/wiki/Compatibility

Download

There are essentially two ways to download MediaWiki: as a "tarball", or a single archive file, and via Git, a version-control system. Using Git is the recommended

9

method, because it's easier to install, and it lets you upgrade your code much more easily later on. But if you don't have Git, you can get the code from here:

> https://www.mediawiki.org/wiki/Download_from_Git#Download

When MediaWiki is downloaded as a tarball, it comes pre-bundled with some number of extensions, contained in the /extensions directory: The exact set depends on the version of MediaWiki: from versions 1.18 to 1.20, the bundled extensions were ConfirmEdit, Gadgets, Nuke, ParserFunctions, Renameuser, Vector and WikiEditor. Since version 1.21, the set of extensions additionally includes Cite, ImageMap, Interwiki, Title Blacklist, SpamBlacklist, Poem, InputBox, LocalisationUpdate and SyntaxHighlight GeSHi; while the Vector extension has been removed, because its functionality is now part of core MediaWiki. Most of these extensions will be discussed in some detail later in the book.

If you have Git installed (and it's at least version 1.7), you can download MediaWiki with the following call:

> git clone https://gerrit.wikimedia.org/r/p/mediawiki/core.git

This will create a directory named "core", which you can (and should) then rename.

Installing

Once you've downloaded the main MediaWiki code, go to the URL for that code in a browser. At that point, assuming you have PHP, a database system and a web server running, the MediaWiki code should get executed correctly, and it will then look for a file called LocalSettings.php – by default, it's not there, and its absence tells MediaWiki that this is a new installation. LocalSettings.php is the initialization file for MediaWiki, holding all the user-modifiable settings for the wiki; we'll get to many of them over the course of this book. Since LocalSettings.php is not there, MediaWiki will guide you on the browser through a series of steps where you have to specify the wiki's name, the name of the database to be created, and other settings, including the username and password for the wiki's first user (by default, the username is "WikiSysop"). This user is important even if you plan to create a different one for yourself later, because it has administrator privileges, so if you want to give yourself administrator privileges (and you will), you'll have to do it via that user.

Once you've completed all the steps, a LocalSettings.php file will be created automatically, and a new database should be created as well on your database system.

Setting the logo

Most, though not all, of MediaWiki's skins include a spot for a logo, at the top left-hand corner of the screen (or top right-hand, if the wiki is in a right-to-left language). In MediaWiki, the logo is the customary way to individualize one's wiki – for better or worse, most skins don't display the name of the wiki anywhere on the page (other than indirectly at the bottom, in the "About ___" link). So the logo should show the name of the wiki, and ideally some representative graphic – though that part is strictly optional; it's much better to have a logo that just states the wiki name than no logo at all.

MediaWiki wikis do have a default logo, which is a grayed-out MediaWiki sunflower logo with the words "Set $wgLogo to the URL path to your own logo image" over it. As the instructions say, all you need to do is set a new value for $wgLogo in your LocalSettings.php file. The logo image can be located either within the MediaWiki directory, or at some arbitrary URL. By default, it's located at /skins/common/images/wiki.png – you shouldn't replace that file with your logo image, because then you run the risk of it being overwritten when you update the MediaWiki code.

Changing the URL structure

By default, MediaWiki URLs appear in a format like:

mywiki.com/mediawiki/index.php?title=Main_Page

However, the preferred format is something more like:

mywiki.com/wiki/Main_Page

This is the format that Wikipedia and other Wikimedia sites use. The "wiki" directory can have any name, though "wiki" makes sense for obvious reasons.

There are various approaches to changing the URL format, based primarily on whether you have root access on the server on which the wiki resides. You can see all the steps required for the various approaches here:

https://www.mediawiki.org/wiki/Manual:Short_URL

We'll just note that there are some cases when users want to have a URL structure that looks simply like:

mywiki.com/Main_Page

It's certainly a clean-looking URL, but this is not recommended, because, among other reasons, it means that your server can't have helper files like robots.txt and favicon.ico. You can see a longer discussion of this approach here:

https://www.mediawiki.org/wiki/Manual:Wiki_in_site_root_directory

Finally, you can also change the name of the start page, which by default is (in English) "Main Page", by changing the contents of the page "MediaWiki:mainpage". This is an example of interface text editable via the wiki, of which there are hundreds of examples – see page 124 for a complete description.

Updating MediaWiki

As new versions of MediaWiki come out, you're generally advised to keep updating to the latest version – there are always bug fixes, interface improvements, and interesting new features. It's generally pretty easy to update, though it depends on whether you're using Git or not. If you are, you can just run a "git pull" in the directory housing your MediaWiki code. Then, you'll need to call the script "update.php", located in MediaWiki's /maintenance directory – it goes through the database and adds or modifies database tables to fit the new DB schema for this version. update.php tends to work very well – it even works when upgrading from extremely old versions.

If you're downloading the new MediaWiki version as a package, instead of via Git, then you'll need to move the /images directory, the /extensions directory (or at least parts of it), and LocalSettings.php into this new directory, and rename both it and the old MediaWiki directory so that the wiki URL will now point to this one. As before, you'll need to call update.php.

And if you're using any extensions besides the ones that come pre-bundled with MediaWiki, then you might have to get the latest versions of those as well. Extensions that don't work with a certain MediaWiki version tend to break pretty easily when you try them out, so it should be fairly straightforward to see if any extensions need updating.

Chapter 3

Editing in MediaWiki

Tabs

In MediaWiki, nearly all page-specific actions are accessible through what are usually tabs, though it depends on the skin: in some cases the "tabs" are just links displayed on the side, and in the case of Vector, the default skin, some of the tab actions are dropdown links, viewable alongside the main tabs. The exact set of tabs/dropdown actions/etc. one sees depends on the type of page it is, the permissions one has, and the extensions installed. Figure 3.1 shows the (nearly) standard view of tabs and dropdown actions that an administrator would see, for a regular page in MediaWiki, with the Vector skin (along with the search interface alongside it).

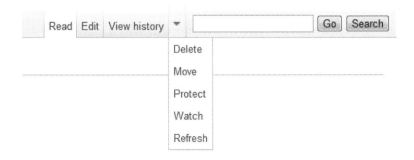

Figure 3.1: Row of tabs in the Vector skin

The "Edit" tab shows up as "View source" instead, if the user isn't allowed to edit the page, in Vector and most other skins.

We'll cover most of these actions in this chapter. The one feature that makes this different from the standard view an administrator would have is the "Refresh" action, which is defined by the Semantic MediaWiki extension – you can read about that on page 146.

Creating and editing pages

In MediaWiki, every page's URL is also its title; there are no URLs that simply look like "?id=123456", of the type that appear in many other content-management systems. That's important, because it means that the creation and renaming of pages can be done in a transparent way, open to all users.

The way to create a new page, and edit an existing page, are basically the same: in both cases, you first have to go to that page. How do you get to a page? Interestingly, for both existing pages and pages that don't exist yet, there are the same three ways to do it:

- Type in the page name in the URL

- Search on that page name, and then either arrive at the page (for existing pages), or follow the link to create it in the search results (for pages that don't exist)

- Follow a link to that page.

A link to a nonexistent page is usually called a "red link". By default, they're red, which easily distinguishes them from links to pages that exist, which are usually blue. The actual MediaWiki term for them, for what it's worth, is "broken link" (though "redlink" is also used, in URLs). Broken/red links are useful for indicating that a page that doesn't exist yet should be created. With Semantic Forms (an extension we'll get to later), you can actually have red-linked pages created automatically in certain cases – but most of the time, this has to be done manually.

Page names

For the most part, page names can contain any Unicode character. The following characters, however, are not allowed in page names:

    # < > [ ] | { }

The underscore character, _, could be added to that list as well, since underscores are simply treated the same as spaces.

By default, page names always start with an uppercase letter: if a page name gets typed in that starts with a lowercase letter, it will simply get capitalized by the system. This can be changed, however, by adding the following to LocalSettings.php:

```
$wgCapitalLinks = false;
```

Page names are restricted to 255 bytes, which, depending on the character set being used, can be as many as 255 characters or as few as 63 characters. Standard Latin characters are one byte each, while most other languages' characters are represented using two or three bytes, and some archaic languages, mathematical symbols, etc. take four bytes.

Editing mode

Once you're at a page, you will see a slightly different interface depending on whether you're allowed to edit it. If you can't edit the page, there will most likely be a tab named "View source", that lets you view the source wikitext of the page (if you're interested in doing that). If you can edit the page, on the other hand, that same tab will most likely be called "Edit" instead. In that case, to edit the page, you just have to click on the "Edit" tab, and start typing. For new pages, the tab is called "Create" instead of "Edit", and there's usually an explanatory message on the page that includes a link to that tab, but otherwise it's the same. In both cases, you end up at a URL that ends with "action=edit", which indicates that you're now in editing mode.

For existing pages, you can most likely also click "Edit" on any page section – usually, every section header will have a link that looks like "[Edit]" near it. This is quite useful – if you have a small change you want to make, it's always better to only edit the section in which it appears, because there's less text to deal with.

The edit page consists of, essentially, one big text area, plus some helper inputs at the bottom, including, most notably, the "Save page" button. The text of the page, or section, being edited goes in the big text area; it's meant to be written in a syntax called wikitext, which is simpler than HTML but which can also include a lot of scripting-like functionality; this is covered in all of Chapter 4. There are various toolbars and utilities that can be used with editing. By default, the top of the text area has a toolbar that looks like Figure 3.2.

Figure 3.2: Standard MediaWiki editing toolbar

You can also use an extension called WikiEditor (we'll cover extensions later), which provides a nicer toolbar, with support for special characters (symbols, and non-Latin characters), and other features. Figure 3.3 shows what it looks like, with the "Advanced" option selected.

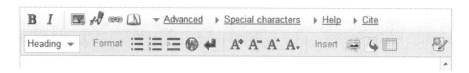

Figure 3.3: WikiEditor extension editing toolbar

You can read more about it here:

https://www.mediawiki.org/wiki/Extension:WikiEditor

There are some extensions that support intuitive, WYSIWYG-style editing, although they all have flaws at the moment; see page 102 for more discussion of these (and a full explanation of "WYSIWYG").

There's also the Semantic Forms extension, which lets you provide a form for editing, in addition to or instead of the standard edit page; this extension is covered in depth in Chapter 17.

Here is what the bottom of the edit page looks like, below the main input for the text:

Summary:

☐ Watch this page

Save page | Show preview | Show changes | Cancel | Editing help (opens in new window)

In the "Summary" field, the user is supposed to summarize their changes in the current edit; this is very useful when looking at the page history later. Clicking "Watch this page" adds this page to the user's watchlist (which we'll get to later in this chapter). "Save page" of course saves the page. "Show preview" shows what the page will look like if it's saved in its current state, while leaving the edit form underneath the preview, so that the user can keep editing. "Show changes" shows the differences between the current text and the saved page, again with the edit form placed at the bottom. It's generally a good idea to hit both of these before saving a page, to make sure that everything looks alright, and that nothing was deleted, or added, accidentally.

"Cancel" and "Editing help" are simply links. "Cancel" takes the user back to the regular page, while "Editing help" brings the user to to the page "Help:Editing", which by default is blank. The latter is a somewhat silly feature – it means that every wiki needs to maintain its own editing help page. The best course of action is to simply put in a link on the local page Help:Editing to the following URL:

https://www.mediawiki.org/wiki/Help:Editing

Page history

The next feature available for every content page in MediaWiki is the history page. You can reach it by adding "action=history" to a page's URL query string, and, as with the edit page, it's available in most skins via a tab, and in some skins as a sidebar link. In English, the tab is called "History" or "View history", depending on the skin.

The history page doesn't usually get much attention, although it is, in a sense, the heart of MediaWiki, because being able to see the page history is what lets wikis function like wikis. Because you can always see the entire set of changes, you can open up editing of your content to any group of people, no matter how large, without fear that important data will be lost.

Here are a few rows from the history page for the article "Paul Broca", on the English-language Wikipedia:

- (cur | prev) ◎   00:27, 14 February 2012 98.81.26.55 (talk) . . (26,275 bytes) (+6) . . (→*Personal life: The term bachelor's degree is a common noun, and it is not capitalized. Likewise for master's degree. Only the abbreviations are capitalized.*) (undo)
- (cur | prev) ◎   19:55, 9 February 2012 Kilom691 (talk | contribs) . . (26,269 bytes) (0) . . (*ref modified*) (undo)

Every row represents a single edit to the page, and all edits are stored permanently. (In MediaWiki nomenclature, an edit is also known as a "revision". It's rarely called a "version"; that word is generally reserved for software.) Each row holds important information and links:

- "cur" and "prev" links, and radio buttons, for showing differences (as described in the next section, "Page diffs")

- the date and time in which the edit was made (configured for the current user's time zone), which link to a page showing that revision

- the name of the user who made the edit, or the person's IP address if the edit wasn't made by a logged-in user

- additional links to the user's talk page and list of contributions

- sometimes, the character "m" (in English), to indicate that the person who made this edit considered it a "minor edit"

- the number of bytes in the page in this revision (for Roman letters, the number of bytes is usually equal to the number of characters, although for other languages, like Chinese, there are often three bytes per character)

- the user's own summary of the edit

- an "undo" link, for all but the earliest row (covered in the upcoming section, "Undoing").

Clicking on the date/time brings you to the page for that specific revision – each one has its own permanent URL. Going to the URL for a specific edit shows you the contents of the page at that time, in addition to some information at the top about that revision:

Paint suppliers

Revision as of 21:20, June 17, 2012 by AAnderson (Talk | contribs)
(diff) ← Older revision | Latest revision (diff) | Newer revision → (diff)

Administrators will also see links for "block" and "rollback" within the rows of the history page. These are both covered in the upcoming section, "Blocking and rollbacks".

Page diffs

The elements at the beginning of each row – "cur" and "prev" links (in English), and the two columns of radio buttons – are used to compare between revisions. Clicking on the "prev" link shows you the change made in this revision, while the "cur" link shows the differences between this revision and the current one. The sets of radio buttons, meanwhile, allow for precise comparison of any two revisions – the first column is meant to select an older revision, and the second column a newer revision (the JavaScript ensures that you can't select a row in the second column older than the one in the first column). Clicking on "Compare selected revisions" will display all the differences between the two revisions.

Figure 3.4 shows an example of one such display, from an edit made on November 21, 2011 to the article "Parallel postulate" on the English-language Wikipedia.

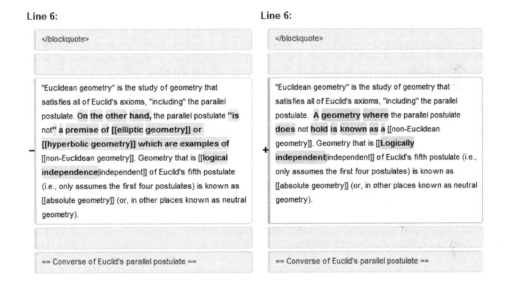

Figure 3.4: A page diff from the English Wikipedia

Colors and bolding are used to show differences. The algorithm used to determine the differences is MediaWiki's own, and it's fairly good, though not perfect. When one or more blocks of text are rearranged on the page, for example, the change is often shown as more dramatic than it actually is: it can be displayed as a massive deletion and addition of text, instead of a simple rearrangement.

Undoing

The "undo" link, after the edit summary, allows any user to undo that one change. An "undo" link also appears in any page showing the difference between two revisions.

Not every difference can be automatically undone, though, and thus not every "undo" link will work, whether it's between a large number of revisions or just two adjacent ones. Clicking on an "undo" link that can't be performed by the system will lead to the error message, "The edit could not be undone due to conflicting intermediate edits."

MediaWiki decides whether or not a change can be undone based on whether the undo would affect any of the edits that have been done since the more recent of the two revisions. The more edits that have been done since the later revision, the smaller the chance that this change can be automatically undone. Conversely, a difference involving the current revision can always be automatically undone, whether it's back to the previous revision or to any revision before that.

If you can't undo a change automatically, you'll have to do it manually, which, for large pages, can be a painful process. In that case, using a text editor can usually make the task easier than editing the text directly within a web page.

Blocking and rollbacks

If you're an administrator, there are a few more links that you'll see on every row in the history page. Next to every username or IP address there will also be a "block" link, to block that person (see page 82). And, in the top row, near the "undo" link, there will also be a "rollback" link. This is a useful link, which automatically undoes the last edit to the page, as well as any edits made by that same user directly preceding the last one; there's no need to go through a second screen. It's especially useful for dealing with vandalism, when you know without a doubt that a certain user's changes are malicious and should all be undone. It should be used with caution in other circumstances, though: if, for instance, you just want to undo the last change you made to a page, if you hit "rollback" you may be surprised to see that more than one of your edits has been reverted, potentially going all the way back to the first revision of the page. (Though it should be noted that the change done by the rollback is simply recorded as another edit, so the rollback can itself easily be undone.)

Deleting revisions

What if a person puts slanderous text, or reveals secret information, like someone's phone number, on a wiki page? Of course, you can revert the edit, but that bad text will remain accessible to anyone who views the page history, and, if it's a public wiki, it could even get linked to from elsewhere. That's a bad outcome, but thankfully there's a way for administrators to hide certain revisions altogether. In LocalSettings.php, you can add the following line:

```
$wgGroupPermissions['sysop']['deleterevision'] = true;
```

This will give the 'deleterevision' permission to all administrators. (We'll get to user groups and user permissions in the next chapter.) You can give this permission to other user groups, although having this exact line is the easiest approach.

If you add this line, any administrator who's logged in will see another checkbox on each row, and another button above the rows, reading (in English) "Show/hide selected revisions". Selecting any number of checkboxes, and clicking the button, will bring you to a page reading "Delete/undelete revisions". Contrary to its name, this page does not actually delete anything, but rather hides certain revisions (though, as we'll see later, regular page deletions don't actually delete any content either). The interface is slightly more complex if more than one revision has been selected. Figure 3.5 shows the interface for one revision, and Figure 3.6 shows it for more than one.

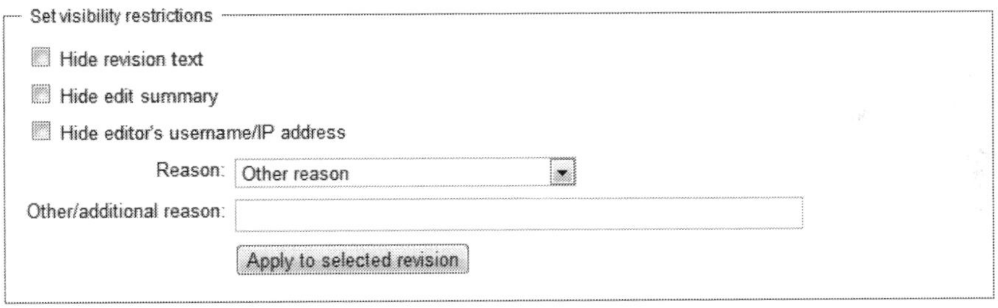

Figure 3.5: "Show/hide selected revisions" interface for one revision

As you can see, in either case, there are three things that can be hidden: the text of the revision (the most important of the three), the revision summary, and the user who made the revision. Once a revision is hidden, neither administrators nor other users will be able to see the hidden elements of that revision; though they'll still be able to see that the revision happened. If all three of the above elements are hidden, here's how that row in the page history will look:

- (cur | prev) ○ ☐ *01:57, June 18, 2012* *(username removed)*

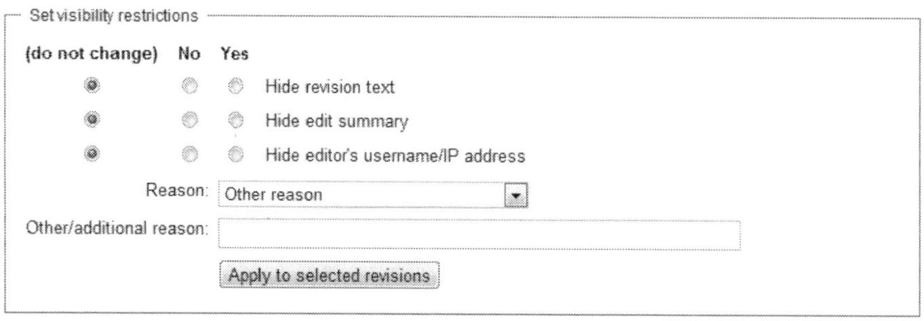

Figure 3.6: "Show/hide selected revisions" interface for more than one revision

The most recent revision cannot be hidden; the inclusion of a checkbox on that row appears to just be a mistake in MediaWiki. Once elements of a revision are hidden, that same interface can be used to unhide any of them. Because this feature is so useful, we recommend enabling it for any wiki, public or private.

Moving pages

Moving a page, in MediaWiki parlance, just means renaming it. The ability to move a page is set by the 'move' permission, which by default is open to everyone in the 'users' group, i.e. all logged-in users.

To move a page, click on the tab or dropdown action labeled "Move". You will then see an interface like this one:

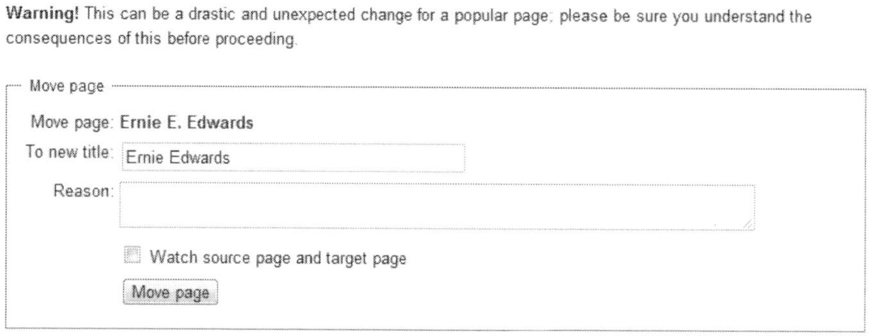

You can choose to either have a redirect from the old page, or not; it's recommended to have one, so that links to the old page name will still work. If there are no links, though, then it doesn't matter.

Moving a page to a title that already exists is effectively the same as deleting the other page; that's why only people with the 'delete' permission, usually administrators, are allowed to do it.

If you have a large batch of pages that all need to be renamed in the same way, the Replace Text extension (page 149) may be helpful.

Deleting pages

By default, administrators can delete any page (except for special pages). On a regular page, among the list of tabs, or dropdown actions, an administrator should see one that says "Delete". Clicking on it will bring you to an interface for deleting the page in question. A page, once deleted, can't be viewed by anyone; but by default it can be restored by any administrator, with all its revisions intact; so in that sense, no content is ever truly deleted.

Deletion and undeletion ability are governed by the 'delete' and 'undelete' permission types, respectively. So, for instance, to allow a user group to only undelete pages, you could add something like this to LocalSettings.php:

```
$wgGroupPermissions['articlesavers']['undelete'] = true;
```

Deletions definitely make sense for the case of pages created by spammers or vandals, since such pages are simply noise. And in the case of Wikipedia, deletions make a certain amount of sense because they give a sense of finality to a community decision to get rid of a certain page. (Though such decisions are sometimes overturned.) But for regular pages on regular wikis, where the contents were just considered unnecessary for some reason, blanking a page (i.e., removing its contents and hitting "save") is often a better strategy.

The advantages of blanking are that anyone can do it, anyone can undo it, and anyone can see what the old contents were, at any time. It's a much less severe way of accomplishing the same goal.

There's a clever extension, PureWikiDeletion, that displays links to blank pages as red, which solves the last part of letting blank pages mimic deleted pages. You can view it here:

https://www.mediawiki.org/wiki/Extension:PureWikiDeletion

Edit conflicts

Edit conflicts are less common than people who don't edit wikis may think, but they do happen. An edit conflict occurs when person A saves a page while person B is still in the middle of editing that same page. When person B goes to save the page, MediaWiki will prevent the save from happening. Instead, Person B will get an error message indicating that there was an edit conflict, and they will see an interface showing both their version of the page and the latest version. At that point the user will have to manually merge their changes into the latest version.

Edit conflicts are another reason why it's a good idea to edit a section of the page, instead of the entire page – if you edit one section, and it's not the section where someone else made their change, then there's a good chance that your edit can go through without a conflict.

Chapter 4

MediaWiki syntax

MediaWiki provides its own syntax, known as "wikitext", for doing standard formatting like section headers, links and tables. It's intended as a simpler alternative to HTML, and one that allows more standardization of display. MediaWiki syntax has caused a lot of angst, especially for new users, but it's not all that difficult once you understand the basic rules. And with the addition of templates, parser functions and the like, MediaWiki gains the ability to have almost unlimited customization of the page content.

Wikitext

MediaWiki allows some HTML within wiki pages, but for the most part all formatting is done using a syntax called "wikitext". Despite its generic name, "wikitext" refers specifically to MediaWiki's markup language; other wiki engines' syntax have their own names. Let's go through the elements of wikitext.

Newlines

First, newlines: a single newline between two lines will be ignored. To make a paragraph break, you need two newlines, i.e. an empty line between the two paragraphs. More than one empty line will lead to a bigger gap.

Pre-formatting

Starting a line with one or more spaces will lead to that line being displayed in a pre-formatted way. So having a line like " This is some text" (note that first space) is equivalent to "<pre>This is some text</pre>". (<pre> is a standard HTML tag.)

Headers

Headers are defined by putting the header text on a line by itself, surrounded by an equal number of equals signs ("=") on both sides. The standard way to create a top-level header is by putting it between two '==', like this:

```
==Instructions==
```

This corresponds to the HTML tag <h2>. You can actually also use <h2>, but then the header won't show up in the page's table of contents, and it won't get an "Edit" link.

Headers for sub-sections, sub-sub-sections, etc. are defined using a progressively higher number of equals signs. You can also use a single pair of equals signs, which creates an <h1> header, but this is not recommended, because only the page title at the top is supposed to have such a header. (Such headers are used, though, with the Header Tabs extension – see page 116.)

Bold and italics

Bold and italics are defined using two and three single-quotes, respectively. They can also be combined together. The following wikitext:

```
Is ''that'' your '''desk''' on my '''''front
lawn'''''?
```

...will produce this display:

Is *that* your **desk** on my ***front lawn***?

Links

There are two kinds of links you can create: internal (to other wiki pages), and external (to outside URLs). To create an internal link, use double square brackets, like this:

```
[[Favorite balloons]]
```

You can modify the link text, by adding more text after a pipe ("|"), like this:

```
[[Favorite balloons|Check out my favorite balloons!]]
```

MediaWiki also has a feature called "link blending", where text placed after an internal link gets incorporated into the link display. This feature is used often on Wikipedia. So if the name of the article is just "Favorite balloon", but you still want the link to read "Favorite balloons", you could do:

```
Check out my [[favorite balloon]]s!
```

Note also that, by default, the first letter in the link is case-insensitive.

External links are done using single square brackets, and there there's no pipe before the link text – you just put in the URL, and add the link text right afterwards. (This is because true URLs don't contain spaces – spaces, like various other special characters, get URL-encoded.) So you could have something like this:

```
[http://geocities.com/joeuser/balloons.html Check out
my favorite balloons from 1996!]
```

Lists and indentation

You can also create numbered and unnumbered lists. Here is text to create an unnumbered list, with bullet points:

```
* These
* are
* some bullet points
```

This will produce the following text:

• These

• are

• some bullet points

You can make hierarchical bullet point lists, by using multiple asterisks together. The following wikitext:

```
* These are
** some nested
** bullet points
```

...will produce this:

- These are
    - some nested
    - bullet points

To display a numbered list, use "#" instead of "*". So the following text:

```
# Buy groceries
# Cook
# Eat
```

...will produce this:

1. Buy groceries
2. Cook
3. Eat

Care has to be taken with numbered lists not to put any extra newlines between one numbered row and the next, because if that is done the numbers will start over at 1.

You can indent text, by putting ":" at the beginning of the line. As with asterisks, putting multiple colons at the beginning of the line will indent further. This comes in very handy in talk pages (see page 55).

Semicolons at the beginning of a line will bold the text; they're meant to be used for definition headers. There's an interesting bit of formatting to them that takes some getting used to – putting a colon on that line splits it up into "term" and "definition". So if you have wikitext like this:

```
;Ray:  A drop of golden sun
```

It will produce a display like the following:

Ray

> A drop of golden sun

Tables

There is also special syntax for defining tables. Here is code for a simple table:

```
{| class="wikitable"
!  10:30 - 11 AM
| style="font-style:  italic" | Snack break
|-
!  11 - 11:30 AM
| Clay sculpting
|}
```

"{|" and "|}" mark the beginning and end of the table. "!" marks a header cell, while "|" marks a regular cell. "|-" separates between rows. And note the presence of the "class" and "style" declarations. You can add such HTML-style attributes to the main table, as well as to any individual cell. If there is also text in a cell, separate the attribute from the text with a "|". This text will produce a table like the following:

10:30 - 11 AM	*Snack break*
11 - 11:30 AM	Clay sculpting

You can also put table cells on the same line within the wikitext, which can possibly make for easier reading. To do that, just use "||", or "!!", to separate the cells. For instance, the following wikitext will produce a table consisting of a single horizontal row of three cells:

```
{| A || B || C |}
```

Transclusion

You can embed pages within other pages – if, for instance, you have a lot of content whose editing you want to break up into multiple pages but still display together. If you have a page like "History of chairs" that you want to embed in a page called "Chairs", you can do that with the following wikitext:

```
{{:History of chairs}}
```

For pages in namespaces other than the main one, you would simply put the entire page name in curly brackets, like:

```
{{Help:How to get started}}
```

Such embedding is also called "transclusion". (You can see an explanation of namespaces on page 47.)

The most important use of such transclusion is to include templates, which, unlike other page types, can take in variables when they're called. Templates are covered later in this chapter.

Within transcluded pages, one can add the markup tags <noinclude>, <includeonly> and <onlyinclude>, all of which affect what shows up when the page is both viewed on its own, and transcluded elsewhere. These three tags are all covered in the section on templates.

Finally, here is a brief listing of all the main elements of MediaWiki wikitext. Some of this syntax won't be covered until later sections and chapters, but it may be helpful to have it all in one place, for easy reference:

```
''italics''
'''bold'''
'''''bold and italics'''''
==standard header==
===next-level header=== (...and so on)
[[Internal link]]
[[Internal link|alternate text]]
[http://example.com text of external link]
[[Category:Example]] (category tag)
[[:Category:Example]] (link to category)
---- (horizontal line)
* bulleted item
# numbered item
:indentation
::double indentation (...and so on)
;term :  definition
[[File:Image-name.jpg|thumb|frame|Caption text]]
{{:Transcluded page name}}
{{Template name}} (call to template)
#REDIRECT [[Page name]]
```

This short reference is based on the Wikipedia syntax "cheat sheet", available here:

https://commons.wikimedia.org/wiki/File:Cheatsheet-en.pdf

If you're planning to do any substantial MediaWiki editing, and you're just starting out, it can be helpful to print that sheet out.

Interwiki links

Interwiki links are basically a way to make external links to other wikis be callable like internal links, with two brackets instead of one. This is helpful for a few reasons: to clarify that some external wiki is a trusted source of information (and is trusted in general), to make linking to such wikis easier for editors, and to allow for linking from the sidebar.

In order to have interwiki links pointing to a particular site, you first need to define an alias for that site, based on its URL structure. For instance, if you want interwiki links to the English-language Wikipedia, you could define a link like "enwp", which looks like the following:

http://en.wikipedia.org/wiki/$1

An interwiki link using this alias could then look like:

```
[[enwp:Rainbow|rainbow]]
```

The text "Rainbow" would get substituted into the URL, where the "$1" is – so the linked URL would be http://en.wikipedia.org/wiki/Rainbow.

And since it's a link, you can include alternate link text (as shown in the example) – this is always recommended, because otherwise the interwiki alias (in this case, "enwp") will show up in the link text.

How do you define interwiki aliases? You can do it directly in the database, by adding to the "interwiki" table, but the recommended way is to use the Interwiki extension:

https://www.mediawiki.org/wiki/Extension:Interwiki

This extension provides a nice graphical interface, at Special:Interwiki, for managing the set of interwiki aliases on a wiki.

Until 2013, interwiki links were also used in Wikipedia to define "interlanguage links": interwiki links placed on the bottom of the page, containing a known language code as the interwiki alias, were displayed as links in the sidebar to the article's equivalents in other languages. Interlanguage links are now defined centrally, via Wikidata. If you want to set up this capability on your wiki, though – if you have a Wikipedia-style setup, with multiple wikis for the same content in different languages – you can do that by adding the following to LocalSettings.php:

```
$wgInterwikiMagic = true;
$wgHideInterlanguageLinks = false;
```

Including HTML

Most HTML tags can be included in wikitext, though they're not usually necessary. Allowed tags include <div>, <span>, <p>, <br>, table tags like <table>, <tr> and <td>, and all the header tags like <h1>, <h2>, etc. Notable tags that aren't allowed are <a>, <img>, <script>, <form>, <fieldset>, and the structural tags like <head>, <title>, etc.

For the most part, the HTML tags that aren't allowed are disallowed for security reasons. If there's specific HTML that you want to include on wiki pages, but can't because of these restrictions, the best approach to including it is to use the Widgets extension (page 257). There are other extensions that allow for embedding HTML, with varying levels of security; you can see a list here:

https://www.mediawiki.org/wiki/HTML_restriction

HTML comment tags can also be included, and that's how comments (explanatory text that you don't want to be displayed) are done in MediaWiki. Here's an example:

```
Jhon<!-- Don't correct!  This is not a typo --> Smith
```

Starting with HTML 5, browsers have supported adding "microdata" within pages, so that search engines and the like can get a better understanding of the nature of the contents – like that a certain text represents a business phone number. This is done via additional HTML tag attributes like "itemtype" and "itemprop". The best-known current schema for microdata is Schema.org. You can have the MediaWiki parser allow these attributes by just adding the following to LocalSettings.php:

```
$wgAllowMicrodataAttributes = true;
```

Templates

Templates are an integral part of the MediaWiki system. Technically, they're nothing more than pages that can substitute in values when they're transcluded, but that simple functionality opens up a world of possibilities. Templates are all stored in the "Template:" namespace (namespaces are described on page 47). At their most basic, templates can simply be a piece of text. For instance, you could have a perfectly valid template called "Hello", whose page, located at "Template:Hello", contains just the following text:

```
Hello, everybody!
```

Once that page was created, you could put the following text anywhere in any wiki page:

```
{{Hello}}
```

Placing double curly brackets around a text makes MediaWiki look for a template with that name, and then place its contents on the page if the template is found. In this case, the call would be replaced by the text "Hello, everybody!".

Here's an example of a more complex template, "Needs work", which looks more like the way templates in MediaWiki usually work. The "Needs work" template is meant to provide a simple way for users to tag pages that have problems. On the page "Template:Needs work", we could have the following code:

```
<noinclude>
This is the "Needs work" template.  You can pass to it
the field "Problem".
</noinclude>
<includeonly>
<div style="border:  1px solid black;">This
page needs work, for the following reasons(s):
{{{Problem|}}}.</div>
</includeonly>
```

Let's go through this code. The `<noinclude>` tag is meant to hold text that is only displayed when users look at the template page itself; it should be text that describes the template. The `<includeonly>` tag, on the other hand, holds text that will only be displayed on the page where the template is transcluded/called. Neither tag is necessary (though they're both recommended); and any text not contained in either tag will be displayed both on the template page and on pages in which it's called. Thus, the page "Template:Needs work" would display just this:

> This is the "Needs work" template. You can pass to it the field "Problem".

A user, seeing a page that needed work, could add a call to the "Needs work" template to the top of such a page, so it looks like this:

```
{{Needs work|Problem=Incorrect information}}
A bat is a kind of bug that lives in caves.  It has
glowing eyes that can shoot lasers!
```

The page would then get displayed as:

> This page needs work, for the following reasons(s): Incorrect information.

A bat is a kind of bug that lives in caves. It has glowing eyes that can shoot lasers!

The value or values passed in to the template are substituted into the corresponding parameters defined in the template's code. Parameters are specified using three curly brackets. Why does the template contain the string "`{{{Problem|}}}`" and not just "`{{{Problem}}}`"? That's because MediaWiki has the unfortunate default behavior of literally displaying parameter strings if values aren't passed in to them. So, if the template contained simply "`{{{Problem}}}`", and the template call looked like "`{{Needs work}}`" (i.e., with no values), the call would get displayed as:

> This page needs work, for the following reasons(s): {{{Problem}}}.

The pipe placed at the end tells MediaWiki to display an alternate string if the parameter isn't set: in this case, nothing. You could also use the pipe to display alternate text: if the parameter tag looked like "`{{{Problem|Unknown}}}`", then a plain call to the "Needs work" template would display this:

> This page needs work, for the following reasons(s): Unknown

Templates can also have unnamed parameters; these are defined by their index, i.e. their order in the set of parameters, starting with 1. Let's take a simple (and rather pointless) example, a template called "Painting" whose relevant section is this:

```
<includeonly>{{{1|}}} is a painting by
{{{2|}}}./<includeonly>
```

A call that looked like "`{{Painting|Composition with Red, Yellow and Blue|Piet Mondrian}}`" would display the following:

Composition with Red, Yellow and Blue is a painting by Piet Mondrian.

Numbered and named parameters can be combined in the same template, which can be useful in certain situations, though it's not usually recommended. If a template is passed both named and unnamed values, then the parameters {{{1}}}, {{{2}}} etc. will get the 1st, 2nd and so on values that do not have a name assigned to them – not necessarily the 1st, 2nd etc. values.

There's one more tag that can be used in templates – <onlyinclude>. This tag is a little trickier than <noinclude> and <includeonly>, because it affects text outside of the tag itself. If you add one or more <onlyinclude> tags to a template page (or to a regular page that's transcluded), then only the text within the <onlyinclude> tags gets displayed in other pages. All other text – whether or not it's part of <noinclude> or <includeonly> tags – is ignored.

Uses for templates

There are generally six main usages for templates within MediaWiki: (1) tags to highlight problems within a page, (2) infoboxes, (3) navigation boxes, (4) structural elements, (5) formatting aids and (6) templates used as formatting aids directly by various extensions.

The "Needs work" template was an example of a **problem-highlighting tag**. **Infoboxes** are well-known to readers of Wikipedia; they usually appear on the right-hand side of the page, and show important information about the page's subject. Figure 4.1 shows one example from the English Wikipedia.

Navigation boxes typically have no parameters; on Wikipedia, they're usually found on either the bottom or the side of the page, and show a large set of links to related pages. You can see an example of it from the English Wikipedia in Figure 4.2.

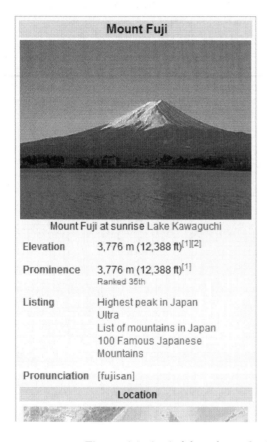

Figure 4.1: An infobox from the English-language Wikipedia

Figure 4.2: A navigation box from the English-language Wikipedia

Templates can also be used to display standard **structural elements** of a page; a common example on the English-language Wikipedia is the "Reflist" template, which is basically just a wrapper around the Cite extension's <references> tag function, providing some additional formatting options.

Templates can be used to do **inline formatting** of text and images, to simplify work for editors. An example is the "Convert" template on the English Wikipedia, which lets you convert a value in a certain unit to another unit – like converting pounds to kilograms. Another interesting example is the "Chess diagram" template, which can display an entire chessboard layout. There are hundreds of other such templates on Wikipedia.

Finally, there are **extensions in which templates are used to format values** – a template name is passed to a function, which then substitutes in to that template other values that it has generated. Semantic MediaWiki is one extension that uses such a trick, with its "template" results format. We'll talk more about that last usage in later parts of the book. And we'll also talk quite a bit about infobox-style templates, which are a key building block for the Semantic MediaWiki system.

Parser and tag functions

Pre-defined calls within MediaWiki are all referred to as "magic words". There are three kinds of magic words: parser and tag functions, variables, and behavior switches. We'll get to parser and tag functions first.

Parser and tag functions are both pre-defined functions that take in a set of inputs and display a result, or otherwise perform some action. The main difference between the two is that parser functions are called by wrapping the function with curly braces, while tag functions are called using angled brackets, in the manner of HTML or XML tags.

As an example, let's take a (fictitious) function, '#reverse', that takes in a string and displays its characters in reverse. If it were a parser function, a call to it could look like:

```
{{#reverse:abc}}
```

...or:

```
{{#reverse:string=abc}}
```

In other words, a parser function can be defined as either taking in named or unnamed parameters. If they're unnamed parameters, they're defined by the order in which they're called.

If 'reverse' were a tag function, on the other hand, a call to it could look like this:

```
<reverse>abc<reverse>
```

...or this:

```
<reverse string="abc" />
```

In all of these cases, the call would produce the string "cba" on the page.

Just as with HTML and XML tags, parameters to a tag function can be either a content string, placed between the start and end tag, or attributes placed within the tag. This means that tag functions can have only one unnamed parameter, all the rest must be named.

How are multiple parameters passed in to parser functions? They're separated using pipes. Here is a call to a real-life parser function, #sub, that displays a substring of a string, starting at a certain location and with a certain length:

```
{{#sub:This is a string.|0|4}}
```

In this case, the #sub function takes the first parameter, the sentence, and returns the substring starting at character 0, with length 4. The resulting displayed string would be "This".

The values passed in to #sub, and to all other parser functions, are separated by pipes.

But what about values that actually contain pipes – how can they be passed in without confusing the function? There is a standard solution to this that's somewhat of a hack: a template called "!" is defined in the wiki, which contains simply the string "|". You could then have a call like:

```
{{#sub:This is{{!}}a string with a pipe.|0|4}}
```

When the parameters are evaluated, the "{{!}}" will change to a "|". (The result will simply be "This", so this is a contrived example, but hopefully you get the idea.)

That brings us to the last difference between parser and tag functions, although it's a difference that's becoming less of an issue. For most of the history of MediaWiki, the big weakness of tag functions was that inputs passed in to them were not first parsed.

To take an example, let's say that there are parser and tag functions named 'spacify', that put spaces in between all the characters in a string (this is a hypothetical example – there's probably no reason why anyone would ever want such a thing). The following calls will both display the string "c b a":

```
{{#spacify:{{#reverse:abc}}}}
{{#spacify:<reverse>abc</reverse>}}
```

The following calls, in most cases, would fail, however:

```
<spacify>{{#reverse:abc}}</spacify>
<spacify><reverse>abc</reverse></spacify>
```

That's because the string that would be "spacified" would be the literal string '{{#reverse:abc}}' or '<reverse>abc</reverse>'. In other words, tag functions don't allow their inputs to be parsed – a weakness that has made them unusable for many situations.

Two features of MediaWiki, though, can help to reduce this difference between tag and parser functions. The first is the #tag function, which is part of core MediaWiki. #tag lets tag functions be called as parser functions, so that their arguments can be parsed. So if only <spacify> were defined and not #spacify, you could call the following, and it would, in fact, display "c b a":

```
{{#tag:spacify|<reverse>abc</reverse>}}
```

The second is that, since version 1.16 of MediaWiki, tag functions can in fact be defined so that they parse their own parameters, just as parser functions do. As of this writing, few tag functions have been defined with this behavior, but hopefully this will become more standard in the future.

Besides #tag, there are a variety of other parser functions defined in core Media-Wiki. There are also a few tags. And some parser functions are called without the '#' character at the beginning – for the most part, this is based on when that parser function was added; older functions do not have it. Here are some of the important parser functions defined in MediaWiki:

- `localurl`, `fullurl`, `canonicalurl` – variants that produce a URL based on a page name and a query string

- `lc`, `lcfirst`, `uc`, `ucfirst` – lower-casing and upper-casing functions

There are a variety of other pre-defined parser functions; you can see the full list here:

https://www.mediawiki.org/wiki/Help:Magic_words#Parser_functions

There are also some tag functions, including <includeonly>, <noinclude> and <nowiki>. <includeonly> and <noinclude> (and <onlyinclude>) were already covered on page 33. <nowiki> is a very useful tag, that prevents MediaWiki formatting from being applied to text. For instance, to display the following on a wiki page:

The way to do *italics* is with "double apostrophes".

You could use this wikitext:

```
The way to do "italics" is with <nowiki>"double
apostrophes"</nowiki>.
```

Variables

A variable is a call that simply outputs something else in its place. Like a template call, it is surrounded by two curly brackets; but its value is set directly from PHP code. The most-used variable is "{{PAGENAME}}", which displays the name of the page. There are dozens of other variables, including variations on the page name ({{FULL-PAGENAME}}), date/time information ({{CURRENTTIME}}), information about the wiki ({{SITENAME}}, {{NUMBEROFPAGES}}), and so on. The full set of variables can be found here:

https://www.mediawiki.org/wiki/Help:Magic_words#Variables

Various extensions also define their own variables. Of special note is the extension MyVariables, which defines the three additional variables {{CURRENTUSER}}, {{CURRENTUSERREALNAME}} and {{LOGO}}, and provides a framework for defining additional variables. You can find it at:

https://www.mediawiki.org/wiki/Extension:MyVariables

Behavior switches

Behavior switches are calls that don't actually display anything, but rather tell the parser to do something, like alter the display, or store some value. Their names are usually written in all-caps and surrounded by two underscores on both sides, and they are usually placed on a page on a line by themselves. The most well-known behavior switch is "__NOTOC__", which tells the parser not to put a table of contents on the page. Another sometimes-useful one is "__NOEDITSECTION__", which removes the "Edit" links that show up by default for each section header.

Some behavior switches take in parameters: these are instead called in the same manner as parser functions. An examples is "DISPLAYTITLE", which sets the display of a page's title to be something different than its actual name. An example call would be:

```
{{DISPLAYTITLE:this is my new title}}
```

Another example is "DEFAULTSORT"; see page 46 for more information about it.

There are about 15 behavior switches altogether defined in core MediaWiki. The current full list is: __NOTOC__, __FORCETOC__, __TOC__, __NOEDITSECTION__, __NEWSECTIONLINK__, __NONEWSECTIONLINK__, __NOGALLERY__, __HIDDENCAT__, __NOCONTENTCONVERT__, __NOTITLECONVERT__, __INDEX__, __NOINDEX__ and __STATICREDIRECT__ (and there are some aliases as well). You can find explanations of all of them here:

https://www.mediawiki.org/wiki/Help:Magic_words#Behavior_switches

Chapter 5

Content organization

Categories

Categories are MediaWiki's basic method of organizing information. On wikis that don't use Semantic MediaWiki, categories are really the only way to tag information about pages. Categories, for that reason, have been used in a large variety of ways – you only have to look at the explosion of categories on Wikipedia to see that. On the English-language Wikipedia, there are at least 6 ways in which categories get used:

- to establish the basic type of the page's subject, e.g. "Space Shuttles"

- to define further characteristics of a page's subject, e.g. "Italian generals"

- to note a larger topic to which this page's subject relates, e.g. "Theosophy"

- to tag temporary information about the page itself, e.g. "Proposed deletion as of September 20, 2014"

- to serve as a container super-category for other categories, e.g. "Symphonies by composer"

- to tag pages other than regular pages or categories, e.g. "Animal templates"

There are better ways of tagging much of this information, which take less work and lead to less redundancy. In fact, Semantic MediaWiki, which we'll get to in later chapters, was first thought up in part in order to remove the need for the profusion of categories on Wikipedia. Still, even with Semantic MediaWiki, categories play an important role.

Let's look at how categories are defined and used. Any content page in MediaWiki can be added to a category, including images and files, as well as category pages themselves. In all cases, adding a page to a category consists of just adding the following text to anywhere in the page:

```
[[Category:category name]]
```

Nothing will be displayed where that text was added. Instead, at the bottom of the page, text that looks like the following will be displayed, showing all the page's categories, in the order they were defined on the page:

Categories: 1899 births | 1957 deaths | 20th-century actors | Actors from New York City | American chess players | American Episcopalians | American film actors ...

Category tags can go anywhere in a page, but to keep things readable, the usual convention is to place them at the bottom of the page, with one tag per line. So the wikitext that would generate the previous set of displayed categories might look like this:

```
[[Category:1899 births]]
[[Category:1957 deaths]]
```

...and so on.

There's one other important place in which categories are declared: within templates. On Wikipedia, the "Proposed deletion..." categories are one example of categories set via templates. (When using Semantic MediaWiki, it is in fact recommended that all category declarations be made via templates; you can see a full explanation of that on page 181.)

Every category has a page in MediaWiki associated with it, which is just the name of that category, preceded by the name of the category namespace, which in English is just "Category:". So the page for a category called "Cars" would be at "Category:Cars".

Let's go through the structure of a category, using a real-life example. Here is the top of the page "Category:Hydraulic engineering" category on the English-language Wikipedia:

Category:Hydraulic engineering

From Wikipedia, the free encyclopedia

*The main article for this category is **Hydraulic engineering**.*

This category is about civil engineering. For mechanical engineering, see Category:Hydraulics.

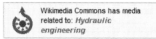

Wikimedia Commons has media related to: *Hydraulic engineering*

The top part of the category page consists of whatever text has been manually placed there. Below that is the set of subcategories, if any, for this category; i.e., categories tagged as belonging to this category. Here is that list, again for the Hydraulic engineering category page:

Subcategories

This category has the following 10 subcategories, out of 10 total.

A

▶ Artificial lakes (1 C, 66 P)

H

▶ Hydraulic engineers (1 C, 46 P)
▶ Hydraulic structures (3 C, 6 P)
▶ Hydrogeology (25 P)

L

▶ London water infrastructure (1 C, 24 P)

R

▶ Reservoirs (3 C, 18 P)

S

▶ Sewerage (3 C, 90 P)

W

▶ Water supply (11 C, 89 P)

W cont.

▶ Water transport infrastructure (16 C, 24 P)
▶ Water wells (1 C, 37 P)

The categories are displayed in alphabetical order, in three columns, with headers for each initial letter. There is also an arrow next to each subcategory name, which can be used to drill down through the hierarchical list of subcategories for each of these subcategories. This arrow functionality is not standard, and comes from the CategoryTree extension (page 101).

Finally, there's the heart of the category page: the listing of all the pages it contains. Here is just the top of that list, again for the same Wikipedia category:

Pages in category "Hydraulic engineering"

The following 126 pages are in this category, out of 126 total. This list may not reflect recent changes (learn more).

A
- Aggradation
- Alpha Hydraulic Diggings
- American Water Works Association

H cont.
- Hardy Cross method
- HEC-RAS
- Hushing
- Hydraulic conductivity

M cont.
- MIKE URBAN
- Mill pond
- MOHID Land
- MOUSE DHI

Pages, like subcategories, are displayed in three columns, with headers for the first letter of the name.

If a category contained any images, below the listing of pages would be a display of the thumbnails of all the images, in gallery format (this is not shown here).

If you click on a category name, and the page for that category hasn't been created yet, you'll see a message saying that the category doesn't exist yet; but it will still list all its pages and/or subcategories. Every category that's used should ideally have a page created for it. You have to add some content to a page in order to be able to save it: a simple sentence explaining the category is usually what's done, although even just a "Category" tag, to establish a parent category for this category, would do the trick.

By default, a category page lists its member pages in alphabetical order. This doesn't always make sense, though: you might want to list people by their last name, you might want to list names that start with "The" under their second word, and so on. You can do that for a particular member page by just adding the indexing string after a pipe in the category tag. For example, to have the page "The Archies" sorted as if it were called "Archies, The", you would place the following in the page "The Archies":

```
[[Category:Musical groups|Archies, The]]
```

Or, if the page belongs a lot of categories, and you want to index it the same way in all those categories, you can use the "DEFAULTSORT" behavior switch on the member page, like this:

```
{{DEFAULTSORT:Archies, The}}
[[Category:Musical groups]]
...etc.
```

"DEFAULTSORT" can be placed anywhere on the page, though it's usually placed right above the set of categories, which in turn are usually at the end of the page.

(That's unless you're using the Semantic MediaWiki system, though, where categories, and default sorting, are usually set via the template.)

Since the "Category" tag looks exactly like a standard wiki-link, how do you actually link to a category page, instead of making a category declaration? You do that by adding a colon at the beginning of the tag, so the text would look like:

```
Also check out [[:Category:Butterflies]].
```

...or, if you want custom text in the link, add a "|" and the text after that, just as you would with a regular link:

```
Also check out the [[:Category:Butterflies|Butterflies]]
category.
```

Namespaces

Namespaces are how different types of content in the wiki are distinguished. A page is defined as being within a certain namespace if the name of the page begins with the name of that namespace, followed by a colon. So, for instance, the page "Talk:UNIX administration" is in the "Talk" namespace.

It's very important to note that a namespace is more than just a prefix: it's a true separate container of content. So the page "Talk:UNIX administration" is actually considered by the system to be the page "UNIX administration" within the "Talk" namespace.

Some namespaces can be represented by more than one string. For instance, in non-English-language wikis, the English-language name for a namespace will always work. So, for example, going to the page "Talk:Paavo Nurmi" on a Finnish-language wiki will redirect you to "Keskustelu:Paavo Nurmi". ("Keskustelu" is Finnish for "discussion".) This can also happen within one language. In most wikis, the project namespace can be accessed with either the name of the wiki, the string "Project:", or, for non-English wikis, the corresponding word for "project" in that language. When settings are changed for individual namespaces within LocalSettings.php, the namespaces aren't referred to by their language aliases, but rather by values like NS_TALK, NS_USER, etc. So if you want to enable subpages for just "User:" pages, for example (we'll get to subpages on page 52), you would add the following line to LocalSettings.php:

```
$wgNamespacesWithSubpages[NS_USER] = true;
```

NS_TALK, NS_USER etc. are actually PHP constants, that in turn simply represent numbers (NS_TALK is 1, for example). Each namespace's number is unique. Pages whose names don't contain a colon are still part of a namespace: that's the "main" or "blank" namespace, denoted by NS_MAIN in LocalSettings.php (which has the numeric value 0). Similarly, pages whose names do contain a colon, but whose string before the colon doesn't correspond to an active namespace, are also in the main namespace: a page named "Happy:Times" is just the page "Happy:Times" in the main namespace, not a page called "Times" in the "Happy" namespace, unless a "Happy" namespace has been defined on this wiki. Namespaces are used for many types of content; below is the listing of each namespace that comes by default in MediaWiki, along with its PHP constant, its actual numeric value, its English-language alias, and its purpose:

Namespace constant	#	English-language alias(es)	Purpose
NS_MEDIA	-2	"Media"	Used for directly linking to uploaded files
NS_SPECIAL	-1	"Special"	Used for special pages defined by the software
NS_MAIN	0	(no text)	Most user-created content
NS_TALK	1	"Talk"	Discussions about pages in the main namespace
NS_USER	2	"User"	Information about the wiki's users
NS_USER_TALK	3	"User talk"	Discussions with individual users
NS_PROJECT	4	"Project" and a specific name for that wiki, usually the name of the wiki	Pages about the wiki itself
NS_PROJECT_TALK	5	"Project talk" and a specific name + " talk"	Discussions about project pages
NS_FILE	6	"File" and "Image"	Uploaded files

NS_FILE_TALK	7	"File talk" and "Image talk"	Discussions about uploaded files
NS_MEDIAWIKI	8	"MediaWiki"	System messages and wiki-wide CSS and JS content
NS_MEDIAWIKI_TALK	9	"MediaWiki talk"	Discussions about those system messages
NS_TEMPLATE	10	"Template"	Holds templates
NS_TEMPLATE_TALK	11	"Template talk"	Discussions about templates
NS_HELP	12	"Help"	Pages meant to help the wiki's users
NS_HELP_TALK	13	"Help talk"	Discussions about help pages
NS_CATEGORY	14	"Category"	Holds categories
NS_CATEGORY_TALK	15	"Category talk"	Discussions about categories

Most of these namespaces will be discussed in greater detail in later chapters.

Extensions to MediaWiki can define additional namespaces of their own: some of the extensions that will be covered later in this book, like LiquidThreads, Semantic MediaWiki, and Widgets, do that.

Administrators can also add their own namespaces to a wiki. When this is done, it's usually in order to separate out types of content. The Wikimedia website Wikisource, for instance, has, in its English-language version, the namespace "Author", which holds all author pages, so that the URL for the poet Robert Frost is:

http://en.wikisource.org/wiki/Author:Robert_Frost

Here, the "Author" namespace seems like it's intended to provide disambiguation, so that a page about, say, a book called "Robert Frost" would automatically have a separate name.

Personally, I tend to argue against using namespaces for disambiguation alone: it adds more complexity (one more rule for the wiki's users to remember), it's a different usage of namespaces than what they were originally intended for, and it's not usually needed as a disambiguation tool – since for all but the largest wikis, there's usually not much need to distinguish between two entities with the same name.

There's at least one compelling reason, though, to create additional namespaces for regular content, which is setting access control. A number of extensions that provide controls on both viewing and editing of content use namespaces to define which pages get which level of security (see page 136). Usually, such extensions allow for defining security levels for categories as well, and sometimes also for individual pages, but namespaces are the most secure approach, since a page is attached to a namespace in a very direct way. For pages that have their security settings defined via categories, there's always the chance that the category declaration will get accidentally removed in one way or another from a page, thus removing its security settings, at least temporarily. To be sure, for pages with namespace-based protection there's the risk that someone will accidentally move the page into another namespace; but this is a smaller risk.

Regardless, for whatever reason, you may want to create one or more additional namespaces for your wiki. In that case, the first step is to choose a number for your namespace; or rather a pair of consecutive numbers, since namespaces almost always come in twos: a namespace for the main content, which has an even number, and the one for its equivalent talk pages, which has the odd number that's one higher. You of course should choose a pair of numbers that haven't already been taken: that includes the IDs of all the default MediaWiki namespaces, as well as namespaces taken by any MediaWiki extensions you use, or may use in the future. For security's sake, you may as well not use namespace numbers taken by any extensions. You can see the complete list of namespace IDs currently used by MediaWiki extensions here:

> https://www.mediawiki.org/wiki/Extension_namespace_registration

Once you've decided on a number, or numbers, for your namespaces, you can register them within LocalSettings.php. For every namespace, you should add two lines, which look like the following:

```
define( "NS_BOOK", 500 );
$wgExtraNamespaces[NS_BOOK] = "Book";
```

The way namespaces are structured can lead to one potential awkwardness. Let's say you create a page called "City:Brussels", and then remember that you haven't yet created a "City" namespace. You do that, and then you discover that the page "City:Brussels" is blank again! That's because the page you created was

"City:Brussels" in the main namespace, whereas the page you're going to now is "Brussels" in the "City" namespace. How can you recover the page that was created before? There are three ways: the first, and probably easiest, way is to temporarily unset the "City" namespace, then move the page "City:Brussels" to any name that doesn't start with "City", then reinstate the "City" namespace, and move the page back to the name "City:Brussels". The second way is to call the script "namespaceDupes.php", available in MediaWiki's /maintenance directory. The third involves going into the database, finding the entry for the page in the 'page' table, and changing both the namespace and the page name via SQL or some other tool. It requires knowledge of database manipulation, and isn't recommended unless you really know what you're doing.

A similar problem can come about if the underlying number gets changed for any namespace. Again, those three previous solutions can also be used in this case.

Redirects

Redirects are another useful basic feature of MediaWiki. Redirects let you point one page toward another, so that if a user goes to the URL for page A, what they'll be shown instead is page B, with a note at the top saying "(Redirected from...".

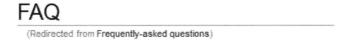

Redirects are generally done for one of three reasons:

- to link a common typo in a page name to its correct spelling

- to link one or more synonyms to a single page (e.g., redirecting "USA" and "United States of America" to "United States")

- to link a topic that's considered not meaningful enough to have its own page, to a general one that's meant to cover that specific topic to some extent (e.g., redirecting "Fax" to "Company communications policy" in an internal company wiki)

A redirect is defined by placing the following text in the page that will be redirecting:

```
#REDIRECT [[target page name]]
```

The "REDIRECT" can actually be written with any casing, though by convention it's usually written as all capital letters.

In most cases that's the only thing that appears on a redirect page, though in theory any other text can appear as well – users just won't see it. The one piece of text that it can be useful to add is category declarations – if you add one or more category declarations to a redirect page, that page will in fact show up as a member in all those category pages, though the name will be in italics. Category declarations are generally only done for the third type of redirect – specific subjects redirecting to more general topics.

Semantic MediaWiki (chapter 16) has its own behavior when dealing with redirect pages: properties that point to a redirect page are treated as if they're pointing to the ultimate destination page; which is useful for the first two kinds of redirects (for typos and synonyms), though not always for the third (subtopics to larger topics).

Subpages and super-pages

Subpages are a handy way to break up a single page into multiple pages, if it gets too big or unwieldy. A subpage is simply a page whose name takes the form "*main page name/additional text*", where "*main page name*" already exists. So if you have a page about the company Ace Motors, and it contains a long section about company's history, you could spin off that section into its own page, named "Ace Motors/History", and link to it from the "Ace Motors" page.

Of course, you could also call the page "History of Ace Motors", which is how it would be done on Wikipedia (Wikipedia doesn't use subpages in its main namespace, though it does use them in other namespaces, like "Wikipedia:" and "Template:"). So are subpages just another naming convention? To some extent, yes, although MediaWiki does offer one important feature that makes subpages feel more like they "belong" to their main page: if you turn on the use of subpages, any page with a slash in its name will include a small "breadcrumb" link at the top, pointing back to the "main" page, i.e., the section before the slash, provided that the main page exists. This small feature goes a long way toward making subpages feel legitimate.

Sub-subpages, and pages further down the hierarchy, are also possible, provided that each page further up in the hierarchy already exists. The "breadcrumb" link at the top will link to each sub-section of the page name in turn. So you could have a page like "Ace Motors/History/Europe/1900-1950", and, if subpages are enabled for the main namespace, the top of the page will look like:

Ace Motors/History/Europe/1900-1950
< Ace Motors | History | Europe

Enabling subpages

Subpages are enabled through the global variable $wgNamespacesWithSubpages, which by default is empty. If you want to have subpages, say, the main namespace and the template namespace, you could add the following to LocalSettings.php:

```
$wgNamespacesWithSubpages = array( NS_MAIN, NS_TEMPLATE );
```

Conversely, if you wanted every namespace to have subpages, you would be best off calling array_fill(), like the following:

```
$wgNamespacesWithSubpages = array_fill( 0, 200, true );
```

(In this case, 200 is an arbitrarily high number, with the assumption that there are no namespaces on this wiki with an ID greater than 200.)

Special pages

There are pages in MediaWiki that do not contain editable content, but rather interface elements, like lists and helper forms. These are called "special pages". They are contained in the namespace "Special:", and unlike other pages, they can't be edited, they have no page history, and they don't have an associated talk page. Instead, the content of these pages is defined by the PHP code. MediaWiki defines a wide variety of special pages, as do many MediaWiki extensions. Among the special pages defined in core MediaWiki are:

- Special:RecentChanges – shows the list of recent edits in the wiki (see page 93)

- Special:Contributions – shows the set of edits made by any one user (when the page is called in the form "Special:Contributions/username")

- Special:Watchlist – shows the most recent change to any page that the current user is "watching" (see page 94)

- Special:Version – shows the current version of MediaWiki, as well as of any extensions that are installed

- Special:SpecialPages – shows the set of all special pages on the wiki; this is a useful starting point (see also page 147 for the Admin Links extension)

- Special:AllPages – shows all non-special pages in the wiki, subdivided by namespace

- Special:RandomPage – brings the user to a random page in the wiki.

There are many more special pages defined by both MediaWiki and its extensions, some of which are intended only for administrators. We'll get to many of these over the course of the book, but the list above is a good one for starting out with MediaWiki.

Chapter 6

Communication

MediaWiki provide a variety of ways for users to communicate with one another. These include talk pages for potentially large-scale discussions, personal communication via user talk pages (and potentially via more social networking-like interfaces in the future), threaded discussions at the bottoms of pages via some extensions, real-time chat, and finally users emailing each other via the wiki. We'll cover all of these in this chapter.

Talk pages

As we saw in the last chapter, every regular namespace for content in MediaWiki has an associated talk namespace, meant to hold pages used to discuss the contents of pages in that regular namespace. In the interface, one of the elements that usually shows up automatically for each page is a link to that page's corresponding talk page; in most skins this is the second tab within the top row of tabs. A page and its corresponding talk page will have the same name, but in different namespaces; for instance, the talk page for "University of Chicago" would be "Talk:University of Chicago", while the talk page for "Category:Universities" would be "Category talk:Universities".

Talk pages in MediaWiki, in general, are intended only for discussion of the corresponding page and how to improve it, and not for discussion of the page's underlying topic – that holds true for both Wikipedia and internal organizational wikis. There are two major exceptions to that, though. Talk pages for users, i.e. pages in the "User talk:" namespace (in English), are usually used for communication with that user, and only rarely to discuss the contents of the user page itself. And on wiki pages meant for documenting some technical topic, like a piece of software, the talk page can often turn into an informal venue for questions and answers about the page's topic.

Let's take a look at a typical usage of a talk page. On a page on an internal wiki, you see the information that the South American division of your company was founded in 1983. This is a surprise to you, since you had always thought that the division was founded in the 1990s. Your first instinct is to simply edit the page and change the information, but then you reconsider, thinking that you've just been misinformed. (The real lesson of this example may be the importance of trying to reference every piece of information; see page 115 for more on that.)

You decide, then, to bring it to the talk page. You click on the page's "Discussion" tab, and then among the tabs will appear one called either "Add topic" or just "+", depending on which skin you're using. You should click that tab. Then you'll see a standard edit interface, but with the addition of a "Subject/headline" field at the top. In that field, you could write something like "Founded in 1983?", and in the body, the following:

```
I had always thought the South American division was
started in the 1990s - I think I heard that during the
employee orientation.  Was it really in 1983?  If so,
is there a source for that?  ~~~~
```

Then you hit "Save", and the new section is created. The "~~~~" at the end is important – the set of four tildes gets changed, when you save the page, into a "signature", containing your username, a link to your talk page, and the date and time the message was posted. You could also put "~~~" instead – three tildes instead of four. This will display everything but the date and time. In practice, there's no good reason to do this; four tildes is always better.

If you're not logged in, your IP address will be displayed instead of a username – which is not very helpful, so you might as well manually type in your name and the data, instead of using the tildes, in that case.

Now it's time to wait – a response could come in the next hour, or in the next month, or of course not at all. You can keep checking the talk page, or monitor it via one of the many ways of monitoring MediaWiki pages – recent changes, watchlist, RSS/Atom, email, etc.

If no response appears within a certain period of time (entirely up to you), you can feel free to make the change you were thinking of making – you can even make the change at the same time as you post the talk page question, so that you don't have to deal with it again until a response comes.

Now, what happens if a discussion does ensue on the talk page? There's a standard syntax that's used. As we saw in the MediaWiki syntax chapter, colons are used for indenting paragraphs, and in the case of talk pages each message is usually intended one further than the previous message. After five or six colons, though, the discussion usually goes back to no colons, for the sake of both sanity and readability, and then the pattern begins again. And if a person's statement is more than one paragraph, each paragraph should begin with the same number of colons.

As before, every statement should end with the user's signature, set by typing "~~~~".

Archiving

If a talk page starts to get very long, the solution is to archive old comments. Unfortunately, there's no way to do that automatically – it has to be done by hand. You do that by copying some or all of the current talk page into a separate page that's a subpage of the main page, i.e. a page with the name "Talk:*name of page/something else*". Then the relevant content is removed from the current talk page, and a link is placed in the talk page to that archive page.

Templates help a lot when archiving talk pages. Usually two templates are used: one to be placed at the top of the talk page, that holds links to all the archive pages for that talk page, and another to be put at the top of archive pages, explaining that this is an archive page and linking back to the talk page.

There's no need to create these two templates from scratch: you can copy them from any wiki that does talk page archiving. On the English-language Wikipedia, for instance, they can be found at the pages "Template:Archives" and "Template:Talk archive", respectively. You could consider going with the two templates at media-wiki.org as well, which have a simpler layout and use a nice file-cabinet image (which itself also would have to be copied over – File:Replacement_filing_cabinet.svg – or you can use the InstantCommons feature to use the image directly; see page 71). You can find these two templates at "Template:Archive box" and "Template:Archive" on the mediawiki.org wiki.

On Wikipedia, archiving is usually done when the talk page reaches over 35 KB or so, and the archive pages are usually given sequential numbers: the first archive page is called "Talk:*page name*/1", the second one is called "Talk:*page name*/2", etc. This works fine, although we recommend an alternate approach for naming: using the date within the name, so that the subpage is called "/2013" or "/May 2013 to January 2014" or "/May 2013", etc., depending on the span of time contained within the archive. This makes it easier for users to find a particular old discussion, if they can remember approximately when it happened. There's no reason, however, to set the frequency of archiving based on this: just because you have archive pages named "2012" and "2013" doesn't mean that you need a page named "2014", if there's not enough content for that one year.

LiquidThreads

This basic setup works fairly well for most discussions, on Wikipedia and many other wikis. However, there are problems with this approach. For one, it's not all that user-friendly: users have to learn a new mini-syntax just to be able to make comments. Second, it lets users modify one another's comments, which is sometimes useful (in the case of vandals), but most of the time should not be done. Third, it doesn't allow for true threaded discussions: if you see a comment halfway through a discussion and you specifically want to respond to that one, it's difficult to do that in a way that makes what you're doing clear to readers of the page, and doesn't interrupt the flow of the previous discussion.

The LiquidThreads extension, in its own way, gets around all these problems. It provides for structured, threaded discussions on each talk page. Figure 6.1 shows how an empty talk page looks if the LiquidThreads extension (also known as "LQT") has been installed.

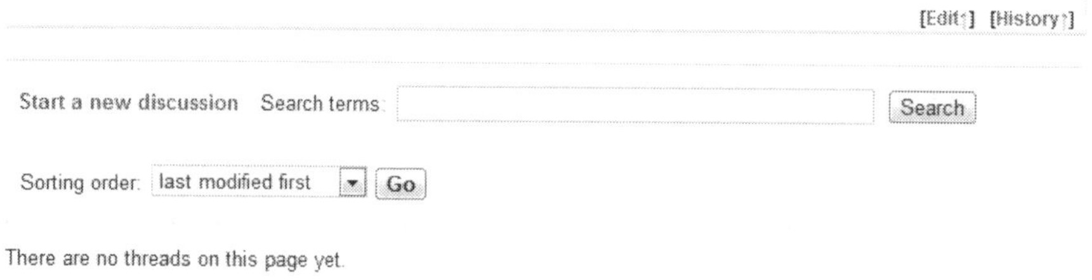

Figure 6.1: LiquidThreads interface

Using LiquidThreads, any user can start a new thread with any title, or respond to any specific comment that's already been made. And users can edit their own comments, but not anyone else's.

With LiquidThreads, users get notified about new messages on talk pages they're watching (see page 94 for an explanation of watching pages) via a link at the top of every page, which reads "My new messages", then the number of new messages that have appeared on all of those talk pages.

It's a setup that some people really like, while others prefer the simplicity of standard wiki-style commenting.

One huge caveat if you're considering using LiquidThreads: though the extension still sees a significant amount of use, the Wikimedia Foundation, which is responsible for its design and development, officially abandoned it in 2013 (in favor of the still-in-progress Flow extension – see next section). LiquidThreads is still maintained by a few developers, and it currently works fine for all recent versions of MediaWiki, but there's no guarantee that it will keep working in the future.

Echo & Flow

Over the longer term, there are two Wikimedia projects that are meant to, among other things, provide a forum-style interface for talk pages, and make communication easier among users. Those are the "Echo" and "Flow" projects:

> https://www.mediawiki.org/wiki/Echo_(Notifications)
> https://www.mediawiki.org/wiki/Flow

Echo is a framework for user notifications in general, which allows a greater range of notifications than MediaWiki otherwise supports, like one user "thanking" another for their edit to some page. Flow, which makes use of the Echo framework, is meant to create a system in which communication happens both within talk pages (using a threaded approach) and outside of pages, allowing individual users to simply "message" one another". Both projects are still in progress, though Echo is already in use on Wikipedia, notifying users when their talk pages are changed, their edits are reverted, etc.

Handling reader comments

It should be noted again that, with both regular talk-page style and LiquidThreads, the talk page is meant, for the most part, to be a place to discuss the contents of the relevant wiki page and not that page's actual subject matter. But what if you want a place for readers (not necessarily even the wiki's own users) to comment on the page's subject matter, or more generally, to place any sort of free-form comments? One solution is to simply use the talk page for that, and avoid wiki-style editing-based discussions altogether. This approach can make sense when the wiki is what's known as a "bliki", or a wiki where pages are generally blog-style, dated posts. Blikis are usually edited by one person, but even if they're not, generally no collaboration happens on the content, so there's no need to use talk pages to aid in collaboration. That frees up the talk pages for use in storing reader comments.

There's an extension that's helpful for that purpose: ArticleComments. It provides a nice blog-style comment-entry form that appears at the bottom of pages, and also displays the resulting comments at the bottom; but, unbeknownst to most readers, the actual storage of the comments is done on the talk page.

For cases when actual collaboration happens, though, and you want both collaboration-related discussions and blog-style comments, we recommend reserving talk pages only for the former. In this case, one solution that works well is to use a third-party commenting tool, and place it at the bottom of pages that require it. At the moment, what seems to be everybody's favorite such tool is Disqus (http://disqus.com). The easiest way to add Disqus commenting to MediaWiki is to use the "Widgets" extension, and add in a Disqus widget – see page 257.

Chat

There are several extensions that display a window, within MediaWiki web pages, that provides a chat room for all the users currently logged in to talk with one another in real time. These extensions are only very rarely used, perhaps because there's generally nothing substantive to be said between two people who both happen to be reading, or even editing, a wiki at the same time. These extensions include the one called Chat, which uses the PhpFreeChat utility:

> https://www.mediawiki.org/wiki/Extension:Chat

The Chat extension provides a new tab, called "Chat", which shows up on every page. In this tab is a chat room interface. The extension can be configured to either have a single chat room across the whole wiki, or to have a separate one for each page.

The other main chat extension is ShoutBox, which uses the Shoutbox chat service. It allows for embedding chat rooms directly within wiki pages:

https://www.mediawiki.org/wiki/Extension:ShoutBox

Emailing users

The page Special:EmailUser lets any user with a confirmed email address email any other user on the wiki with a confirmed email address. The user can set anything for the email's subject and body. The email that is sent will have the sender's username and email address appear as the "From" in the email, so you shouldn't use this page if you want to hide your email address from the recipient.

MediaWiki does not offer a way for administrators to email all of the wiki's users at once. There is an extension that does this, "STGS MassMailer", but it is currently insecure.

There are several extensions that allow the wiki to have a contact form, where users can enter comments that will then be emailed to one or more administrators. You can see the full set here:

https://www.mediawiki.org/wiki/Category:Contact_form_extensions

Chapter 7

Images and files

MediaWiki should never be mistaken for a real document-management system, but it does have a reasonable amount of support for managing files. True document-management systems have integration with the file system of the computer or network they're on, and usually let you edit documents inline – neither of which MediaWiki allows. (Though there's discussion about enabling the latter for MediaWiki, for SVG and some video formats, in the future.) MediaWiki does, however, let you upload files, and display them within other pages in a variety of ways – and it keeps a version history for each file, which is a very useful feature.

Uploading

The standard interface for uploading files to MediaWiki is the page Special:Upload, which lets you upload one file at a time.

When you upload a file, you are asked to select its name on the wiki, which, by default, is the file's name on the local system. You can also provide a summary of the file, and finally you are asked to specify a copyright type for that file, based on the set of allowed copyrights for the wiki (more on this later). The copyright choice assumes that the person doing the uploading was responsible for generating the file; or, at the very least, knows the copyright wishes of the person who generated the file – and often, neither of these is the case. This book will not get into issues of copyright, legal or otherwise; but you should know that there are a lot of options for allowed copyright type, and the best solution may depend on a variety of circumstances, including

```
┌─ Source file ──────────────────────────────────────────────────┐
│  Source filename: [                                ]  [ Browse... ]
│  Maximum file size: 2 MB (a file on your computer)
│           Permitted file types: png, gif, jpg, jpeg, pdf.
└────────────────────────────────────────────────────────────────┘

┌─ File description ─────────────────────────────────────────────┐
│  Destination  [                                            ]
│   filename:
│   Summary:   [                                            ]
│              [                                            ]
│              [                                            ]
│              [                                            ]
│              [                                            ]
└
```

Figure 7.1: Special:Upload page

whether the wiki is public or private.

Once a file is uploaded, several things happen: the file gets placed in the wiki's /images directory (the directory is called "images", even though it can hold uploaded files of all types); a page in the "File:" namespace is created for that file (the full name of the page will be "File:*page-name*", like "File:Cat.png"); and, if it's an image, and the image is bigger than the standard thumbnail size, a thumbnail is created for that file and is placed in the directory /images/thumb.

The /images directory

The /images directory can take two structures. By default, the directory is subdivided into two levels of subdirectories, where the first level consists of folders whose name is a single hexadecimal digit, from "0" to "f"; and the second level has folder names whose name consists of the parent folder's number or letter, plus a second hexadecimal digit. In other words, a file can be placed in a directory like "/images/8/8b" within the MediaWiki directory. There are 16 * 16 = 256 such possible sub-subdirectories. This default approach is also known as the "hashed" approach. It is used to try to prevent directories from getting too large – some file systems have a limit on the number of files any one directory can contain.

The other approach is to simply store every file in the /images directory. This approach has the advantage of simplicity, and for smaller wikis it's just as good a solution. To enable this approach, add the following to LocalSettings.php:

```
$wgEnableHashedUploads = false;
```

If you're going to use this setting, you should ideally do it before any files are uploaded. If, however, you want to change this setting for a wiki that already has uploaded files, you'll probably have to re-import the files (see page 263).

Thumbnails

A thumbnail is a small image meant to represent an uploaded file. For files that are images, these are simply smaller versions of the original image (or, for images that are already small, versions of the same size). For non-image files, these tend to just be an icon: for PDF files, for instance, it's the Adobe Acrobat logo.

Thumbnails are used to represent images in various places within the wiki. Most importantly, they can be used to display the image on wiki pages – we'll get to the syntax and options for displaying images later in this chapter. Thumbnails are also used to show the version history of each file, within its own page. They are also used in the Special:ListFiles page (see page 88), in image galleries, and in category pages, and they're used when querying images in Semantic MediaWiki, with formats such as "table" and "gallery" (see pages 169 and 230, respectively).

Troubleshooting uploading

It could be that, when you try to upload files on a wiki, you're not allowed to. That could be for any of the following reasons:

- PHP on the server is blocking uploads

- The /images directory is not writable by MediaWiki

- MediaWiki itself has uploading disabled

- your user account is not allowed to upload.

If it looks like PHP is blocking uploads, add the following line in php.ini:

```
file_uploads = On
```

If the images directory is not writable, the solution depends on the web server and file system in question – this page holds more information:

https://www.mediawiki.org/wiki/Manual:Configuring_file_uploads

Uploading also needs to be enabled in MediaWiki itself – make sure that you have the following line in LocalSettings.php:

```
$wgEnableUploads = true;
```

By default, every logged-in user is allowed to upload files, but unregistered users aren't. This can be changed in LocalSettings.php, via the 'upload' permission. (There's also a second relevant permission type, 'reupload', for uploading files that already exist on the wiki and thus overwriting their contents.) To prevent regular users from uploading, for instance, you could add the following to LocalSettings.php:

```
$wgGroupPermissions['user']['upload'] = false;
$wgGroupPermissions['sysop']['upload'] = true;
```

And it may be that you're allowed to upload files in general, but the specific file you have can't be uploaded. That could be for two reasons: the file's size, or its file type.

Every wiki has a limit on the allowed size of uploaded files, which is set by a combination of four PHP and MediaWiki settings. Essentially, the smallest of these dictates what is allowed to go through, so you may need to change all four to increase the allowed limit on file sizes. There are two PHP settings: "post_max_size" and "upload_max_filesize", both of which would need to be changed in php.ini. The two MediaWiki variables are $wgUploadSizeWarning and $wgMaxUploadSize – both represent a number of bytes. $wgUploadSizeWarning sets only what file size results in a warning to the user, so it doesn't actually affect which files go through and which don't – but it should be made consistent with what the actual limits are. So, to change the allowed file size to 30 megabytes, you would change the following in php.ini:

```
post_max_size = 30M
upload_max_filesize = 30M
```

...and add the following to LocalSettings.php:

```
$wgUploadSizeWarning = 30 * 1024 * 1024;
$wgMaxUploadSize = 30 * 1024 * 1024;
```

File type restrictions

As for file types – only a limited set is allowed by default, because certain file types, like Microsoft Office documents (Word, Excel and the rest) can contain viruses, which unsuspecting users can end up installing on their systems if they download the file. The default set of file extensions allowed is very short: only "png", "gif", "jpg" and "jpeg" (with the last two both representing JPG files).

What if someone tries to upload a .doc file simply by renaming the file's extension to, say, ".gif"? Thankfully, MediaWiki guards against that by looking at the file's internal file type, which the web server determines – the allowed set of file suffixes is really just shorthand for the allowed set of file types.

To add to or change the allowed set of file types, use the "$wgFileExtensions" variable in LocalSettings.php. The most common addition is allowing PDF files – to do that, you would add the following line:

```
$wgFileExtensions[] = 'pdf';
```

Extensions for uploading

A MediaWiki extension, UploadWizard, provides a nicer approach to uploading than the standard one, by guiding users on a step-by-step process that explains all the different options, like the copyright license used. It was developed for use on Wikimedia Commons (the wiki that holds the uploaded files for Wikipedia and other Wikimedia projects), but it can also be used on standard wikis; though some of the wording is unfortunately Wikimedia-specific, and can't easily be customized away. You can read more about the extension here:

https://www.mediawiki.org/wiki/Extension:UploadWizard

There's another extension, MultiUpload, that lets users upload more than one file at the same time; which can be useful when there's a large set of images to be added. At the moment, this extension is somewhat unmaintained, and may have problems depending on your MediaWiki version, but when it works it's quite useful:

https://www.mediawiki.org/wiki/Extension:MultiUpload

Finally, uploads are possible via Semantic Forms. Uploading from within a form has the advantage that the name of the file gets automatically placed on the page after it's uploaded, so that users don't need to do the second step of inserting a tag to display the image/file on the wiki page after they've uploaded it. For more on this option, see Chapter 17.

Displaying images

Images are generally displayed by simply linking to the image – which is a somewhat unexpected syntax. Let's say there's an image on the wiki called "Easter Island.png". The simplest way to display it is to just have the following:

```
[[Image:Easter Island.png]]
```

Alternatively, you could have this instead, since "Image" and "File" are aliases for the same namespace:

```
[[File:Easter Island.png]]
```

For the rest of this example, we'll just use "Image".

There are various additional settings you can apply to images: the height and width, the horizontal and vertical alignment, the caption, where the image links to, whether to place a border, etc. These are all parameters that can be added to the image tag, separated by pipes. Some are named, while others are unnamed.

Here's an example of an image display with more parameters set:

```
[[Image:Easter Island.png|100px|x150px|right|link=Easter
Island info|This is Easter Island.]]
```

The parameters can be passed in in any order, so the parser determines what parameter each value corresponds to, based on the specific text in each (except for a few named parameters like "link="). A "px" value without an "x" at the beginning sets the width, while one with an "x" at the beginning sets the height. "right" here controls the horizontal alignment of the image – the other options are "left", "center" and "none".

The "link=" parameter sets the location that the image links to – it can be either a wiki page or a URL. By default, an image links to its own page.

The last parameter, unless it's obviously something else, sets the caption for the image.

The only other very important setting for images is being able to display a thumbnail – most of the time, when images are displayed, it's actually a thumbnail that's shown, rather than the full-size image. To display an image as a thumbnail, just add the parameter "|thumb" to the image tag.

What if you just want to link to an image, rather than display it? You can either link to the wiki page for the image, or to the image itself. To link to the image's wiki page, just add a colon at the beginning of the link, so it looks like:

```
[[:Image:Easter Island.png]]
```

If instead you want to link directly to the image, use the "Media" namespace instead, which exists just for this purpose. You could do:

```
[[Media:Easter Island.png|Click here to see a great
picture.]]
```

There's more customization that can be done of image display. This page has all the details, as well as a lot of helpful demos:

https://www.mediawiki.org/wiki/Help:Images

Image galleries

The built-in MediaWiki tag <gallery> lets you display a group of images in one place. It takes in a group of image names and, optionally, their captions (which can include wikitext); a call to it would look like the following:

```
<gallery>
Image:Monkey.png
Image:Rhesus monkey.jpg|This is a [[rhesus monkey]]
Image:Large monkey.gif|This is a ''large'' monkey
</gallery>
```

Newlines here separate the names of the images.

In addition, if you're using Semantic MediaWiki, the "gallery" query format defined in the extension Semantic Result Formats lets you display a similar result via a semantic query, so that you don't have to hard-code the image names; see page 230.

Slideshows

You can also display images in a JavaScript "slideshow", which is an interface where a series of images and/or text appear one after another in the same spot. The switching from one display to the next can be done manually, using links or arrows so that the user can flip through the images, or by simply cycling through them automatically. There are several extensions that do this; the most reliable standalone extension currently seems to be Javascript Slideshow, which also lets you include text within each slide:

> https://www.mediawiki.org/wiki/Extension:Javascript_Slideshow

If you're using Semantic MediaWiki, you can also display a slideshow using the Semantic Result Formats extension's "gallery" format (see page 230).

This slideshow functionality should not be confused with a PowerPoint-style slideshow presentation. There actually is an extension that lets you turn wiki pages into individual slides, suitable for a presentation – S5SlideShow:

> https://www.mediawiki.org/wiki/Extension:S5SlideShow

And similarly, Semantic Result Formats also offers a format that enables slideshow presentations: the "pagewidget" format.

The capability to run a slideshow presentation directly from the wiki is nice, because it lets you create a presentation collaboratively, in the manner of Google Docs.

Displaying outside images

By default, images from outside the wiki cannot be displayed. That's for several reasons, the most important of which is that a malicious user can place an external image on a wiki page, then collect information about all the visitors to that page; which would be a violation of privacy. You can change this default by adding the following to LocalSettings.php:

> $wgAllowExternalImages = true;

If this is set, placing the URL of an external image in a page will display that image there.

You can also, instead, use the variable $wgAllowExternalImagesFrom to only allow images from certain trusted domains. Here is one example:

```
$wgAllowExternalImagesFrom    =    array(    'http://upload.wikimedia.org',
'http://www.flickr.com' );
```

However, if you're planning to use images from Wikimedia Commons (whose URL always starts with upload.wikimedia.org), the best approach is to use the "Instant-Commons" feature – which lets you directly use the standard image syntax to display images found on Wikimedia Commons. If you have InstantCommons enabled, and have a call that looks like "`[[Image:Rocking horse.jpg|...]]`", MediaWiki will first look for an image named "Rocking horse.jpg" on your wiki; and, if it doesn't find one, will look for that file name on Wikimedia Commons, and display that one if it finds it there. You can enable InstantCommons just by adding the following to Lo-calSettings.php:

```
$wgUseInstantCommons = true;
```

Chapter 8

User registration and management

Registration

By default, user registration in MediaWiki is fairly simple: for users who are not logged in, at the top of each page is either (for MediaWiki 1.20 and up) two links, reading "Create account" and "Log in", or one link reading "Log in / create account". It's a fairly small difference, since each of those two pages links to the other anyway.

If you click on either "Log in" or "Log in / create account", you'll see a screen that looks like Figure 8.1.

If you click on the "Create account" link, either from this screen or (if it's there) from the top of any page, you'll see something like Figure 8.2.

There is no demographic or questionnaire information solicited; just the essential fields of username and password, plus optional fields for email address and real name (and, if you're using MediaWiki 1.22 or later, a bit of automatic promotional text). And if you have the anti-spam ConfirmEdit extension installed (see page 132), you will probably also see some form of CAPTCHA there.

The email address field is recommended for all users to fill in, since it allows for notification and messaging. As an administrator, you can require users to enter and confirm an email address before they can read or edit on the wiki, if you want, by using the "emailconfirmed" group (see next section).

What about the "Real name" field? That's not a very important field, but it can

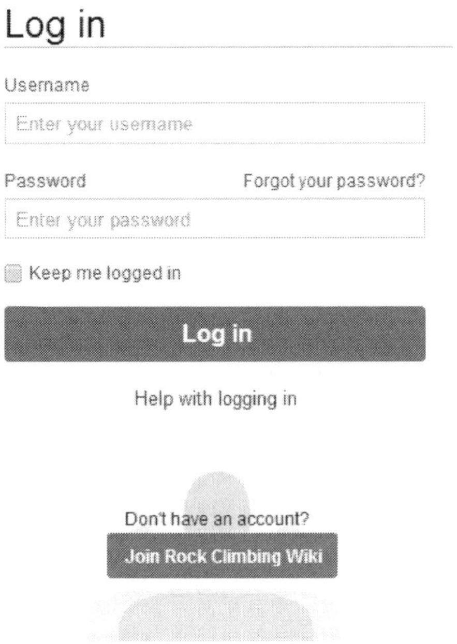

Figure 8.1: Login screen for a fictional wiki

be nice to fill in if your username is different from your real name, but you still want people to know what your real name is. Other users can view it if they go to the "action=credits" URL for a specific page (this has to be typed in manually; it's not linked from anywhere). On Wikipedia and other Wikimedia sites, this action is disabled, for privacy reasons. (Most likely the disabling was done using the $wgActions setting.)

There are also various extensions that allow for displaying real names in different formats; you can see listing of these extensions here:

> https://www.mediawiki.org/wiki/Category:Real_name_display_
> extensions

If, as an administrator, you want users to fill in more information about themselves when they register, there's at least one extension that allows that: SemanticSignup, which also requires the Semantic MediaWiki and Semantic Forms extensions. You can read more about SemanticSignup here:

> https://www.mediawiki.org/wiki/Extension:SemanticSignup

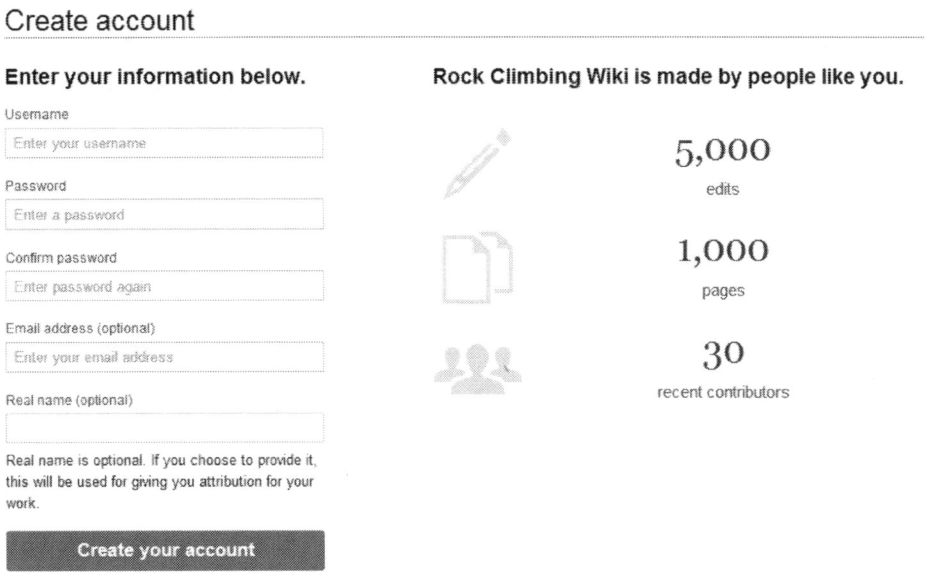

Create account

Enter your information below.

Username

[Enter your username]

Password

[Enter a password]

Confirm password

[Enter password again]

Email address (optional)

[Enter your email address]

Real name (optional)

[   ]

Real name is optional. If you choose to provide it, this will be used for giving you attribution for your work.

Create your account

Rock Climbing Wiki is made by people like you.

5,000

edits

1,000

pages

30

recent contributors

Figure 8.2: "Create account" screen for a fictional wiki

Another extension, ConfirmAccount, requires potential users to fill in more information about themselves – for the purpose of getting approval to become a user. See page 79 for more detail.

Usernames

In general, MediaWiki is very flexible about the username users can choose – it can include nearly any Unicode character, including spaces. There are some restrictions, though: usernames of course have to be unique, and they can't contain any of the reserved characters that page names can't contain, plus a few more. Here is the main list of characters not allowed in usernames:

< > [ ] | { } / @

There are also various control characters, and unusual whitespace characters, which usernames can't contain. And you can't create a username that spoofs a MediaWiki page name with a namespace, like "Help:Contents", or spoofs an IP address, like "123.45.67.89" (the latter is because the IP address is used as an identifier for users who are not logged in).

Also, a username cannot be longer than 40 characters.

Finally, usernames cannot start with a lowercase letter – if you register a username that stars with a lowercase letter, the first letter will get automatically capitalized. That holds true even if lowercase first letters in page names are enabled, using "$wgCapitalLinks = true".

User groups and permissions

All user-rights management in MediaWiki is done via "groups", and not for individual users. You can't assign permissions to an individual wiki user – instead, you put users in different groups, with each having its own set of permissions.

Default user groups

By default, there are three defined groups to which users can be added: "sysop", "bureaucrat" and "bot".

"sysop" is a misnamed group – sysops don't do anything with administering the server on which the wiki resides, as you might think from the name; instead, they simply administer wiki content. "administrator" would be a much more accurate name, and in fact the term "administrator" is how it is referred to in the web interface, but behind the scenes it's still called "sysop". Sysops/administrators, by default, can perform the main administrative tasks on wikis: deleting pages, "protecting" pages (so that some or all non-sysop users can't edit them), blocking users, etc.

The main right of the "bureaucrat" group, by default, is to be able to assign users to different groups.

The "bot" group is meant to be reserved for user accounts that are actually automated scripts, which perform various actions. Bots are prevalent on Wikipedia, but are rare on most smaller wikis. You can read about bots on page 151.

There are three more implicit groups, which users can't be added to or removed from but simply belong to: "user", "autoconfirmed" and "emailconfirmed". Once a user registers with a username, they're defined as a "user"; once they've been in the system for long enough and have made enough edits (both values are settable) they're also in "autoconfirmed", and once they confirm an email address, they're in "emailconfirmed" as well.

When a wiki is first set up, an initial account is created: by default it's called "Wiki-Sysop". This account initially belongs to both the "sysops" and "bureaucrats" group, so anyone logged in as WikiSysop can make other users administrators and bureaucrats as well, thus setting up the whole user structure.

The page Special:UserRights is the page with which bureaucrats (by default) can change any user's group memberships. Figure 8.3 shows one example of how it could appear.

User rights management

```
┌─ Manage user groups ──────────────────────────────────────────────┐
│                                                                    │
│   Enter a username: [Gina Gonzalez        ]   [ Edit user groups ] │
│                                                                    │
└────────────────────────────────────────────────────────────────────┘

┌─ Edit user groups ────────────────────────────────────────────────┐
│                                                                    │
│   Changing user rights of user Gina Gonzalez (Talk | contribs)     │
│   You may alter the groups this user is in:                        │
│     • A checked box means the user is in that group.               │
│     • An unchecked box means the user is not in that group.        │
│     • A * indicates that you cannot remove the group once you have added it, or vice versa. │
│   Member of: Bureaucrats                                           │
│   Implicit member of: Autoconfirmed users                          │
│                                                                    │
│   Groups you can change                                            │
│     ☐ bot                                                          │
│     ☐ administrator                                                │
│     ☑ bureaucrat                                                   │
│     ☐ Widget editor                                                │
│                                                                    │
│   Reason: [                                              ]          │
│           [ Save user groups ]                                     │
│                                                                    │
└────────────────────────────────────────────────────────────────────┘
```

Figure 8.3: Special:UserRights page

Setting permissions

How are the permissions of each user group set? That's done through the LocalSettings.php file, and the variable $wgGroupPermissions. Every permission that can be set has its own name, which is usually the name of the action that would be performed. To set whether the a certain user group can perform a certain action, the general form in LocalSettings.php is:

$wgGroupPermissions['*group name*']['*action name*'] = *true/false*;

For instance, by default, only sysops/administrators can delete pages. The action for deleting pages is called, as you would expect, 'delete'. So, to allow bureaucrats to also delete pages, you would need to add the following line to LocalSettings.php:

```
$wgGroupPermissions['bureaucrat']['delete'] = true;
```

Creating new groups

And how do you add a new group? That's actually very simple: as soon as a group is referred to in LocalSettings.php, within a "$wgGroupPermissions" call, it gets defined within the system if it wasn't defined already. So, for instance, suppose you want to create a new user group, "blocker", whose only special rights are the ability to block and unblock users. You would just have to add the following to LocalSettings.php:

```
$wgGroupPermissions['blocker']['block'] = true;
```

When they're first created, new groups don't have any members. So, once you created the "blocker" group, you would presumably use the page Special:UserRights to start adding users to that group.

Common permissions settings

In addition to specific group names, you can use the value '*' to refer to everyone, including non-logged-in users, if the wiki has them. This comes in handy when removing rights that by default are available to everyone. So if you want to make editing of pages available only to logged-in users (a common setting), you can just add the following two lines:

```
$wgGroupPermissions['*']['edit'] = false;
$wgGroupPermissions['user']['edit'] = true;
```

Similarly, to disallow viewing of the site by anyone not logged in, you would add:

```
$wgGroupPermissions['*']['read'] = false;
$wgGroupPermissions['user']['read'] = true;
```

Another somewhat-common setting is to turn off user registration on the wiki, so that only administrators can add new users. This is again accomplished with just two lines:

```
$wgGroupPermissions['*']['createaccount'] = false;
$wgGroupPermissions['sysop']['createaccount'] = true;
```

There are actually dozens of settable MediaWiki permissions, defined within both core MediaWiki and many of its extensions. Some of these are covered in this book, but a complete list of all MediaWiki permissions can be found at:

> https://www.mediawiki.org/wiki/Manual:User_rights

Restricting the viewing and editing of specific pages or sections in the wiki is covered on page 136.

Creating user accounts

This section does not cover standard MediaWiki registration, but rather existing users creating additional user accounts. For public wikis in which anyone can sign up, or private wikis in which anyone within the relevant network can sign up, that's not a very important feature – if someone wants an account on the system, they can just create one themselves. However, there are cases when you want closed registration – where only existing users, or only administrators, can create an account. The way to create an additional account, when you're logged in, is to simply go to the "Create an account" page. If you're logged in, that page is not linked from the top of pages, but you can reach it by going to Special:UserLogin and clicking on "create an account" – or going directly to the URL "Special:UserLogin?type=signup". And if you have the Admin Links extension installed (see page 147), this URL is included directly in that page of links.

The permissions around creating user accounts are governed by the 'createaccount' right. So, for instance, to allow only administrators to create new user accounts, you would add the following to LocalSettings.php:

```
$wgGroupPermissions['*']['createaccount'] = false;
$wgGroupPermissions['sysop']['createaccount'] = true;
```

If you did that, you should presumably include at least an email address on the wiki, for people to write to to request an account – this makes sense whether the wiki is public or internal. But the best approach is probably to use the ConfirmAccount extension, which provides a form to let potential new users request a user account. As part of the request, they can supply some information about themselves. When a request happens, an administrator can be notified by email; once an admin approves the request (from within the wiki), the new account is created automatically. The whole process works quite well in practice. You can find download and installation information about ConfirmAccount at its homepage:

> https://www.mediawiki.org/wiki/Extension:ConfirmAccount

Another extension which can be used either instead of or in addition to ConfirmAccount is InviteSignup, which lets administrators, and potentially regular users as well, send out invites to other people to join the wiki, using just their email address. Invitees can then go to the site and automatically sign up, choosing their own username and password:

> https://www.mediawiki.org/wiki/Extension:InviteSignup

InviteSignup is somewhat the mirror image of ConfirmAccount: they both require both a wiki user and an outsider to agree to the outsider's joining, but with ConfirmAccount the process is initiated by the potential new user, while with InviteSignup it's initiated by the existing user.

OpenID and other login integration systems

OpenID is an exciting technology that aims to solve a chronic issue on the web: the proliferation of user accounts and passwords. The concept is that a user can associate their accounts on websites with a standard "identity provider", like Google, Yahoo! etc.

OpenID was invented in 2005, but it only started to gain real acceptance a few years later, with companies like Google, Microsoft and Yahoo! starting to offer support for it in 2008. It has been seen steadily increasing in usage since then, although it remains a relatively unknown technology. In 2014, a more powerful version was released, called "OpenID Connect". The software remains in flux, and hopefully, its best days are yet to come.

You can use OpenID on your MediaWiki website, by installing the extension that's appropriately also called "OpenID":

> https://www.mediawiki.org/wiki/Extension:OpenID

If you install it, users who are not logged in will see an OpenID link at the top of every page – next to the "Log in / create account" link will be a link that reads "Log in / create account with OpenID". If they click on that, they will see the interface shown in Figure 8.4.

Figure 8.4: OpenID login/registration screen

This interface allows users to easily create a MediaWiki account that's associated with an account from one of the 12 OpenID providers whose icons are shown (the bottom set of icons includes sites such as LiveJournal and Flickr). Users just have to click the relevant icon and follow the instructions.

A user who creates an account can choose any username within MediaWiki (provided it's not taken already) – there doesn't have to be a connection between their username in the OpenID provider system and the one they choose for the wiki.

There are a number of OpenID configurations that one can make, but the most important one is to be able to set OpenID as the only login option; so that users will not see the regular "Log in / create account" link. You can do this by adding the following to LocalSettings.php:

```
$wgOpenIDOnly = true;
```

The "OpenID only" setting has a very useful benefit, which is that it seems to stop spammers entirely (provided one also restricts editing to logged-in users).

You can also use the OpenID extension to turn your wiki into an OpenID provider/server, not just an OpenID consumer, but this is very rarely done.

In addition to OpenID, there are other protocols that can be used to allow users to log in using existing accounts, available via different extensions:

- The **LDAP Authentication** extension lets users log in via LDAP accounts:

  https://www.mediawiki.org/wiki/Extension:LDAP_Authentication

This is especially helpful for internal wikis that want to make use of an existing LDAP server (most commonly, using Microsoft's Active Directory) that stores a personnel directory.

- The **Facebook Open Graph** extension lets users register and log in to MediaWiki with their Facebook accounts:

    https://www.mediawiki.org/wiki/Extension:Facebook

- The **TwitterLogin** extension lets users register and log in with their Twitter accounts:

    https://www.mediawiki.org/wiki/Extension:TwitterLogin

  To use this extension, you need to register your site with Twitter as a Twitter app.

- The **Persona** extension lets users log in using Mozilla Persona, which is a generic authentication protocol similar in concept to OpenID:

    https://www.mediawiki.org/wiki/Extension:Persona

- The **OAuth** protocol is similar in spirit to OpenID, but differs in some key ways. It's not yet possible to log in to MediaWiki via OAuth, but there's a project in place to allow this. You can see its current status here:

    https://www.mediawiki.org/wiki/OAuth

Blocking and deleting users

Administrators can block other users from editing, which is extremely useful when dealing with spammers, vandals, and (to a more limited extent) people who make too many poor edits. Blocking is governed by the 'block' permission.

Blocking is done at the page Special:Block, which you can go to directly, although for administrators it's also linked to from each row in both the RecentChanges page and in history pages. Figure 8.5 shows the interface viewable at Special:Block.

You can specify either a username or an IP address to block; if the user in question is making edits without being logged in, then you will of course have to specify

Block user

Use the form below to block write access from a specific IP address or username. This should be done only to prevent vandalism, and in accordance with policy. Fill in a specific reason below (for example, citing particular pages that were vandalized).

```
┌─ Block user ──────────────────────────────────────────────────────┐
│                                                                    │
│    IP address or  ┌──────────────────────────────────┐            │
│       username:   └──────────────────────────────────┘            │
│                                                                    │
│         Expiry:   ┌Other time: ▾┐                                 │
│                   └─────────────┘                                  │
│                   ┌──────────────────────────────────┐            │
│                   └──────────────────────────────────┘            │
│                                                                    │
│         Reason:   ┌Other                        ▾┐                │
│                   └──────────────────────────────┘                │
│                   ┌──────────────────────────────────┐            │
│                   └──────────────────────────────────┘            │
│                                                                    │
│              ☑ Prevent account creation                           │
│              ☐ Prevent user from sending e-mail                   │
│              ☑ Automatically block the last IP address used by this user, and any │
│                subsequent IP addresses they try to edit from      │
│              ☐ Watch this user's user and talk pages              │
│              ☐ Prevent logged-in users from editing from this IP address │
│   ┌─────────────────┐                                             │
│   │ Block this user │                                             │
│   └─────────────────┘                                             │
└────────────────────────────────────────────────────────────────────┘
```

Unblock a username or IP address | View existing blocks | Edit block reasons

Figure 8.5: Special:Block page

their IP address. In reality, it shouldn't matter which you do, as long as you keep the "Automatically block the last IP address used by this user..." checkbox checked (which you should, assuming that this is a true malicious user and not just someone that you temporarily want to send a message to).

The checkbox defaults are generally good; however, it's usually a good idea to check the last checkbox as well, "Prevent logged-in users from editing from this IP address". Spammers can sometimes register hundreds of accounts, then wait until months or even years later to attack with them. If you select that checkbox, all those accounts could potentially be neutralized, which would be a big win.

Sometimes, spammers and malicious users can use a whole range of IP addresses, such as any address that starts with "123.45", or "123.45.67". (Even if they're always logged in when making edits, you can still find out their IP address if you're an administrator – see page 150.) If that's the case, blocking individual IP addresses will probably be ineffectual. Thankfully, the Block page also lets you block an entire range of IP addresses, which can end up being a real lifesaver. To do that, you can simply specify a range instead of a single IP address in the "IP address or username" field. For the first example, you could enter "123.45.0.0 – 123.45.255.255".

For what it's worth, there's a whole syntax you can use for IP range blocks, beyond the simple "a – b" formulation – it's all described here:

https://www.mediawiki.org/wiki/Help:Range_blocks

The "Expiry" field dictates how long the user will be blocked for – this can always be changed later. With spammers and egregious vandals, the best approach is to block them "Indefinitely", i.e. forever.

Conversely, if you want to unblock a user, IP address or IP range, you should go to the page Special:BlockList - that will show the complete list of blocks that have been made on this wiki, in chronological order; with links to undo any of them.

On wikis with closed registration, blocking a user would ideally prevent them from being able to read any of the contents as well. Unfortunately, that's not the case – and there's no "block from reading" or "block from logging in" action, nor does there appear to be an extension to do it. But if you have a closed wiki, and want that ability, adding the following to LocalSettings.php should do the trick:

```
$wgHooks['UserGetRights'][] = 'blockFromReading';
static function blockFromReading( $user, &$rights ) {

    if ( $user->isBlocked() ) {

        foreach ( $rights as $i => $right ) {

            if ( $right === 'read' ) {

                unset( $rights[$i] );
                break;

            }
            return true;

        }

    }

}
```

For obviously malevolent user accounts – like when spammers register with lots of accounts in quick succession – it would be great to not just block these accounts but delete them. Unfortunately, there's no extremely easy way to do it. MediaWiki itself doesn't offer the ability to delete accounts at all; for that, you'll need the UserMerge extension:

> http://www.mediawiki.org/wiki/Extension:UserMerge

It lets you merge two user accounts together, with one of the accounts then getting deleted. So to delete a group of accounts, you would need to keep merging them in, one at a time, into a single account – a manual process that may be too slow to run for a large group of accounts.

Chapter 9

Browsing and searching

Viewing the set of all pages

MediaWiki provides a standard way of seeing the entire set of pages in the wiki: the special page Special:AllPages. It lets you view an alphabetical list of pages in the wiki for each namespace, other than "Special:" – that includes all the namespaces, so you can also view categories, templates, files, etc. Figure 9.1 shows the top of the page Special:AllPages for mediawiki.org.

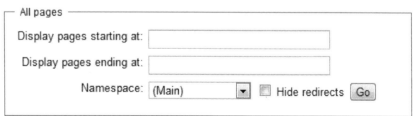

Figure 9.1: Special:AllPages on mediawiki.org

The listing of page ranges in Figure 9.1 keeps going like that for another 10 lines.

Clicking on any of those names will display a list of all the pages within that row's alphabetical range; that list is separated into three columns.

You can also use the form at the top to display a manual list of pages within a certain alphabetical range.

For pages in the "File:" namespace, i.e. pages for uploaded files, there's an alternate way to see them listed: the page Special:ListFiles. This special page has an advantage over Special:AllPages in that it also shows a thumbnail image for each file.

Figure 9.2 shows how the page Special:ListFiles looks on mediawiki.org.

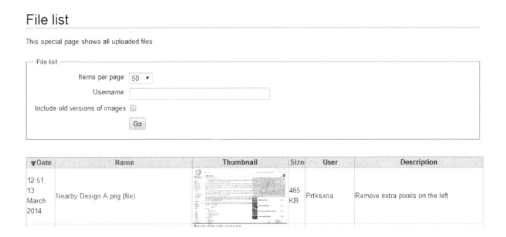

Figure 9.2: Special:ListFiles on mediawiki.org

For each file, the following information is shown: the date it was uploaded, or last uploaded if more than one version has been uploaded; a thumbnail of the file if it's an image; its size; the user who last uploaded it; and a description of the file, if one was submitted during the upload. The name of each file is a link to that file's page in the "File:" namespace, while the subsequent "(file)" link is a link directly to that file.

Searching

MediaWiki search functionality is available via its search bar, which in the Vector skin shows up on the top of the page (Figure 9.3).

When a user does a search, they are sent to the page Special:Search, which handles all the actual search functionality. This page lets the user modify their search term, as well as change the set of namespaces that are being searched.

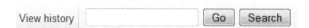

Figure 9.3: Search bar in the Vector skin

Within Special:Search, assuming you're using the Vector skin, if the user runs their search and then clicks on the "Advanced" link, they will see an interface like the one shown in Figure 9.4.

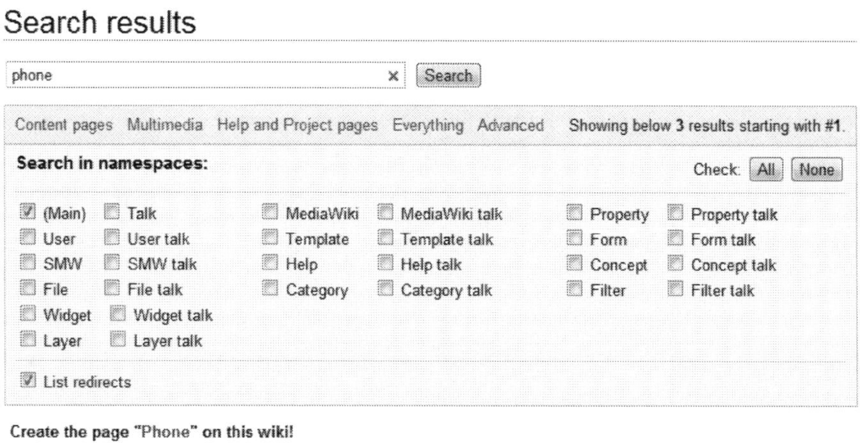

Search results

phone   × Search

Content pages Multimedia Help and Project pages Everything Advanced   Showing below **3** results starting with **#1**.

Search in namespaces: Check: All None

☑ (Main)   ☐ Talk   ☐ MediaWiki   ☐ MediaWiki talk   ☐ Property   ☐ Property talk
☐ User   ☐ User talk   ☐ Template   ☐ Template talk   ☐ Form   ☐ Form talk
☐ SMW   ☐ SMW talk   ☐ Help   ☐ Help talk   ☐ Concept   ☐ Concept talk
☐ File   ☐ File talk   ☐ Category   ☐ Category talk   ☐ Filter   ☐ Filter talk
☐ Widget   ☐ Widget talk
☐ Layer   ☐ Layer talk

☑ List redirects

Create the page "Phone" on this wiki!

Figure 9.4: Special:Search page

Searches always start out being done only for namespaces defined as being "content namespaces", which by default is just the main (blank) namespace. As an administrator, you can change that by adding to $wgContentNamespaces. For instance, to also get pages in the "Help:" namespace to be searched, you would add the following to LocalSettings.php:

```
$wgContentNamespaces = array( NS_MAIN, NS_HELP );
```

Each link changes the set of namespaces being searched. MediaWiki's search interface is case-insensitive. If a user enters text in the search box that exactly matches the name of a page, they will be sent directly to that page. Which is usually the right behavior; but what if the user wants to instead search on that text? This could be more obvious in the interface, but the way for the user to do it is to type in the search string, then wait

for the autocompletion dropdown to show up, and select the last item, "containing…
search-string".

There's another nice feature related to search: having autocompletion within the
search input, based on page names in the wiki. You can see this behavior in Wikipedia,
if you start typing text in the search box. Starting with MediaWiki 1.20, this is the
default behavior. For earlier versions of MediaWiki, you can enable it by adding the
following to LocalSettings.php:

```
$wgEnableMWSuggest = true;
```

Installing another search engine

MediaWiki's default search simply uses SQL querying. It's not bad, although it is
sometimes criticized as primitive. Notably, it lacks the ability to find alternate spellings
of words. It also ignores any advanced search-engine syntax, though it does support
the most common syntax, of putting phrases in quotations to indicate that they should
show up exactly as written.

There are three search engine applications that can be be substituted in to Media-
Wiki in place of the default one: Lucene, Sphinx and Elasticsearch. All three have
features that the regular MediaWiki search doesn't, like checking for misspellings, and
all three are open source. Lucene is the best-known one, and it's the one used by default on Wikipedia. Sphinx is less powerful, but easier to install. Elasticsearch is the
newest (to MediaWiki, that is), and in terms of its handling within MediaWiki, it may
be the best. It has some advantages in terms of speed and support for non-Latin characters, but its biggest advantage over the other solutions is that it searches on the text
of pages when the templates are fully expanded, not on the raw wikitext. It's currently
available as an optional "beta feature" on Wikipedia.

If you want to use Lucene, there are two ways to add it to MediaWiki. The standard
way is by installing the extensions Lucene-search and MWSearch. Lucene-search is
not really an extension, though it's billed that way: it's just the code for Lucene itself,
installed on Wikimedia's code repository. Lucene is written in Java, so you'll need Java
installed as well. MWSearch is the actual MediaWiki extension that connects the search
input to the Lucene back end.

The other way is to install the SolrStore extension, which works with Apache Solr (a
search platform that includes Lucene), as well as with Semantic MediaWiki. SolrStore
allows for both free-text searches and SMW property-based searches. Unfortunately,

the extension doesn't currently allow for searching on misspellings and synonyms, as Lucene/MWSearch does.

You can see the three extensions here:

> https://www.mediawiki.org/wiki/Extension:Lucene-search
> https://www.mediawiki.org/wiki/Extension:MWSearch
> https://www.mediawiki.org/wiki/Extension:SolrStore

To add Sphinx instead, you need to install Sphinx, as well as the SphinxSearch MediaWiki extension. You can view that one here:

> https://www.mediawiki.org/wiki/Extension:SphinxSearch

Finally, there's the Elasticsearch engine, which is available via the MediaWiki extension called CirrusSearch:

> https://www.mediawiki.org/wiki/Extension:CirrusSearch

CirrusSearch was only released in June 2013, but given its advantages, it may well become the standard MediaWiki search extension before too long.

One common request is the ability to search through uploaded files, such as Word documents and PDFs. This functionality is available, although currently it's tricky to set up, and costs money. You have to install the SearchBlox application (not open source, and not free), and then use the SearchBlox extension:

> https://www.mediawiki.org/wiki/Extension:SearchBlox

Both the Lucene and Elasticsearch engines natively provide support for searching through such documents, though, so perhaps it's just a matter of time until such functionality is easily available through one or more of the extensions above.

Using an outside search engine

The other possibility for search is to use an outside search engine, and the overwhelming favorite for this option is Google. Google provides an easy-to-install "custom search" functionality, which is documented at:

> http://www.google.com/cse/

The usual approach to installing it in MediaWiki is to use the extension "Google Custom Search Engine", which lets you place the input for this custom search anywhere on the page, including in place of the existing search input:

https://www.mediawiki.org/wiki/Extension:Google_Custom_Search_
Engine

There are a few advantages to using Google's search in place of an internal one: Google's search interface is top-notch, and it's also very well-known to people. And instead of searching through the wikitext, as most internal MediaWiki search options will do, a Google search will look at what's actually displayed on the page – which in some cases could be quite different, especially if extensions like Widgets or External Data are used.

There are also some downsides, though: this setup only works for public wikis, unless you're willing to pay to install a local Google search engine on your site. And it will take some time for Google (or any other outside engine) to see changes to your wiki, so recent edits will most likely not show up in search results.

Chapter 10

Monitoring the wiki

Recent changes

The page Special:RecentChanges is extremely important; as you might guess, it shows the latest set of changes to the wiki. By default, it's linked to from the sidebar, and it's publicly-viewable. And by default, it shows the latest 50 changes, over the last seven days, and changes made by bot users (page 151) are not shown. These settings can be changed within the interface itself, and the defaults can be modified by an administrator, though in general these defaults work fine.

Minor edits are shown with an "m", and newly-created pages are shown with an "N"; and for every edit, the page name, revision time, user, edit summary (if any) and the number of bytes that were added or removed in this revision are shown. The display is similar to the history page (page 17).

You can make the display of the Recent Changes page slightly more sophisticated, by going to your Preferences page, selecting the "Recent changes" tab, and then checking the option "Group changes by page in recent changes and watchlist" (and saving). This will group together all recent changes to any one page on one line – so that, if there are many edits to a single page, it doesn't end up overwhelming the Recent Changes display.

The Recent Changes page is crucial for monitoring recent activity. Conveniently, it's also available as a feed, using Atom, which means that you can just add the feed to your RSS reader (if you use one, that is – and if you don't, they're highly recommended). Then you will be automatically notified of all new edits at the same time that you check your news, etc. You can just go to the Recent Changes page and get the URL of the "Atom" link from the sidebar.

Watchlist

For larger wikis, monitoring recent changes is unwieldy – if there are more than, say, 10-20 edits a day, it becomes untenable to try to monitor all activity, every day. That's when another page becomes crucial: the Watchlist page, at Special:Watchlist.

Every user has their own watchlist, which others can't see. You can add pages to your watchlist in various ways:

- There's a "watch" tab at the top every page, which lets you add that page to the watchlist (or, if it's already on your watchlist, remove it). On Wikipedia, this is instead just a clickable star icon – that's a nice interface enhancement available by adding the following to LocalSettings.php:

    ```
    $wgVectorUseIconWatch = true;
    ```

    It only works when using the Vector skin, however.

- When you edit a page, you can check the "Watch this page" checkbox, which adds that page to your watchlist. This checkbox is checked by default if you're creating a new page.

- You can directly edit the set of watched pages at Special:EditWatchlist/raw. You can also use the interface at Special:EditWatchlist, although that one only allows for removing pages, not adding them. Both pages are linked to from the top of Special:Watchlist.

Logs

Most of the non-editing administrative changes, like the blocking of users, are logged, so that the history of those changes is preserved. (In most cases, these actions also show up in the Recent Changes page.) Each type of action is contained within its own log. You can see all of the logs at the page Special:Log, which is publicly-viewable.

Actions that are logged include creation of user accounts, blocking of users, page moves, page deletions, page protections, page imports, and file uploads. Some extensions also define their own additional logs, including Approved Revs, FlaggedRevs and LiquidThreads.

Statistics

The Statistics page, at Special:Statistics, holds some nice top-level information about the wiki: the number of pages, the number of edits, the number of users in the various user groups, and so on. Figure 10.1 shows the top of the Statistics page for media-wiki.org.

Statistics

Page statistics	
Content pages At MediaWiki.org, only the main, manual and extension namespaces are counted as content namespaces.	13,854
Pages This includes "talk" pages, pages discussing the site, minimal "stub" pages, redirects, and others that probably don't qualify as content pages. (All pages in the wiki, including talk pages, redirects, etc.)	158,312
Uploaded files	2,333
Edit statistics	
Page edits since MediaWiki was set up	1,049,079
Average edits per page	6.63
User statistics	
Registered users	1,390,442
Active users (list of members) (Users who have performed an action in the last 30 days)	1,093
Bots (list of members)	29
Administrators (list of members)	158
Bureaucrats (list of members)	30

Figure 10.1: Special:Statistics page on mediawiki.org

Note the distinction between "Content pages" and regular "Pages". The text that explains the two here is specific to mediawiki.org, though it's fairly similar to the default text. This is often a cause of confusion, because the number given for "Content pages" tends to undercount the true number of content pages. This number only includes pages within the "content namespaces" (by default, this is only the main namespace, though that's settable via $wgContentNamespaces). And it only counts pages that contain at least one wiki-link. Pages that don't are considered "stubs", and not counted. It's not a perfect system, and it can end up undercounting severely, depending on the type of content you have.

Chapter 11

Extensions

A crucial part of the MediaWiki system is the plugins, or extensions, that have been developed to be added to the MediaWiki core application. Over 1,500 publicly-released extensions exist in some form currently; though many of these are obsolete or redundant, and many never fully worked in the first place, so the number of extensions that could conceivably be used at any one time is probably closer to several hundred. Extensions in MediaWiki cover a very wide range of functionality. Some of it is rather essential functionality, which could easily belong directly within MediaWiki but was never added for one reason or another. An example is the Cite extension, which defines tags that can be used to show footnoted references; it's heavily used on Wikipedia, and there's no strong reason why it's not part of core MediaWiki.

Almost all MediaWiki installations include at least a few extensions; Wikipedia uses dozens of them.

The core MediaWiki code is structured in a way that makes it easy to install extensions, and develop them: the key element is the widespread use of hooks. Hooks are lines in the code that outside functions can register themselves to be called at. When a hook runs, every function that has registered itself with that hook is called, and each one can then perform its own actions. A simple example of the use of hooks would be an extension that displays ads on each wiki page. The extension would most likely register with one or more hooks in the code that are called when the the display of the page is generated, in order to add its own snippets of HTML to the page. The big advantage of hooks is that they let extensions run without the administrator having to modify the core MediaWiki code – something that makes installing and upgrading the code much easier.

Some extensions define their own special pages; some define their own parser functions, tags, behavior switches, etc.; and some add their own tables to the database. The more involved extensions may do all of these things: use hooks, add tables to the database, define special pages to (in some cases) display and modify their data, and define various commands, like parser functions and the rest.

Finding extensions

This book covers a fairly large number of extensions, but it doesn't cover all of them – and the "ecosystem" of extensions keeps changing, with new extensions being created, others becoming unnecessary due to changes in MediaWiki, and others becoming unusable as they stop being maintained. So it's important to know how to find extensions, and how to determine which ones are useful.

The site mediawiki.org is the main resource for finding out about extensions. Every extension is meant to have a page there, so you can do text searches to find specific functionality you're looking for. You can also use the "Extension Matrix", which is actually a collection of pages, which hold different views of the full collection of extensions:

> https://www.mediawiki.org/wiki/Extension_Matrix

If you do find an extension, it's useful to know whether it will work on your system. There are a few clues you can use for that. Every extension page should have an infobox, listing important information about that extension. One of the fields is "Status", which can be either "Experimental", "Unstable", "Beta", "Stable" or "Unknown", with "Stable" of course being the preferred one. This status is usually just set by the extension's authors, though, so it may be out-of-date, and it may not have been reliable in the first place.

Extension pages usually also list what versions of MediaWiki the extension is compatible with. This information can again be out of date (especially if it reads something like "MediaWiki 1.11 and higher"), but it can also be useful information.

A good way to check the viability of an extension is to look at its talk page. If the extension hasn't worked with versions of MediaWiki from the last two years, there will probably be at least a few messages to that effect. You can also get a sense from the talk page of how committed the authors or maintainers are to maintaining the code and supporting users.

Conversely, if there are no or few talk-page messages, that's quite possibly a sign that people don't find the extension useful (or comprehensible).

Finally, whether or not an extension's code is contained on the MediaWiki Git repository is to some extent, for reasons of both cause and effect, an indicator of how well-maintained it is.

Installing extensions

Once you've found an extension that you want to use, the next step is of course to install it. Many applications make it easy to install extensions or plugins, directly from within the user interface – that includes both consumer applications like Firefox, and server-side applications like WordPress. MediaWiki, unfortunately, is not one of them – code has to be downloaded and installed manually. Adding a simple extension installation system to MediaWiki is something that many people have talked about, including both users and developers, and there have even been a few attempts to create such a system, but none of them have worked out yet. Hopefully such a thing will be created before too long.

So for now you will have to get the code for each extension yourself, in one way or another. How you do this depends on the extension, as well as on your system. Until 2012, MediaWiki and most of its extensions were stored on a repository that used the version-control software Subversion, otherwise known as SVN. In 2012, MediaWiki moved to a repository that uses Git, an alternate version-control system. Most of the MediaWiki extensions have moved as well, including nearly all of the actively-maintained ones. Still, a few extensions remain on SVN, and there are some extensions whose code is elsewhere – hosted with GitHub, Google Code or SourceForge, or in many cases (though this is not recommended), directly on the extensions' wiki pages on mediawiki.org

If you have Git on your server, and the extension you want to install can be downloaded with one of those, then that's the ideal way to do it. If you don't have Git and thus can't automatically download an extension, there are a few alternatives. One is to get the extension as part of a package or bundle. There are several bundles of MediaWiki extensions; of special note is Semantic Bundle:

https://www.mediawiki.org/wiki/Semantic_Bundle

It's a package of around 15 extensions, based around Semantic MediaWiki. Many, though not all, of the extensions described in detail in this book are contained in Semantic Bundle.

Other packages of extensions include:

- BlueSpice (https://www.mediawiki.org/wiki/Extension:BlueSpice)

- semantic::apps (https://www.semantic-apps.com/en/Main_Page)

Besides downloading packages, you can also usually download extensions directly. One easy way to download extensions was via the "Extension Distributor":

> https://www.mediawiki.org/wiki/Special:ExtensionDistributor

It's a page on mediawiki.org that creates a downloadable file on the fly, for any extension that's in the SVN MediaWiki repository, and any applicable version of MediaWiki. However, for most extensions, these files represent a random snapshot that may not actually hold a working set of code (for instance, if someone made some bad change to the code right before the snapshot was made).

For extensions on the MediaWiki Git repository, though, Wikimedia provides a standard web-based Git code-review tool, called Gerrit, which lets you download a "snapshot" version of the code at any moment in time, including the latest version. This is a very convenient feature. This book won't get into the details of Gerrit, but it's a powerful tool for dealing with versioned code, if unfortunately not always the most user-friendly.

Finally, some extensions, especially ones not hosted on a MediaWiki repository, provide a downloadable file directly.

For the next part of this chapter, we'll go over some of the useful MediaWiki extensions that didn't fit in anywhere else in this book. This is far from a comprehensive list.

Gadgets

"Gadgets" is one of the extensions that come pre-bundled in MediaWiki. It lets an administrator define pieces of JavaScript that users can then make use of, usually for help with editing or other wiki tasks. You can see the full list of gadgets installed on any wiki by going to that wiki's Special:Gadgets page, which lists all the gadgets and a brief description of each.

To install a gadget on a wiki, if it already exists on another wiki, go to that wiki's Special:Gadgets page, click on the gadget's "Export" link, and follow the instructions.

Any user can then use any installed gadget by going to the "Gadgets" tab within their Preferences page, checking the gadgets they want installed, and hitting "Save".

There are many gadgets defined; two notable ones, both available on Wikipedia, are:

- **Navigation popups** – lets users see the top contents of a page, and a menu of action items for that page, when they hover over a link to it. (This functionality is also available via an extension, "Hovercards" (https://www.mediawiki.org/wiki/Extension:Hovercards).)

- **HotCat** – provides autocompletion when adding or editing categories for a page.

You can read about the Gadgets extension here:

> https://www.mediawiki.org/wiki/Extension:Gadgets

There is a plan in place to make the installation of gadgets more automatic, via a central repository of gadgets – this may happen sometime in 2014. You can read more about this effort here:

> https://www.mediawiki.org/wiki/RL2#Gadget_Manager

CategoryTree

CategoryTree extension is another popular extension. It adds the ability to drill down into large category trees from within a single category page – it's used on Wikipedia for that purpose. Earlier there was an image of the default listing of subcategories in a category page; but Figure 11.1 shows that same display, with some of the subcategories "opened up" to show their own subcategories.

CategoryTree also lets you put, on any page, a similar collapsible, hierarchical list of categories, but this one also listing the pages that each category holds.

The CategoryTree homepage is at:

> https://www.mediawiki.org/wiki/Extension:CategoryTree

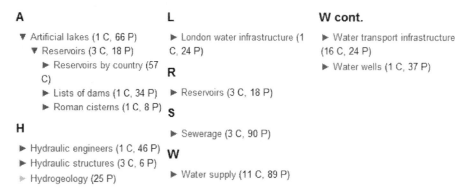

Figure 11.1: Hierarchical display of subcategories, enabled by CategoryTree extension

WYSIWYG editing extensions

Every software has its weaknesses, and for MediaWiki, there's very little question what the number one weakness is: the lack of a good WYSIWYG editor. WYSIWYG, which is pronounced "WIZ-ee-wig" and stands for "what you see is what you get", simply means that the content, when being edited, looks identical, or nearly identical, to how it appears when being viewed. This has been the standard approach in word-processing applications, like Microsoft Word or Google Docs, for decades; but for wiki applications, including MediaWiki, the track record is a lot spottier.

In reality, true WYSIWYG editing is impossible for MediaWiki, because its wikitext can include template calls and parser functions, two scripting-like features that, when displayed, can take almost any appearance – there's no way to mimic that display in the editing screen while still making the contents editable.

A WYSIWYG-style editor for MediaWiki, then, would have to take a split approach: true WYSIWYG for regular wikitext (including handling of bold, italics, headers, tables and the like), and some alternate approach for template calls, either by keeping them as straight text or by using some helper mechanism, such as forms, to let users add and edit them. (The Semantic Forms extension, discussed in detail in Chapter 17, provides a form-based approach for editing template calls.) Such an editor might better be described with the alternate acronym WYSIWYM, for "what you see is what you mean", which implies a looser connection between what's on the editing screen and what shows up on the page, though changes in the display are still done via the interface instead of by writing in syntax. Though it's less well-known, WYSIWYM is a standard approach for word-processing software; this book was in fact created with a WYSIWYM editing tool, LyX.

There's another complication when trying to implement WYSIWYG – or WYSIWYM – editing for MediaWiki, which is that the rules for MediaWiki's wikitext parsing have never been fully defined. Yes, we know that two single-quotes around text means italics, and three means bold, but what if a line of wikitext contains, say, a string of three single-quotes, then some text, then four single-quotes, then some other text, then five single-quotes? Currently, the handling for these kinds of cases is not precisely defined. The MediaWiki parser at the moment is an amalgam of rules, exceptions and counter-exceptions, and for a WYSIWYG editor to match the exact behavior of MediaWiki's parser in all cases would be quite difficult.

So, there are two big obstacles to getting such editing working in MediaWiki: scripting-style elements, and the lack of well-defined parsing rules. Still, there are some extensions that try to achieve it.

Until 2012 or so, the most well-known, and popular, WYSIWYG solution for MediaWiki was FCKeditor. FCKeditor was a general-purpose WYSIWYG application for web editing that was created in 2003 by Frederico Caldeira Knabben (hence the name).

There have been two MediaWiki extensions that support FCKeditor, both called "FCKeditor": one that was created in 2005 and was maintained until 2007; and the "official" FCKeditor extension, which was created in 2007 by the FCKeditor team. This official version is the one that has been widely used. FCKeditor itself, though, is a defunct application: in 2009, development on it ended, and its developers forked the software to a new application, called CKEditor (which apparently stands for "Content and Knowledge"). In 2011, the developers decided to stop maintaining the MediaWiki extension, on the grounds that FCKeditor is obsolete. The FCKeditor extension already doesn't work with more recent versions of MediaWiki, and seems doomed to become increasingly incompatible. There is an extension that supports CKEditor, appropriately called "WYSIWYG", which is part of the SMW+ software bundle. The development and maintenance of it, too, appears to have stopped, however (see page 244).

In any case, the FCKeditor- and CKEditor-based extensions share a common problem: they trip up when dealing with too much wikitext. Using any of them to edit a template page, for instance, will usually destroy the page beyond recognition.

VisualEditor

There's bright news on the horizon, though, with the VisualEditor extension, an ongoing project by the Wikimedia Foundation to create a true, built-in WYSIWYG/WYSIWYM solution within MediaWiki. This project is even more ambitious than it sounds, because VisualEditor is meant to be a standalone utility, that can be used by other web applications like WordPress.

Work on the VisualEditor extension began in May 2011, by a team consisting of some of the WMF's most experienced programmers. In July 2013, VE was made the default editing tool for the English-language Wikipedia, in a massive test of the software. Users experienced problems, however, with both slowness of loading time and occasional errors in the output, and after two months the old, standard editing was restored as a default, and VE became an "opt-in" editor instead. Over December 2013 and January 2014, it became the default, "opt-out" editing option for most of the small and mid-sized language Wikipedias, a situation that continues to this day.

Figure 11.2: The row of tabs in the Portuguese-language Wikipedia (pt.wikipedia.org)

Figure 11.2 shows the row of tabs for the Portuguese-language Wikipedia; "Editar" ("Edit") brings the user to the VisualEditor interface, while "Editar código-fonte" ("Edit source code") brings the user to the standard editing textarea.

Figures 11.3 and 11.4 show different aspects of VisualEditor in use, on the same article in the English-language Wikipedia: the standard editing interface, here used to edit a link (note how similar VE's display looks to standard MediaWiki page appearance), and the interface to edit a template call, here for the main infobox for the page.

VisualEditor has remaining problems in terms of speed, accuracy and browser coverage – at the time of this writing, Internet Explorer is not supported at all (the plan is to support IE 9 and higher). Nonetheless, it seems safe to predict that VisualEditor will become the default editing tool on the remaining Wikipedias – including the English-language one – within the next few years.

As for the usage of VisualEditor outside of Wikimedia wikis, at the moment it's minimal but growing. The page for the extension currently states, "Use at your own risk; it's not ready for production deployment except for experts!" That's in large part because the development of VE is tightly coupled with development on core Media-

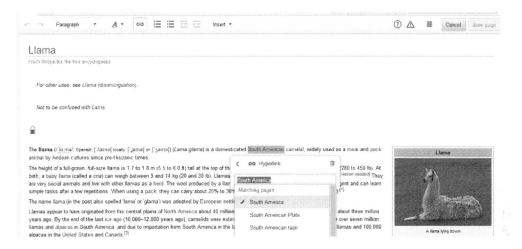

Figure 11.3: VisualEditor interface for editing a link

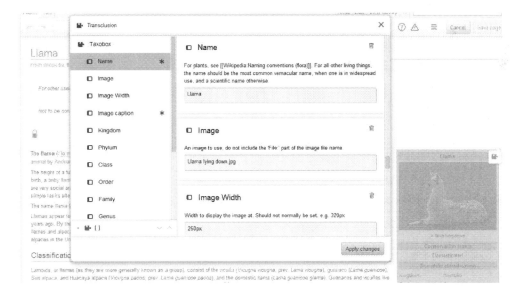

Figure 11.4: VisualEditor interface for editing an infobox template

Wiki. However, there may be a stable release of the extension by the end of 2014.

You can read more about VisualEditor and its current status here:

> https://www.mediawiki.org/wiki/VisualEditor

SocialProfile

Social networking in the enterprise is big business, with lots of companies wanting to add replicas of Facebook and the like to their internal network. Social networking can in theory encompass a lot of different features: messaging, user profiles, user groups, blogging, microblogging/"status updates", and so on. There are some that MediaWiki already has natively; talk pages are arguably one example.

The SocialProfile extension adds a variety of additional social networking features, and it has a number of spinoff extensions that add even more. These extensions were all originally developed for ArmchairGM, a site that was purchased by Wikia in 2006, and the code for most of them was made public in 2011.

The SocialProfile extension family is in somewhat of a messy state at the moment: not all of the extensions work well with the latest versions of MediaWiki, and the distribution of functionality across the various extensions seems somewhat haphazard – there are currently 21 extensions tied in with SocialProfile, many of which are very small and look like they could be merged in with others. Still, there is an effort in place to improve all of these extensions, and some wikis have found the SocialProfile functionality useful.

Here are the main features of the core SocialProfile extension:

- **User profile** – a wizard lets users easily create a detailed user profile, including uploading an avatar image that is then used in discussions.

- **Public and private messaging** – users can write both private messages to one another, and public messages on a shared "user board".

- **Friending/"foeing"** – users can publicly specify the other users that they know.

- **User status** – users can set their current status, and users' status history is preserved, allowing for Twitter-style microblogging.

- **Rewards system** – you can assign points to different actions, like editing a page and friending someone, and then set ranks that users are publicly given when they reach a certain number of points.

And here are some of the additional SocialProfile-based extensions:

- **BlogPage** – lets users create (non-wiki-page) blog posts.

- **PollNY** – lets users create polls.

- **QuizGame** – lets users create quizzes.

- **VoteNY** – lets users vote on articles.

- **SiteMetrics** – shows administrators various metrics related to usage of Social-Profile tools.

You can read more about SocialProfile, its current status, and all its related extensions here:

> https://www.mediawiki.org/wiki/Extension:SocialProfile

UrlGetParameters

UrlGetParameters is an extension that can read and display the values of parameters from the URL query string. For instance, if the URL for a wiki page contains "&abc=def", you could have the following call on the page:

```
{{#urlget:abc}}
```

...and it would display "def". It also works for array values, so that, if there's a string like "vegetables[1]=cauliflower" in the query string, the call `{{#urlget:vegetables[1]}}` will display the right thing ("cauliflower").

UrlGetParameters isn't usually necessary, but at times it can be very helpful, because it lets wiki pages pass information to one another. For instance, you could create a page that functions as a "wizard", guiding users through a list of choices and offering them advice based on their inputs. The user's inputs can be embedded in the query string via either links (the #fullurl parser function could help), or a mini-form (the Widgets extension could be used for that – see page 257). Then, the resulting page, which could be the same page or a different one, could use #urlget, in conjunction with #if or #switch from ParserFunctions, to display the right text.

The #urlget function can also be used in conjunction with Semantic Forms, especially with SF's "run query" option (page 215), which similarly can be used to display a wizard.

For more information about UrlGetParameters, see:

https://www.mediawiki.org/wiki/Extension:UrlGetParameters

Ratings extensions

People have become used to being able to provide quick feedback on content on the web, whether it's "liking" a post, giving a thumbs up or thumbs down to a comment, rating a movie, etc. So not surprisingly, tools exist for doing the same within wiki pages. Such ratings extensions are always somewhat awkward in a wiki, though, because the content can change at any time. What if a page is poorly written, and you give it a low rating, and then the next day someone rewrites it and makes it a lot better? You might be able to change your rating at that point, but until you do, your rating is a meaningless metric that's just confusing.

(To be sure, in many cases blog and social networking posts can be rewritten too, making votes on such pages awkward as well – but wholesale rewriting of a post is rarely done.)

There's the added awkwardness where it may not be totally clear whether users are supposed to rate the page, or the topic that the page applies to – like in a wiki page about a restaurant. This is the same confusion that can affect commenting functionality on wiki pages (see page 59).

Nonetheless, there are various ratings and article feedback extensions, and some have been considered useful in some circumstances. Here are a few of them:

- **ArticleFeedbackv5**   (https://mediawiki.org/wiki/Extension: ArticleFeedbackv5) – provides users with a simple interface, asking "Did you find what you were looking for?", with a text box to allow additional feedback. This extension is used on a small percentage of articles in Wikipedia. It replaces the now-defunct "ArticleFeedback" extension, which was more complex, letting users rate pages on a variety of metrics, like "Objective" and "Well-written", and which was used fairly extensively for a while on Wikipedia.

- **W4G Rating Bar** (https://mediawiki.org/wiki/Extension:W4G_Rating_Bar) – provides an input to let users rate pages, and then shows the results, on the pages themselves and elsewhere.

- **CommunityVoice** (https://mediawiki.org/wiki/Extension:CommunityVoice) – lets users give star ratings to arbitrary things on a wiki page; any page can have any number of such inputs.

- **VoteNY** (https://www.mediawiki.org/wiki/Extension:VoteNY) – lets users vote on pages, then shows the highest-rated pages elsewhere. This is part of the SocialProfile family of extensions; see page 106.

- **Semantic Rating** (https://www.mediawiki.org/wiki/Extension:Semantic_Rating) – used in conjunction with Semantic MediaWiki (Chapter 16); lets users enter ratings within forms, and then allows for displaying individual and aggregated ratings, all using a five-star display.

Chapter 12

Extended MediaWiki syntax

There's a variety of other syntax, available through extensions, that can be used for specific purposes: displaying specialized content, handling logic, and displaying page elements such as tabs and footnotes. We'll get to some of it in this chapter.

ParserFunctions

The single most indispensable MediaWiki extension, and likely the most popular, is the ParserFunctions extension. As you may be able to guess from its name, Parser-Functions defines a collection of parser functions (see page 37 for an explanation of those). The functions it defines are useful in a variety of circumstances. Since 2010, ParserFunctions has included all the code for what used to be a separate extension, StringFunctions. The original ParserFunctions function are all programmatic in nature: there's #if, the most important of them, which does conditional display, #expr, which evaluates mathematical expressions, and others along similar lines; the full listing is below. The functions that came from StringFunctions all do typical string-manipulation actions, like getting substrings, and replacing certain substrings with others.

In practice, almost all of the usages of functions defined by ParserFunctions are in templates, because that's the one case where you don't know in advance what all the values passed in will be. That's why most of the examples later on for ParserFunctions functions take place within the context of a template, with passed-in parameters.

ParserFunctions comes bundled in with the downloadable version of MediaWiki. But why, given that it's so popular, isn't its functionality directly a part of core Media-

Wiki? That's because ParserFunctions is a bit of a hack. Functions like #if, for all their helpfulness, can be cumbersome to use, and you only need to look at the code for some of the templates in Wikipedia to see how such functions can quickly turn wikitext into an unreadable mess of curly braces. Here's a small example, from the English Wikipedia's "Infobox settlement" template:

```
{{#ifeq:{{{parts_style|}}} | para | <b>{{{parts|}}}
{{#if:{{both | {{{parts|}}} | {{{p1|}}}}}} |
&#58; |}}</b> {{#if:{{{p1|}}} | {{{p1}}}
{{#if:{{{p2|}}} |, {{{p2}}} {{#if:{{{p3|}}} |,
{{{p3}}} {{#if:{{{p4|}}} |, {{{p4}}} {{#if:{{{p5|}}}
|,
```

It goes on like that for a while.

Almost as soon as ParserFunctions was created, discussions began about replacing it with true scripting functionality, including "if-then" statements, "for" loops, and the like, which would be both more powerful and more elegant than the current approach. This finally came about in 2013 with the Scribunto extension, which allows for creating "modules", written in the scripting language Lua, which can include sophisticated logic and text processing:

https://www.mediawiki.org/wiki/Extension:Scribunto

Scribunto is intended to be a powerful framework, by the way: though its default scripting language will be Lua, it's designed to allow other languages as well, such as JavaScript (server-side, not client-side).

Nevertheless, ParserFunctions is still in widespread use, even on Wikipedia. Below is the listing of the original functions it defines, along with a description of each.

- #expr – displays the result of a mathematical or logical expression.

  Example: `{{#expr:2 + 3}}`

- #if – displays different strings depending on whether some value is blank.

  Example:

  `{{#if:{{{height|}}}|The height is {{{height|}}}.|No height entered.}}`

- #ifeq – displays different strings depending on whether two values are equal.

- #iferror – displays different strings depending on whether a call to another such function returned an error.

- #ifexpr – displays different strings depending on whether a mathematical expression is correct.

- #ifexist – displays different strings depending on whether a given page exists.

- #rel2abs – displays a page name, based on a directory-like view of subpages.

- #switch – displays different strings depending on some specific value (there can be multiple options).

  Example:

  ```
  {{#switch:  {{{Season|}}}} | Summer = How nice, it's summer!
  | Winter = Brr, it's winter!  | It's some other season!  }}
  ```

- #time – displays a specific time, in a specified format.

- #timel – displays the current local time, in a specified format.

- #titleparts – displays one or more parts of a page name, based on splitting up the page by slashes.

  Example: `{{#titleparts:  A/B/C/D/E | 2 | 3}}`

  (returns "C/D" – call returns 2 segments, starting at segment #3)

And here are the ParserFunctions functions that came from StringFunctions:

- #len – shows the length of a given string.

  Example:

  ```
  {{#ifexpr:  {{len:  {{{Zip code|}}} }} = 5 | The zip code
  is {{{Zip code|}}}.  | The zip code ({{{Zip code|}}})
  should be 5 characters long.}}
  ```

- #pos – finds the numerical character position of one string within another.

- #rpos – similar, but finds the last occurrence of a string.

- #sub – shows the substring of a string, given a start and end location.

- #pad – pads out a string to a certain length, using a character or longer string as padding.

- #replace – shows a string that has had a substring replaced with another string.

- #explode – shows a substring, based on splitting up a string by a delimiter.

  Example:

  ```
  The third name in your list is {{#explode:{{{List of
  names|}}}|,|3}}.
  ```

- urldecode – URL-decodes a string, e.g. turning '%20' into ' ', etc.

- urlencode – URL-encodes a string; sometimes useful for creating links.

Note the lack of a "#" at the beginning of both urldecode and urlencode.

You can read more about ParserFunctions, including many additional examples, here:

> https://www.mediawiki.org/wiki/Extension:ParserFunctions

Displaying code

You may want to display source code in some programming or markup language on a wiki page, if it's, say, part of a software-related wiki. The awkwardly-named Syntax-Highlight GeSHi is the recommended extension for doing that. It uses the third-party GeSHi library, whose name itself stands for "Generic Syntax Highlighter". The extension defines the tag <syntaxhighlight>, which takes in the parameter lang=, which can hold any of over 100 language names, and can then display any set of code. Here's one example call:

```
<syntaxhighlight lang="java">
System.out.println( "Bonjour, monde!" );
</syntaxhighlight>
```

And here is the resulting output:

```
System.out.println( "Bonjour, monde!" );
```

<syntaxhighlight> can take in some other parameters, which modify the display; these are only rarely used, but here are some of them:

- line – adds a line number at the beginning of each line.

- `start=` – if `line` is used, sets the line number for the first line (by default it's 1).

- `highlight=` – specifies a line to highlight.

- `enclose=` – specifies the HTML tag used to enclose the entire text. By default it's `"pre"`, but it can also be `"div"` or `"none"`. Using `"div"` allows for line wrapping, which is helpful when there are long lines of code.

See the SyntaxHighlight GeSHi homepage for more information on how to download and use this extension, including the full set of languages allowed:

> https://www.mediawiki.org/wiki/Extension:SyntaxHighlight_GeSHi

Displaying math

The Math extension lets you display mathematical formulas on the page in a nicely-formatted way, by placing them within the `<math>` tag. This functionality was formerly part of core MediaWiki, until it was spun off into an extension in version 1.18. You can see more information here:

> https://www.mediawiki.org/wiki/Extension:Math

Cite

The Cite extension should be well-known to anyone who has read Wikipedia – it's the extension that lets users create footnotes. It's not used often outside of Wikipedia and other Wikimedia sites, but it can, and probably should, be used more often, because providing citations for facts is always a good idea. To add a footnote after a statement on a page, you can add something like the following afterward:

```
<ref name="USA Today interview">
[http://usatoday.com/1234567.html Interview with a
Screen Legend], Dana Douglas, ''USA Today'', January
1, 1980.  Page retrieved February 2, 2014.</ref>
```

The citation style is up to you, and you can use a template to set the formatting; that's how it's often done on Wikipedia, using templates like "cite news" and "cite web". On Wikipedia, you could do, in place of the former,

```
<ref name="USA Today interview">{{cite
news |url=http://usatoday.com/1234567.html
|title=Interview with a Screen Legend |first=Dana
|last=Douglas |work=USA Today |date=January 1, 1980
|accessed=February 2, 2014}}</ref>
```

This will guarantee a consistent display of citations.

The "name=" attribute within the <ref> tag is optional – it's useful if you cite the same source more than once. If that happens, every additional citation can simply look like this:

```
<ref name="USA Today interview" />
```

Finally, at the bottom of the page, you need the following tag to display the full set of footnotes:

```
<references />
```

The English Wikipedia has a "{{Reflist}}" template that displays this tag, and applies some custom formatting around it.

Header Tabs

Header Tabs is a cool extension that lets you place tabs within a wiki page (separate from, and below, the editing-based tabs provided by the skin), thus letting you break up the content of what might otherwise be overly-long pages. It's fairly limited: it can only create one set of tabs on a page, with no sub-tabs. Still, that by itself is enough to make pages a lot more readable in a variety of circumstances.

To create a tab with Header Tabs, just print the tab name as a top-level section header, i.e. with one '=', like this:

```
=Tab name=
```

This takes advantage of the fact that top-level headers are usually unused; two equals signs ('==') and higher are recommended for regular page headers in almost all cases.

Here's an example of the display of tabs, for a page about an athlete:

This display would just require having lines like "=Biography=", "=Statistics=", etc. within the wikitext.

Even if you have Header Tabs installed, such headers won't automatically get turned into tabs unless you do one of two things. The first option is to place the tag <headertabs /> somewhere below the set of tabs for the page; wherever it goes marks the end of the contents of the last tab, and everything below the <headertabs /> will show up below the tabs structure.

The other option is to designate one or more namespaces as automatically getting tabs, so that headers with a single equals sign around them will get turned into tabs, without the need for a <headertabs /> tag. You can do this by adding to the global variable $htAutomaticNamespaces, within LocalSettings.php. So to make tabs automatically show up for every page in the main namespace, you would add the following line, below the inclusion of Header Tabs:

```
$htAutomaticNamespaces[] = NS_MAIN;
```

(If you don't know PHP, this line adds the value "NS_MAIN" to the array of values that $htAutomaticNamespaces already held.)

This approach is certainly more convenient; its downside is that you can't have a section of the page below the tabs area – everything from the last tab name down to the end will become part of the last tab's contents. (Although you can still manually insert a <headertabs /> tag in the right place to get around this problem.)

In either case, you also need to have at least two such headers on a page for tabs to show up – unless you add "$htRenderSingleTab = true;" to LocalSettings.php.

Tabs are useful for a variety of purposes; though we've most often seen them in structured pages, defined by templates and editable with forms (using Semantic Forms – Chapter 17). The structured, data-centric nature of such pages makes splitting them into tabs a very natural fit. In this case, it makes sense to have the set of tabs be the same for the page and for the form.

There other customizations you can do, also within LocalSettings.php, to modify some of the other aspects of Header Tabs. By default, every click on a tab adds another page to the browser history, so that hitting the "back" button will bring you back to the previous tab you were on. You can disable this behavior, so that tabs won't show up in the browser history, by adding the following:

```
$htUseHistory = false;
```

Every tab also gets an "edit" link that shows up on the right-hand side. You can remove this link by adding the following:

    $htEditTabLink= false;

You can also change the display of the tabs, using the "$htStyle" global variable. The default display is also the nicest-looking one, but you can, for instance, switch to the default display that jQuery UI provides, by adding the following:

    $htStyle = 'jquery';

Header Tabs also provides a parser function, #switchtablink, that produces a link to a specific tab, from within either the page on which the tab is located or another page. It is called in the following format:

    {{#switchtablink:*Tab name*|*Link text*|*Page name*}}

If the tab is on the same page as the link, only the first two parameters are needed; if it's called from another page, the third parameter is needed as well.

More information about Header Tabs can be found at:

https://www.mediawiki.org/wiki/Extension:Header_Tabs

Chapter 13

Display and customization

MediaWiki allows for a lot of customization of its look-and-feel, including changing the text of the interface itself. Such customization is available for both for administrators and users – we'll get to both in this chapter.

User preferences

Every logged-in user on a wiki can change many of their settings via the Special:Preferences page. This page is available conveniently through a link at the top of the page (in most skins), called "Preferences". This page is split up into tabs, and lets you change a wide variety of settings: the skin you use (see the next section), your language of choice, your time zone, your preferred way to display the time, and a variety of other settings relating to the look-and-feel of the rest of MediaWiki's functionality. You can choose which "gadgets" you want to use, out of the ones installed on this wiki (see page 100).

From this page, you can also make changes to your basic user account – your password and email address. Users cannot change their username, though – usernames can't be changed at all within core MediaWiki, though the Renameuser extension, which comes bundled in with MediaWiki, lets administrators do it.

Skins

In MediaWiki, a "skin" is the set of PHP and CSS files used to specify the display a wiki. MediaWiki, like any good content-management system, separates out the content of the display from its look. The files for all the skins are stored within the /skins directory. Each skin is represented by a file within that directory, and, in most cases, a sub-directory as well.

Every installation of MediaWiki has a default skin, that users see if they're either not logged in or haven't changed their settings. Additionally, users, if they're logged in, can change the skin that they view the wiki with, by going to Special:Preferences, then going to the "Skins" tab – there they can select among any of the skins installed on that wiki. Unlike most good content-management systems, MediaWiki makes it rather difficult to create and maintain good skins. Part of the problem is that the set of functions that need to be defined and called by the skin keeps changing with new MediaWiki versions; although the rate of change seems to have subsided in more recent versions.

If you do want to create a custom skin, by the way, this is a good tutorial, by Daniel Friesen, that explains the basics:

http://blog.redwerks.org/2012/02/08/mediawiki-skinning-tutorial/

Before 2010, MediaWiki's built-in skins were, all-in-all, underwhelming. The default skin until then, MonoBook, was criticized for its lackluster design and (to some) difficulty of navigation. But MonoBook itself shines in comparison with the older skins that were created for MediaWiki, a small and dwindling number of which remain bundled with the application. The Wikipedia Usability Initiative, which ran during all of 2010, took a methodical approach to the problem of the interface, hiring interface designers and, for the first time, doing large-scale usability testing. The most important result of the initiative was the creation of the current default skin, Vector. This is a clean, functional skin that has gotten high marks from users.

The current best place to find alternative MediaWiki skins, or at least to be inspired by the possibilities, is the "Gallery of user styles", here:

https://www.mediawiki.org/wiki/Manual:Gallery_of_user_styles

At the moment, many or most of the skins listed there are out of date, though.

One notable skinning framework that has been gaining a lot interest recently is Bootstrap, which was originally created for Twitter. It makes modifications like changing around colors easy to do, and the skins it generates are responsive (see section below).There are a few different MediaWiki-based implementations for Bootstrap; the most commonly-used one at the moment is the "Bootstrap" extension:

> https://www.mediawiki.org/wiki/Extension:Bootstrap

At least one skin, Chameleon, makes use of this extension already:

> https://www.mediawiki.org/wiki/Skin:Chameleon

One interesting, unconventional usage of skins is as a way to turn a wiki into a more standard content-publishing system. The idea is that users who can edit the wiki (of whom there will be relatively few), and who are logged in, will see the wiki with a normal skin; while the majority of users/readers, who aren't logged in, will see the wiki with a custom skin that doesn't show the history and edit tabs, the standard sidebar, etc.: it's a lightweight method of making a regular-looking website with the editing convenience of a wiki. The custom actions are usually still there, if users manually type in URLs that end with "action=history" and the like; but the absence of links on the screen will mean that the vast majority of users will never know that there's a wiki behind the scenes, let alone see the history of page, the set of recent changes, etc. If you go with this approach, you would still most likely want to block non-logged-in users from being able to edit the wiki, but that's easy to accomplish (see page 78).

Mobile display

Until 2012 or so, mobile support for websites meant one of two things: either dedicated mobile apps showing the website's content, or a mobile-friendly version of the site, sometimes located at a subdomain like "m.". However, in 2012 the concept of responsive web design began to really catch on. The term (which was invented in 2010) refers to websites that, through a clever use of HTML and CSS, manage to look good in all screen browser widths. As the browser width shrinks, horizontal image sets become more vertical, formerly-visible menu options get hidden within dropdowns, and text widths of course become smaller.

There is already a framework for developing responsive MediaWiki skins: Bootstrap (see previous section). It could be that in the future, Bootstrap-based skins will become not just more popular, but the dominant form of display for MediaWiki.

Another responsive MediaWiki skin – that isn't based on Bootstrap – is Refreshed, which looks great in both standard tablet and standard cell phone widths:

https://www.mediawiki.org/wiki/Skin:Refreshed

What about the old style of mobile support – native apps and device-specific display? For both of those, support is still at an early stage. There are a variety of apps for viewing Wikipedia for both iOS and Android, including an official one, Wikipedia Mobile, developed by the Wikimedia Foundation. However, there don't appear to be any apps for viewing an arbitrary MediaWiki wiki.

On the other hand, there are ways to get a mobile-friendly display from within the browser itself. If you go to Wikipedia on a smart phone, you'll see a minimized, easy-to-read display even without a Wikipedia app. That's accomplished through the MobileFrontend extension:

https://www.mediawiki.org/wiki/Extension:MobileFrontend

This extension can be installed on any MediaWiki site. Unfortunately, it seems to require using a proxy server (like Varnish), which detects the device making each web request, and modifies the request accordingly if it's a mobile device, so that MediaWiki can know to return a different display. This is a rather substantial amount of extra work. And the resulting display lacks some important functionality – most notably, there's no way to edit the page.

There is a Wikimedia Foundation project, named "Athena", that is meant to overhaul the display of MediaWiki, including the creation of a mobile-friendly skin, which may also end up being called "Athena", and which could be responsive. It is a project without a clear end date, but you can see more about it here:

https://www.mediawiki.org/wiki/Athena

Ads

If you run a public wiki, you may want to to put ads on it. Ads can be a good fit for wikis, because wikis tend to hold targeted content, and appeal to a targeted community. That's certainly the case if your wiki is about a high-ad-revenue topic like insurance, lawyers or mortgages, but it can be true even if your wiki is about, say, model airplanes – or even Greek philosophers.

In MediaWiki, ads are usually placed either at the top of the page, or in the sidebar, or in both places. The easiest way to add ads to the wiki is to simply add the code directly to the skin you're using: once you've signed up with the ad service (assuming you're using an ad service), and gotten the HTML/JavaScript code snippet(s) for your site, you can just add them to the relevant parts of the skin, and everything should work automatically. There are two downsides to this approach, though: it means you'll have to re-add that code every time you upgrade MediaWiki (assuming that the upgrade involves a skin upgrade as well), and it means that ads will only show up in one skin, or at least only on the skins you add the ad code to.

There are several extensions that handle the display of ads. Oddly, there is no one definitive extension that's easy to set up, and allows you to put horizontal banner ads at the top and bottom of the page, and a vertical one in the sidebar (ideally using Google AdSense, the most popular ad service. There are extensions that do subsets of this, though, and hopefully sometime soon an extension that handles all of it will come along. You can see the entire set of ad-displaying extensions here:

> https://www.mediawiki.org/wiki/Category:Advertising_extensions

One notable extension in that group is AdManager, which allows setting of specific sidebar ads in specific pages, or groups of pages – it's a more complex approach than that offered by the other ad extensions. You can read about it here:

> https://www.mediawiki.org/wiki/Extension:AdManager

jQuery and ResourceLoader

MediaWiki has fairly sophisticated handling for JavaScript and CSS. Bundled within MediaWiki are the entire jQuery and jQuery UI JavaScript libraries; and MediaWiki has a component, ResourceLoader, that handles the display of JS and CSS intelligently. For MediaWiki developers, it's very helpful to know about these components of MediaWiki, and they're indispensable if your code contains any JavaScript or CSS. But even for MediaWiki administrators and users it can be helpful to know about them, so we'll cover them in brief here.

jQuery is a third-party JavaScript library that simplifies a lot of typical JavaScript tasks considerably. Since its release in 2006, it has become, to some extent, a standard on the web. There are many other JS libraries available, but jQuery at the moment dominates the field: according to an ongoing survey at w3techs.com, jQuery is currently in use on an astounding 58% of all websites, and on 94% of websites that use any JavaScript library.

jQuery UI is a sibling library that adds to jQuery a large variety of standard interface utilities: drag-and-drop, animations, form inputs like date pickers, and so on.

MediaWiki and some of its extensions make significant use of jQuery, and sometimes of jQuery UI as well – the Semantic Forms and Semantic Forms Inputs extensions (pages 181 and 218) notably make significant use of jQuery UI.

ResourceLoader, or "the Resource Loader" as it's sometimes known, is a component of MediaWiki that handles the addition of JavaScript and CSS onto the page. In regular web pages (and how it used to be in MediaWiki, until 2011), all the relevant JavaScript and CSS files are simply included on the page, usually on the top. But with ResourceLoader, MediaWiki and its extensions are meant to register all the JavaScript and CSS files they use, in the form of "modules", and then ResourceLoader is responsible for placing the necessary JavaScript and CSS on the page. For both JavaScript and CSS, the content is displayed to the browser as one big file, and for JavaScript, the code is also minimized, or "minified". In most cases, it's also placed at the bottom of the page, instead of at the top. Because of the way browsers work, all of these changes make the display of pages significantly faster.

For the most part, the presence of ResourceLoader shouldn't be noticed by users. The one exception to that is that, because by default the JavaScript and CSS is loaded at the end of the page instead of the beginning, users can sometimes see bare-looking text before formatting is applied to it. This sort of initial display is not unique to MediaWiki; it happens for every page where the JS and CSS are loaded last, and it's referred to by web designers as a "flash of unstyled content", or FOUC, which can be distracting to users. Specific modules can in fact be registered as being displayed on the top and not the bottom, and many already are, so this problem may go away entirely in the future.

A second version of ResourceLoader, ResourceLoader 2, is under development: its major planned new feature is the addition of JavaScript gadgets, defined using the Gadgets extension (page 100), into the loading system. However, its development has been superseded by that of VisualEditor and other development priorities for the WMF, so there is no estimated completion date for the project.

You can read more about ResourceLoader, how it's structured and its current development process, here:

   https://www.mediawiki.org/wiki/ResourceLoader

MediaWiki: pages, and modifying the interface text

One relatively little-known feature of MediaWiki is the fact that you can modify the text of almost any part of the interface, directly through the wiki itself. You just need to find out the identifier of a particular piece of text (referred to in MediaWiki as a "message"), then go to the page named "MediaWiki:*message-name*". Take, for example, the "Summary" label that shows up at the bottom of the edit page. This turns out to be confusing for some users, who think that what they're being asked to summarize is the entire page, not their most recent change. You may consider a label like "Description of edit" to be more useful. If you go to the page "MediaWiki:summary", and enter in the value "Description of edit", that's how it will show up from then on to all users. To revert, you can simply delete the page.

Wikipedia itself contains some customizations. In MediaWiki the main tab for each page in the main namespace is called, by default, "Page". In the English-language Wikipedia, however, this tab instead appears as "Article". The name of the message holding that value is "nstab-main", and the content of the Wikipedia page "MediaWiki:Nstab-main", is the word "Article". (Looking at the page history, it appears that this value has been changed a number of times, most recently (at the time of this writing) on January 7, 2009.)

A downside of making such a modification is that it's hard-coded to one language: if someone is viewing your wiki and has another language specified in their user preferences, they'll normally see the entire interface in their language. But any messages that you modify will show up as that exact text to everyone, regardless of their language. (Whether it's useful to view a wiki's interface in one language if all the content is in another language, is a separate issue). But you can in fact set translations at the same time that you set a new value; that's covered in the next section.

The most common usage of this functionality is to modify the sidebar. The sidebar, as odd as it sounds, is represented by a single "message". Here is the default value of the sidebar in the English language, in MediaWiki 1.22:

```
* navigation
** mainpage|mainpage-description
** portal-url|portal
** currentevents-url|currentevents
** recentchanges-url|recentchanges
** randompage-url|randompage
** helppage|help
* SEARCH
* TOOLBOX
* LANGUAGES
```

The last three lines are standard elements that have special handling, so their connection to the display is not obvious, but Figure 13.1 shows how that appears in the sidebar within the standard Vector skin (and with the Semantic MediaWiki extension installed, which adds the "Browse properties" link).

Figure 13.1: Default sidebar display, in the Vector skin, with Semantic MediaWiki installed

The structure is fairly simple: a single asterisk indicates a section header, while two asterisks indicate an item within that section. Each item can be thought of as a MediaWiki link: it can either be a single string, in which case the link text and the linked page are the same, or it can be two strings separated by a pipe, with the first string as the page being linked to and the second, the link text. The only difference between the strings in the sidebar and regular MediaWiki links is that strings in the sidebar can be (and often are) language messages themselves. Note the "recentchanges" string in the sidebar, for instance: when displaying the sidebar, the system searches for a language value for "recentchanges" – it finds it ("Recent changes"), and substitutes that in. If no value had been found, the text "recentchanges" would simply have appeared as is.

Another popular usage of this functionality is to change the copyright text in the edit page, at MediaWiki:copyrightwarning. By default it looks like:

```
Please note that all contributions to {{SITENAME}}
are considered to be released under the $2 (see $1
```

```
for details).  If you do not want your writing to be
edited mercilessly and redistributed at will, then
do not submit it here.<br /> You are also promising
us that you wrote this yourself, or copied it from a
public domain or similar free resource.  '''Do not
submit copyrighted work without permission!'''
```

Whenever you see values like $1, etc., it means that they're placeholders to be filled in by the PHP code that displays those messages. In the case of the copyright warning, the values $1 and $2 are filled in with values derived from a combination of various global variables, settable in LocalSettings.php: $wgRightsPage, $wgRightsText and $wgRightsUrl.

How can you find out the name of a certain message? Fortunately, MediaWiki offers a clever way to do it – if you add "?uselang=qqx" to the URL of any page in the wiki (or "&uselang=qqx", if there was already a question mark in the URL), it will show the *name* of every message, in place of the value. So all you have to do to find the name of a message is go to a page that contains that message, add the "uselang=qqx" to the URL, and see what shows up in place of that message.

A special page, "Special:AllMessages", also exists, that shows the full set of message names and their values in the wiki's current language.

Deleting a message page will revert that message back to its original value.

Customizing the site's CSS and JavaScript

Some pages in the MediaWiki namespace are used for something other than defining interface text: adding additional JavaScript and CSS to the wiki's pages. The most important of these are MediaWiki:Common.css and MediaWiki:Common.js. MediaWiki:Common.css contains CSS that is applied to every page in the wiki. Very often, this file is used to define 'prettytable' and 'wikitable', two CSS classes that are usually defined as synonyms of one another, used to make tables look nicer than the HTML default (MediaWiki skins rarely apply any special display to tables, for some reason.)

MediaWiki:Common.js, as you could guess, is meant to contain custom JavaScript that will be added to every page. It is often used to add additional functionality to help with the viewing or editing experience. The more standardized way to add such functionality is via the Gadgets extension (page 100), although there you're restricted to the gadgets that the administrator has selected for the wiki (this may change in the future).

In addition to Common.css and Common.js, there are pages that you can use to define custom JavaScript or CSS to be used only for one skin, or only for one user group. These follow a standard naming convention: to add CSS only for the MonoBook skin, for instance, you would add it to the page MediaWiki:monobook.css, while to add CSS only for the "bureaucrat" group, you would add it to the page MediaWiki:group-bureaucrat.css.

Site notice

You can set a message to be displayed at the top of every page; this is useful when you want to make a general announcement, such as that there will be an upcoming site outage, or that the wiki has some new feature, or that volunteers are needed for some task, etc. This can be done in a variety of ways:

- Setting the global variable $wgSiteNotice in LocalSettings.php.

- Modifying the page "MediaWiki:sitenotice".

- Modifying the page "MediaWiki:anonnotice" – this displays a notice only for anonymous, non-logged-in users.

- Using the extension CentralNotice – this is a fairly heavy-duty extension, that allows for coordinating an entire "campaign" of banner ads and the like among a group of wikis; it is used by the Wikimedia Foundation during its annual fundraising drive:

    https://www.mediawiki.org/wiki/Extension:CentralNotice

- Using the extension DismissableSiteNotice – this extension displays a site notice that users can dismiss by clicking on a link, after which they won't see it again:

    https://www.mediawiki.org/wiki/Extension:DismissableSiteNotice

Language support

MediaWiki's support for different written languages is a major point of pride; it appears to be unsurpassed by any other software. MediaWiki has been translated, at least to some extent, into over 400 languages, from Abkhazian to Zeeuws, including variants you might not think of as separate languages, such as Austrian German and Latin American Spanish. Its secret weapon in this effort is the excellent site Translatewiki.net (http://translatewiki.net), which itself runs on MediaWiki, and which serves as a platform for an army of volunteer translators around the world to translate every displayed piece of text in both MediaWiki and its extensions. You can see the impressive full list of languages at:

> http://translatewiki.net/wiki/Special:SupportedLanguages

Translatewiki.net has taken on a life of its own, and is now used by additional, non-MediaWiki applications, including OpenLayers and Mifos.

MediaWiki's messages are divided into two types: user messages and content messages. A user message is any piece of text that is simply displayed, and has no impact on the content of wiki pages, or their URLs. A content message, by contrast, is any piece of text that does show up in either page contents or URLs. You can see the difference in, for instance, the "Random page" link in the sidebar, which by default is defined by the text "randompage-url | randompage". Assuming the wiki is in English, the text reads "Random page", and points to the page "Special:Random". The link text is defined by the message "randompage", which is a user message, while the page name is defined by "randompage-url", which is a content message.

Every MediaWiki wiki has a default language, which is determined by the value of $wgLanguageCode in LocalSettings.php (this variable takes in the IETF language tag for the language, which is often, though not always, a two-letter abbreviation – see http://en.wikipedia.org/wiki/IETF_language_tag). This is the language used for both content messages and user messages, by default. A logged-in user, however, can choose to display user messages (though not content messages) in any other language, if they click on the "User preferences" link and change their language within the main "User profile" tab. So a user can view a wiki with content messages in one language and user messages in another.

All of these messages can be modified within the wiki, via pages in the "MediaWiki:" namespace, as described previously. But modifying a page like "MediaWiki:*message-name*" will actually override that message's value in every language: if it's a user message, that means that even if someone views your wiki in another language, they'll still see that exact text you entered. You may not want that to happen; if not, you can set translations to only apply to one language, by using the structure "MediaWiki:*message-name/language-code*" instead. This will set the value for the language specified by that language code (again, usually a two-letter value). For instance, to change the sidebar only for Italian speakers, you would edit the page "MediaWiki:summary/it". Unfortunately, this can be done for every language except for the wiki's main language: if your wiki is in English, changing the value of "Media-Wiki:summary/en" will have no effect.

What about running multi-language wikis, though, where the page contents can themselves be in different languages? That is covered in the section "Multi-language wikis", on page 155.

Chapter 14

Protecting content

Handling spam

The web 2.0 revolution of user-generated content, for all its positive impact, has also been a godsend for spammers. Never before in human history has it been so easy to sell dubious merchandise or services, whether it's prescription drugs, life insurance, college essay writing, or more of those prescription drugs. So spam has infiltrated countless blog comments, Twitter feeds, and wiki pages. If your wiki is not public, or is public but has closed registration, then you have nothing to fear and you can skip ahead to the next chapter. If, however, your wiki allows contributions from the general public, then chances are good that, at some point, one or more groups of wiki-spammers will find it and will start trying to turn it into a free advertising platform.

MediaWiki already does an important task in preventing spam, which is to add a "nofollow" tag to the HTML of every external link – this tells search engines not to go to that link, thus greatly minimizing the benefit that adding links can provide to spammers. You can undo that behavior, by the way, by adding the following to LocalSettings.php, though you really shouldn't:

```
$wgNoFollowLinks = false;
```

Still, for whatever reason, some spammers really like to hit MediaWiki sites. Thankfully, there are a number of effective extensions that let you fight back against spam. The two most important ones, which are recommended for every publicly-editable wiki, are ConfirmEdit and SpamBlacklist; we'll get to those in the next sections.

ConfirmEdit

The ConfirmEdit extension comes bundled in with every MediaWiki install. Its documentation can be found here:

> https://www.mediawiki.org/wiki/Extension:ConfirmEdit

It sets up a CAPTCHA tool for page edits, user registration and user login. A CAPTCHA (which stands for "Completely Automated Public Turing test to tell Computers and Humans Apart") is any input that's designed so that a human can enter but a software program can't: its most common variety is those now-ubiquitous tests in online forms that ask you to look at an image with distorted numbers and letters and type them in. ConfirmEdit provides, at the moment, six different CAPTCHA options. They are:

- **SimpleCaptcha** – the default option. Displays a simple math problem.

- **FancyCaptcha** – displays an image of stylized set of letters that users have to decipher (this option is most like the standard CAPTCHAs).

- **MathCaptcha** – like SimpleCaptcha, but the math problem is displayed as an image.

- **QuestyCaptcha** – asks a question, out of a pre-defined set (the administrator has to create the questions, and their allowed answers).

- **ReCaptcha** – uses the reCAPTCHA service, which uses distorted text from scanned-in books.

- **Asirra** – asks users to select only the cat photos out of a list of 12 photos of cats and dogs.

All of these options, including SimpleCaptcha, are better than nothing; though there's a big range of effectiveness among all of them. For a while, the ReCaptcha option was a very popular anti-spam tool (as was the reCAPTCHA service in general, on non-wiki sites). It's the nicest-looking of the ConfirmEdit options, it performs a useful service (helping to digitize old books), and it's also the only one that provides an alternate, audio-based CAPTCHA, for use by blind or visually-impaired users. However, it may have become a victim of its own popularity: sometime around 2010, spammers apparently figured out en masse how to get around it, and now it's no longer very useful.

At the moment, the two most effective of these options appear to be QuestyCaptcha and Asirra. With QuestyCaptcha, there's no automated software that can figure out the right answer to your questions, so even simple questions are generally effective. (Though it's helpful to replace the set of questions every once in a while, if spam starts getting through.) Asirra appears to be effective in that there's currently no software that can easily distinguish between cats and dogs – that presumably won't be the case forever, but it is at the moment.

Whichever CAPTCHA module you go with, ConfirmEdit offers the same standard set of additional options. First, it lets you customize which user groups will see CAPTCHAs, using the 'skipcaptcha' permission type. By default, only the 'bot' and 'sysop' user groups are exempted from CAPTCHAs (in other words, they have 'skipcaptcha' set to true). If you want to, say, exempt registered users as well, you could add the following to LocalSettings.php:

```
$wgGroupPermissions['user']['skipcaptcha'] = true;
```

That may seem like a reasonable change, but actually it's not necessary or recommended, as we'll see soon.

ConfirmEdit also lets you configure which actions result in a CAPTCHA test. The relevant actions are:

- 'edit' – any attempted page edit

- 'create' – the creation of a new page

- 'addurl' – any edit which results in a new URL being added to the page

- 'createaccount' – user registration

- 'badlogin' – when a user tries to log in after already having given an incorrect password (this is useful to guard against bots that try to guess passwords)

By default, 'addurl', 'createaccount' and 'badlogin' are checked, while 'edit' and 'create' are not. Why is that – surely every edit is worth checking? Actually, it's not usually necessary, because of the presence of the 'addurl' action. Spam almost always involves the addition of one or more URLs. (Not always, though, because, bizarrely, some "pseudo-spammers" like to just add random text to pages.) Meanwhile, in regular wiki editing, new external URLs get added to pages only occasionally. So checking the addition of URLs works to ward off most automated spammers, while being only a minor inconvenience to real users.

In an ideal world, a CAPTCHA system would block all spam. But spammers have figured out how to bypass CAPTCHAs, most likely by hiring humans to enter the inputs (the going rate, according to Wikipedia, is an absurd 0.1 cents for every completed CAPTCHA). Still, ConfirmEdit does seem to cut down significantly on spam: it stops the waves of automated spam that spammers sometimes like to unleash, where hundreds of spam pages can be created in a few hours.

SpamBlacklist

Another, complementary tool is the SpamBlacklist extension, which can block edits based on two criteria: what URLs they add to the page, and what IP address they originate from. URLs that spammers add tend to be to members of a very large, but finite, set of known websites. The SpamBlacklist extension lets you use as many URL "blacklists" as you want, each containing a set of domains (actually, it's a set of regular expressions for domains, so that, for instance, every domain containing the string "casino-online" can get blocked with one line). By default, SpamBlacklist uses a single blacklist – the Wikimedia Meta-Wiki blacklist, located at:

> http://meta.wikimedia.org/wiki/Spam_blacklist

It's an impressively long list, and it seems to be fairly effective at blocking the spam edits that ConfirmEdit doesn't. The set of websites that spammers use, though, is always growing, but thankfully there's no shortage of additional blacklists available – the SpamBlacklist documentation lists a number of these.

There's more functionality in SpamBlacklist, including the ability to create "whitelists", of domains that match some anti-spam criteria but are actually fine. You can read more on the extension's web page:

> https://www.mediawiki.org/wiki/Extension:SpamBlacklist

Other anti-spam tools

Even ConfirmEdit and SpamBlacklist, as helpful as they both are, don't block all spam. Most perniciously, some spammers simply link to the URLs of pages they've created on other wikis, which themselves contain spam. There's no real way to block such URLs, since they point to innocent domains. There's a third way of guarding against spam, though, which is to check attributes like the IP address and email address (assuming they've registered) of the user making the edit. Two extensions that do that are "Bad Behavior" and "Check Spambots":

> https://www.mediawiki.org/wiki/Extension:Bad_Behavior
> https://www.mediawiki.org/wiki/Extension:Check_Spambots

If you do get hit with spam, there are three useful tools for getting rid of it quickly and easily: "Nuke", "Block and Nuke" and "DeleteBatch".

Nuke is an extension that's bundled in with MediaWiki that lets you delete all the pages created by a single user or IP address. If a spammer sticks to just a few user accounts or IP addresses, and they only create new pages, Nuke will work very well. You just need to enter the username or IP address, and it does the rest. You can get the extension here:

> https://www.mediawiki.org/wiki/Extension:Nuke

An extension that's probably more useful overall is "Block and Nuke", which, instead of going after one account, goes after all of them, except for usernames that have been added to a whitelist file (it's the "guilty until proven innocent" model). In most cases, wiki spammers seem to create many accounts, abandoning each one after only one or two edits; and "Block and Nuke" will work much better in those cases:

> https://www.mediawiki.org/wiki/Extension:BlockandNuke

Unfortunately, there's no current extension that does something similar with bad edits to pages that already existed – in other words, does a mass revert instead of a mass deletion. The closest thing is this JavaScript code, which you can add to Media-Wiki:Common.js, which lets you do that via JavaScript – it's not nearly as efficient, but it's certainly better than nothing:

> http://en.wikipedia.org/wiki/User:John254/mass_rollback.js

MediaWiki has a script, deleteBatch.php, that provides a different approach to undoing spam and vandalism – it lets administrators delete a large group of pages at once, by supplying a text file containing all the page names:

> https://www.mediawiki.org/wiki/Manual:DeleteBatch.php

Additionally, there's the DeleteBatch extension, which lets you do essentially the same thing from the browser interface:

> https://www.mediawiki.org/wiki/Extension:DeleteBatch

mediawiki.org has an entire "Combating spam" page, that lists these and other extensions, as well as other, more involved ways of avoiding spam. You can see it here:

> https://www.mediawiki.org/wiki/Manual:Combating_spam

Restricting registration

Finally, there's an alternate approach to preventing spam, which is to control users'
ability to register, and then to restrict editing to just logged-in users. It makes registration more difficult for users, but it may well be the most foolproof approach against
spam.

There are two extensions that can be used for this purpose: OpenID and ConfirmA-
ccount. The OpenID extension lets users register and log in via the OpenID protocol,
and can be set to only allow registration via OpenID. OpenID, until now at least, seems
to have been impossible for spammers to crack. You can see page 80 for more information.

The other extension is ConfirmAccount, in which every user registration has to be
approved by an administrator; which also works quite well against spam. You can
read about it on page 79.

Access control and protecting pages

There are two kinds of access control: restricting the ability of certain users to read
certain content, and restricting their ability to edit certain content. In MediaWiki, these
are very different from one another, and we'll handle them in two separate sections.

Controlling read access

MediaWiki was never designed, and never re-designed, to allow for restricting read-
access. If you go to the page on mediawiki.org for almost any access-control extension,
you will see the following friendly message:

> *If you need per-page or partial page access restrictions, you are advised to in-
> stall an appropriate content management package. MediaWiki was not written to
> provide per-page access restrictions, and almost all hacks or patches promising to*

add them will likely have flaws somewhere, which could lead to exposure of confidential data. We are not responsible for anything being leaked, leading to loss of funds or one's job.

In reality, there are hooks in the MediaWiki code to allow extensions to restrict viewing of pages – using any of the access-control extensions, a user who is not allowed to view a page will most likely only see an error message if they go directly to the page. However, the warning is still appropriate, because, for whatever reason, there are places in the MediaWiki code that ignore these read restrictions. Currently there are two known ones: the search page, and the "Recent changes" page. If a user does a search on text contained in a restricted page, they will be able to see the name of the page, the fact that it contains the search text, and the text fragment around the search text. And any changes to restricted pages will show up in the "Recent changes" page, where at least the edit summary will be viewable by everyone.

In addition, for those using the Semantic MediaWiki extension, SMW poses a third security gap, because it, too, ignores read restrictions – so any data stored semantically within a restricted page will be viewable by everyone.

It could be that all of the current issues will be fixed in future versions of the software. Nevertheless, even then, trying to restrict people's ability to access content in MediaWiki still seems like it would be a bad idea. This being a wiki, anyone who can read a certain protected page can easily copy over its contents to another, unprotected, page; or make some mistake in editing the page that leads to it no longer being in a protected category; etc. Even if the mistake lasts for no more than five minutes, that's still enough time for someone to see the material and have a permanent copy of it. And you might never find out if such a breach happens.

The other big issue is that every extension you use has to restrict read-access permissions. If even one doesn't, like Semantic MediaWiki, then all your restriction work may be in vain.

So what do you do if you want to store confidential information in your wiki? Probably the most foolproof solution for that case is to simply have a second wiki, one which is restricted to only the small group of people with preferred access (most likely, top-level managers or the like), which will hold all the confidential data. Then you can have an additional element of "security through obscurity" – people who don't have access to the wiki may not even know about it, or may not know its web address; so there's less chance of any sort of breach. It's much safer to prevent someone from reading a wiki entirely, than reading only certain parts of it.

How do you prevent people from getting to a wiki? If you're on an internal network, and there's already some server that only the people you want to restrict access to, have access to, then the easiest solution is to put the wiki on that server. Otherwise, the best way to restrict viewing of the wiki is via LocalSettings.php settings – that's covered on page 78, but here are the relevant lines again:

```
$wgGroupPermissions['*']['read'] = false;
$wgGroupPermissions['user']['read'] = true;
```

The variable $wgWhitelistRead can also be useful in this case, because it lets you define certain pages that non-logged-in users can see, even if they can't view the rest of the wiki. If you want everyone to be able to see the front page, for instance, you could add the following:

```
$wgWhitelistRead = array( 'Main Page' );
```

And if you're using the ConfirmAccount extension (page 79), which lets people request a user account, then at least the following would be necessary if the wiki is private:

```
$wgWhitelistRead = array( 'Special:RequestAccount' );
```

In addition to using $wgGroupPermissions, there are also general web-based solutions, like using an .htaccess file.

What about more complex requirements – like, for instance, if you want to implement some system where regular users can only read and edit their own contributions, while administrators can read and edit everything? There may be extensions intended to support specific configurations, but good general advice is to echo the warning message: "you are advised to install an appropriate content management package."

Controlling write access

Thankfully, all the many issues related to restricting reading ability don't apply to restricting writing ability. Unlike read restrictions, write restrictions in MediaWiki work quite well; and even if a security breach occurs, it can be easily undone. If you're an administrator, you can restrict the writing of any particular page just via the "Protect" tab (or dropdown selection). In Figure 14.1, you can see an example of the interface shown after clicking on that tab/selection. As you can see, an administrator can set different protection levels for editing and moving pages, and they can set expirations on that protection.

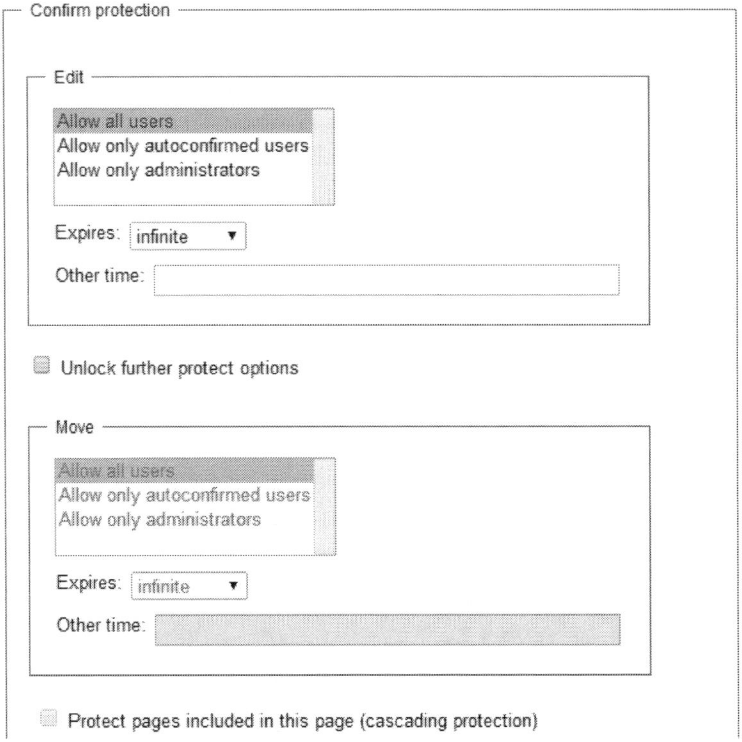

Figure 14.1: "Protect page" interface

All of the access-control extensions also let you restrict write access. These generally provide a way to restrict all pages in a category and/or namespace to editing by one or more user groups. Of these, the safest choices at the moment seem to be the extensions Lockdown and SemanticACL; they both work with the most recent versions of MediaWiki. You can view them here:

> https://www.mediawiki.org/wiki/Extension:Lockdown
> https://www.mediawiki.org/wiki/Extension:SemanticACL

In addition, you can practice a "nicer" form of write-restriction, by using one of the extensions that let you mark a certain revision of the page as approved; anyone can then modify the page further, but the newer edits won't be displayed to users until they, too, are approved. We'll cover the two extensions that allow that in the next section.

FlaggedRevs and Approved Revs

Running a wiki can be a frightening experience: you're in charge of a set of documents that are meant to reflect some sort of official view of things, but sometimes many people, and sometimes everyone, can change anything on the wiki at any time. Which means that you can check the wiki in the morning and find out that a page about some software utility has, for the last four hours, held nothing but a string of obscenities, or some incorrect information about the software, or a nice recipe for chocolate mousse. Or perhaps you find that that bad edit has been in place for a week.

This fear tends to be overblown, because (a) with the (major) exception of spam, edits that are malicious or obviously incorrect are usually pretty rare, (b) to the extent that users are reading the wiki and have editing power, they can usually be trusted to find and revert such changes on their own. Still, the threat is there; and beyond that, some administrators simply want to have final control over what gets displayed at all times. Editorial control, in many cases, can be a nice thing to have.

The natural solution to this problem is one that has its roots in software version control: having one or more versions of a wiki page that are certified as "stable" or approved, and then having the most recent stable version be the one shown by default to users. That way you don't interfere with the process of wiki-editing, while at the same time ensuring a certain level of security for the content.

FlaggedRevs

This view of things has reached to Wikipedia, where vandalism has always been a problem. The FlaggedRevs extension (sometimes also referred to as PendingChanges) was developed for that purpose. It was first used on the German-language Wikipedia in 2008, and it is currently used on some other language Wikipedias, though not yet on the English-language one.

FlaggedRevs can be used on any MediaWiki-based wiki, though it takes some effort to install and use it because it's a substantial piece of software. It does more than simply enable setting a stable revision of a page: it provides a whole framework for users to review different revisions of a page according to different criteria, so that the decision about which revision(s) to go with can be made by consensus.

You can read more about FlaggedRevs here:

https://www.mediawiki.org/wiki/Extension:FlaggedRevs

Approved Revs

FlaggedRevs makes sense for Wikipedia, although it may be overkill for small-to-medium-sized wikis, where decisions can just be made by one or a few people without the need for a full, open discussion. In such a case, the Approved Revs extension may be the better solution.

Approved Revs is an extension that essentially was created to be a much simpler alternative to FlaggedRevs. It basically just lets administrators do one thing: select a single revision of a page as the approved one. When a user goes to a page that has an approved revision, that approved revision is what they will see by default (though they can still see any other revision if they go the "history" page).

If a page has no approved revision, users will, by default, just see the latest revision – Approved Revs will have no impact. However, the wiki can be set to instead show a blank page if there's no approved revision – this can be done by adding the following to LocalSettings.php:

```
$egApprovedRevsBlankIfUnapproved = true;
```

If normal users edit a page that already has an approved revision, their changes won't show up on the default page until another approval happens. But by default, if anyone who has revision-approval permission edits a page, their edit (and thus, the latest revision of the page) will automatically be marked as approved. That usually makes sense, since such editors presumably wouldn't make changes that they wouldn't themselves authorize. However, you can change that default behavior by adding the following to LocalSettings.php:

```
$egApprovedRevsAutomaticApprovals = false;
```

Besides protecting content, Approved Revs can also be used to turn MediaWiki into more of a publishing platform, or a traditional CMS, where "draft" versions of a wiki page exist before the page gets "published". For this case, the $egApprovedRevs-BlankIfUnapproved setting becomes quite useful. It's different from standard publishing schemes because readers can still see all the draft versions, through the history page (although those can be hidden if necessary – see page 20), but the basic concept of a page that's kept hidden until it's reviewed and approved is there.

You can also set the group of namespaces for which Approved Revs is applied, via the $egApprovedRevsNamespaces variable. By default it comprises four namespaces: NS_MAIN (the main namespace), NS_HELP (help pages), NS_TEMPLATE (templates) and NS_PROJECT (the project namespace). And you can set Approved Revs to apply to specific individual pages, using the "__APPROVEDREVS__" behavior switch. This is best done via a template.

As an example, let's say you only wanted approval to apply to the set of pages in the category "Essays". You would first turn off Approved Revs in general, by adding the following to LocalSettings.php:

```
$egApprovedRevsNamespaces = array();
```

You would then create an infobox template, to be used for every "essay" page, that defines pages as being in the "Essays" category; and you would add to that template the "__APPROVEDREVS__" behavior switch, so that it was added automatically to every such page.

Approved Revs also defines a new special page, Special:ApprovedRevs, that provides several lists of pages: all pages that have an approved revision, all the ones that don't, and all the ones whose approved revision is not their latest.

You can read more about about Approved Revs on its homepage:

https://www.mediawiki.org/wiki/Extension:Approved_Revs

Chapter 15

MediaWiki administration

Administering a MediaWiki wiki is generally not that hard, once you've done the initial setup. It involves both actions done via the web interface, and actions done on the back end, like editing LocalSettings.php and installing extensions. Usually there are just one or a handful of people with access to the back end, and the same or a slightly larger group of people with administrative access on the wiki itself.

This entire book is geared in large part toward MediaWiki administrators, so in a sense most of this book could be fit under the topic of "MediaWiki administration". But this chapter is meant to hold some of the tools and actions that are relevant only to administrators, that didn't fit in elsewhere.

Configuration settings

There are many settings for core MediaWiki that can be modified in LocalSettings.php – essentially, all the variables that start with "$wg". Some are covered in this book, though it's a very small percentage of the total set. You can see the full listing here, grouped by functionality type:

> https://www.mediawiki.org/wiki/Manual:Configuration_settings

Here are some of the more useful ones, that aren't mentioned elsewhere in the book:

- $wgCategoryPagingLimit – sets the maximum number of pages listed in every category page; default is 200

- $wgReadOnly – sets the entire wiki to be read-only, with the specified string given as the reason; useful for temporary site maintenance

Debugging

MediaWiki is software, and software unfortunately can go wrong. The issue may be file directory permissions, database user permissions, missing files, missing database tables, bad settings in LocalSettings.php, incompatible versions, or even (perish the thought) bugs in the code. (Which, by the way, are much more likely to happen in extensions than in core MediaWiki.)

Generally, the source of the most confusion in MediaWiki comes when users see a blank page in the browser at any point while on the wiki. This happens if there's an error, and if PHP is configured to show a blank page, instead of the error message, when that happens. It's almost always better to see the error on the screen; so if that happens, the best solution is to add the following line, either to LocalSettings.php or to PHP's own php.ini file:

```
ini_set( 'display_errors', 1 );
```

If it's being added to LocalSettings.php, it should be near the top of the file, right under the "<?php" line.

By far the best tool for any kind of debugging is the MediaWiki debug toolbar. It puts all the necessary information (SQL calls, warnings, debug displays) in one easily-accessible place at the bottom of the browser. For those of us used to having done MediaWiki debugging the old-fashioned way, it's a remarkably useful tool. You can enable it by adding the following to LocalSettings.php:

```
$wgDebugToolbar = true;
```

However, you may not want everyone to see the debugging toolbar, during the time it's enabled (if you enable it, everyone will see it). Or it may not be available, if you're using a version of MediaWiki before 1.19. In either case, there are other options. If you see an error message that contains the text "(SQL query hidden)", and you want to see the SQL that was called, you can see it by adding the following to LocalSettings.php:

```
$wgShowSQLErrors = true;
```

And if the error that's happening seems to be complex, you can turn on MediaWiki's own debug logging, and then examine the contents of that file. To turn it on, add the following to LocalSettings.php:

```
$wgDebugLogFile = "/full/path/to/your/debug/log/file";
```

This file needs to be writable by your web server.

Often, the easiest solution, as with a lot of software, is just to do a web search on the text of the error message – it could well be that others have come across, and maybe diagnosed, this problem. If you believe that the problem is coming from a specific extension, it's a good idea to check that extension's main page, or its talk page, to see if there's any mention of it.

Improving MediaWiki performance

This is not a web performance book, but if you feel your wiki is too slow, or you're worried about the results of increased traffic in the future, here are some helpful tips:

- Make sure your web server and PHP have enough memory assigned to them.

- There are a variety of caching tools that can be used in conjunction with Media-Wiki (and with each other), like Squid, Varnish and memcached. Of all the available tools, the most useful is probably APC, a PHP caching utility that often dramatically improves MediaWiki's performance. You can see all the options for caching here:

  https://www.mediawiki.org/wiki/Manual:Cache

- There's an effort in place to get MediaWiki to work with HipHop, a PHP compiler developed by Facebook engineers, that is supposed to have even more dramatic performance benefits. This is still an ongoing project (as is HipHop itself). You can see the current status of this effort here:

  https://www.mediawiki.org/wiki/HipHop

- If you're using Semantic MediaWiki, there are various ways to guard against queries slowing down the server; these are covered in some detail here:

  https://semantic-mediawiki.org/wiki/Speeding_up_Semantic_MediaWiki

The MediaWiki cache

MediaWiki does extensive caching of pages: when you go to a wiki page, chances are that it wasn't generated on the spot, but rather is a cached version that was created sometime in the previous day or so. (This doesn't apply to pages in the "Special" namespace, which are generated anew every time.)

Users can always see a "live" version of any page by adding "action=purge" to the URL.

The MagicNoCache extension lets you mark some pages as never to be cached, via the "__NOCACHE__" behavior switch. See here:

> https://www.mediawiki.org/wiki/Extension:MagicNoCache

Caching becomes an issue when Semantic MediaWiki is installed, because pages that are cached don't automatically show the latest set of query results; this can cause confusion to users if they add some data and it then doesn't appear in query results elsewhere. The best workaround for this problem is to install the MagicNoCache extension, using it on every page that contains a query. (The 'calendar' query format already disables caching on pages where it's displayed, in order for the layout to display correctly.)

Another option is to use the Approved Revs extension (page 140) – although it's not intentional, pages that have an approved revision don't get cached. This may change in the future, but at the moment it's a side effect that one should be aware of.

SMW actually provides a new tab/dropdown, which only administrators see, called "Refresh", that points to the "action=purge" URL, preventing admins from having to type it in manually.

The job queue

There are certain tasks that MediaWiki has to run over an extended period of time, in the background. The most common case comes when a template is modified. Let's say that someone adds a category tag to a template – that means that every one of the pages that include that template need to be added to that category. This process can't be done all at once, because it would slow down the server considerably, or even temporarily crash it. Instead, the process is broken down into "jobs", which are placed in a "job queue" – and then those jobs are run in an orderly way.

Behind the scenes, the job queue is really just a database table called "job", which holds one row for each job. These jobs are run in sequential order, and once a job is run its row is deleted.

Jobs are run every time the wiki gets a page hit. By default, one job is run on every hit, but this number can be modified to make the running of jobs slower or faster, by changing the value of $wgJobRunRate. To make the running of jobs ten times faster, for instance, you would add the following to LocalSettings.php:

```
$wgJobRunRate = 10;
```

Conversely, to make it ten times slower, you would set the value to 0.1. (You can't actually run a fraction of a job – instead, having a fractional value sets the probability that a job will be run at any given time.)

You can also cause jobs to be run in a more automated way, instead of just waiting for them to be run (or hitting "reload" in the browser repeatedly to speed up the running). This is done by calling the script runJobs.php, in the MediaWiki /maintenance directory. You can even create a cron job to run runJobs.php on a regular basis – say, once a day.

There are various parameters that runJobs.php can take, such as setting the maximum number of jobs to be run, or, maybe more importantly, the type of job to be run. To enable the latter, each job type has its own identifier name, which can be found in the database, if nowhere else. You can read about all the parameters for runJobs.php here:

https://www.mediawiki.org/wiki/Manual:RunJobs.php

In addition to core MediaWiki, extensions can create their own jobs as well. Some extensions that do are Data Transfer, DeleteBatch, Nuke and Replace Text.

Admin Links

One feature common in web-based applications, which MediaWiki has always lacked, is a "dashboard" area, that lets the administrator(s) view statistics and perform administrative tasks from one place.

To a limited extent, the page Special:SpecialPages does that already; it simply lists most of the available special pages, grouped by categories. It's certainly better than nothing, but not all the pages listed in Special:SpecialPages are specifically useful to administrators, and conversely, not all administrative tasks are done via special pages (editing the sidebar, for instance, is not).

The extension Admin Links provides something closer to a real administrator dashboard. It defines a single page, Special:AdminLinks, which holds links that are useful to administrators, separated by functionality type. Other extensions can add their own links to the Admin Links page, if they choose to, via hooks, and a handful do. Figure 15.1 shows what the page looks like when various of the extensions described in this book, like Semantic MediaWiki, Semantic Forms, and Nuke, are installed.

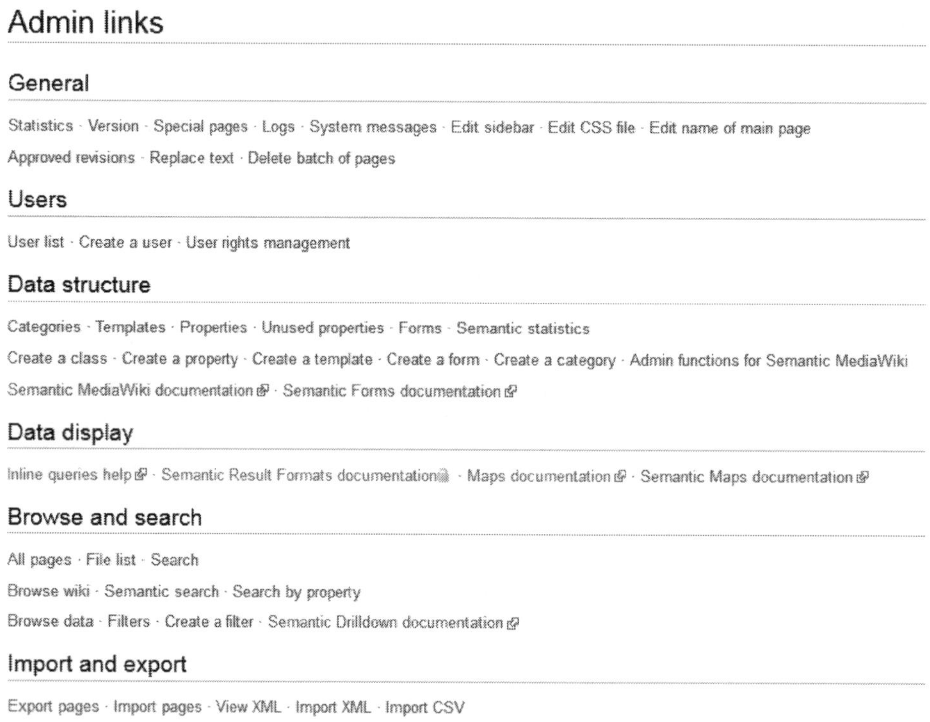

Admin links

General

Statistics · Version · Special pages · Logs · System messages · Edit sidebar · Edit CSS file · Edit name of main page
Approved revisions · Replace text · Delete batch of pages

Users

User list · Create a user · User rights management

Data structure

Categories · Templates · Properties · Unused properties · Forms · Semantic statistics
Create a class · Create a property · Create a template · Create a form · Create a category · Admin functions for Semantic MediaWiki
Semantic MediaWiki documentation ₫ · Semantic Forms documentation ₫

Data display

Inline queries help ₫ · Semantic Result Formats documentation₪ · Maps documentation ₫ · Semantic Maps documentation ₫

Browse and search

All pages · File list · Search
Browse wiki · Semantic search · Search by property
Browse data · Filters · Create a filter · Semantic Drilldown documentation ₫

Import and export

Export pages · Import pages · View XML · Import XML · Import CSV

Figure 15.1: Admin Links page

The other nice feature of Admin Links is that it provides a link to the "Admin links" page within the user links at the top of every page, so that the dashboard is always just a click away. Here is how the top of the page looks in the Vector skin, with Admin Links installed:

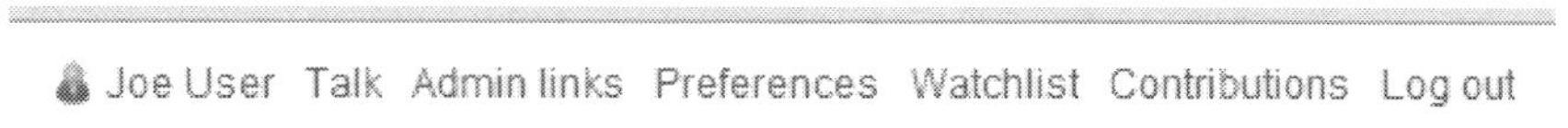

   🔒 Joe User   Talk   Admin links   Preferences   Watchlist   Contributions   Log out

Replace Text

MediaWiki lacks an innate way to do global search-and-replace of text, a feature that would come in handy when, for instance, the name of a certain template parameter changes, and many pages that call that template have to be modified. On Wikipedia and some other large-scale wikis, bots are used for that purpose, but having a way to do it from within the wiki is a lot more convenient. Thankfully, the Replace Text extension makes it possible to do site-wide text replacements. Replace Text can handle both the contents of pages and their names; if content in a page title is replaced, it means that the page gets "moved". Every change made by Replace Text shows up in page histories, with the user who initiated the replacement appearing as the author of that edit.

To run a replacement, go to Special:ReplaceText. This action is governed by the 'replacetext' permission, which by default is given to administrators.

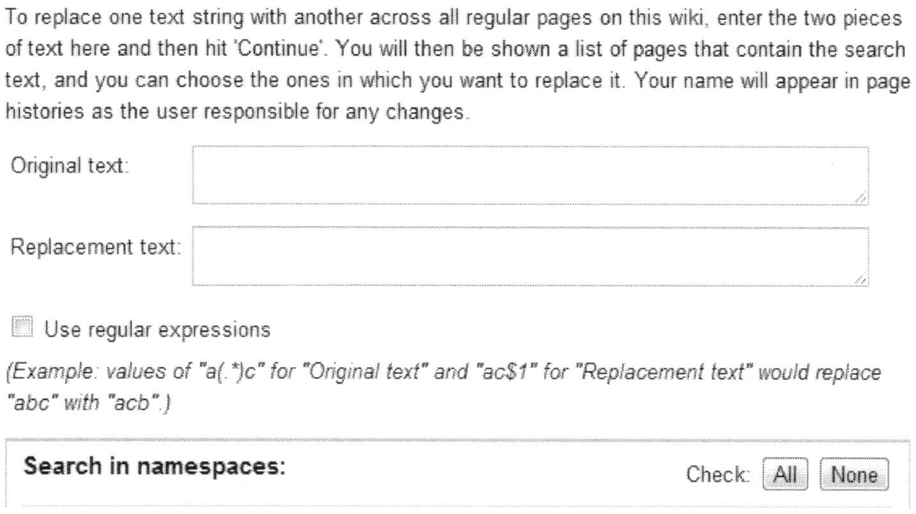

To replace one text string with another across all regular pages on this wiki, enter the two pieces of text here and then hit 'Continue'. You will then be shown a list of pages that contain the search text, and you can choose the ones in which you want to replace it. Your name will appear in page histories as the user responsible for any changes.

Original text: _____

Replacement text: _____

☐ Use regular expressions

(Example: values of "a(.)c" for "Original text" and "ac$1" for "Replacement text" would replace "abc" with "acb".)*

Search in namespaces: Check: [All] [None]

Figure 15.2: Top of Special:ReplaceText

You can see the top of the Special:ReplaceText page in Figure 15.2. What follows below that is a list of namespaces that the user can select from; then below that are some additional options for the replacement, which are shown in Figure 15.3.

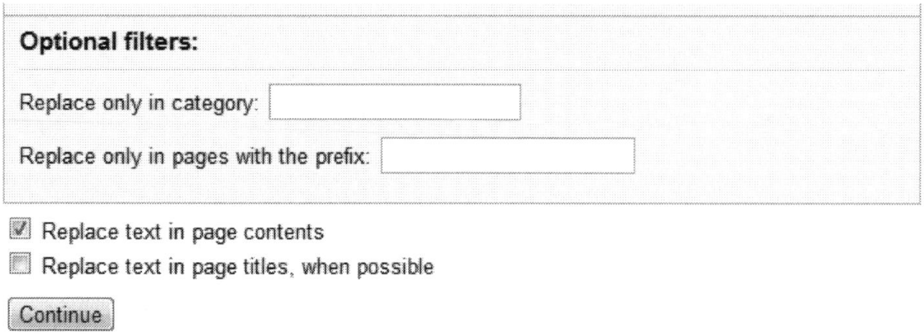

Optional filters:

Replace only in category:

Replace only in pages with the prefix:

☑ Replace text in page contents
☐ Replace text in page titles, when possible

Continue

Figure 15.3: Bottom of Special:ReplaceText

Hitting the "Continue" button brings the user to a second page, listing the exact matches for the search string, so that the user can manually select which pages will have their contents and/or titles modified.

For more complex transformations, you'll probably have to rely on bots and the MediaWiki API, which we'll get to next.

Getting user IP information

In rare cases, it can be useful to get IP address information about users who are logged in – for example, if a user's password is stolen, and someone else starts editing the wiki as them; or if you suspect that a single user is vandalizing the wiki from multiple accounts; or if you suspect that a single user is creating multiple accounts to try to give the illusion of widespread consensus on some issue (this is known as "sockpuppeting"). An IP address is actually stored for each change that happens in the wiki, though it's not visible anywhere in the wiki. If you have access to the database, you can view this information in the "rc_ip" column of the "recentchanges" table.

If you don't want this information stored, for privacy reasons, you can disable storage by adding the following to LocalSettings.php:

    $wgPutIPinRC = false;

Conversely, the CheckUser extension lets administrators view this information from the wiki itself, for easier access:

    https://www.mediawiki.org/wiki/Extension:CheckUser

Bots and the MediaWiki API

There are various tools for making automated changes to the wiki's contents, like the Replace Text extension. But in many cases the set of edits required is too specific to be handled by an automated tool. For all those cases, there are bots, and the MediaWiki API.

A bot, in MediaWiki terminology, is a script that does one or more specific kind of edits, or retrieves one or more pieces of data. A bot can be written in any programming language: it just has to connect with the MediaWiki API, which does the actual work of writing and reading data. Most of the major programming languages have one or more MediaWiki API libraries written for them, which take care of the details of logging in to the wiki and connecting to the API. But even without a library, it's not that hard to create a MediaWiki bot – the script just needs to hit some MediaWiki URLs.

If a bot makes any edits on a wiki, it should ideally be logged in as a user – and ideally that user should be a separate account, which gets added to the "bots" group. You can see these kinds of accounts all over Wikipedia – they're the ones fixing broken `<ref>` tags, renaming categories, adding signatures to unsigned talk-page messages, etc. On other wikis, they're quite a bit less common, but some smaller wikis do make significant use of them.

This page holds some information, and helpful links, on creating and running bots:

> https://www.mediawiki.org/wiki/Manual:Bots

The MediaWiki API

The MediaWiki API is essentially a set of URLs that one can access in order to read from and write to the wiki. They all involve different parameters passed in to the file api.php. That file is located in the same directory as index.php; so, for instance, if your wiki has URLs of the form mywiki.com/w/index.php?title=..., the main API URL can be found at mywiki.com/w/api.php. (For more recent versions of MediaWiki, the API is linked from the Special:Version page.)

If you go that main URL, you'll see a fairly exhaustive (automatically generated) explanation of all the API actions available. API actions are defined by both core MediaWiki and a number of extensions. You'll also see a listing of the different formats that the results can be displayed in, including JSON and XML. For example, adding "format=jsonfm" to the URL will display results in a pseudo-JSON format that users can read on the screen, while "format=json" will result in actual raw JSON.

We won't get into the details of all the API functionality available here, but you can see it at api.php – and you can also read more about it at:

https://www.mediawiki.org/wiki/API:Main_page

Search engine optimization

Search engine optimization, or SEO, is the practice of attempting to get the pages of one's web site to show up as high as possible in search-engine results, most notably on Google. It's a controversial field: to its proponents, it's an indispensable way to get web traffic, while to its detractors, it's at best tacky, and at worst the domain of hucksters, spammers and scammers. Nevertheless, for people who run public wikis, showing up high in search results can be important.

First of all, MediaWiki is already well-geared for doing well in search results in a number of ways. Wikipedia, which is of course MediaWiki-based, is the number one best-performing site for search results, by any metric: it's usually in the top three, and often #1, for a search on any topic it covers. That's mostly just because it gets linked to so often from other sites about those specific topics, but it's also in part due to MediaWiki's own design.

In MediaWiki, the subject of every page is also: the page's name, a part of its URL, the text in the top-level header, and the text that shows up in internal links to that page. That sort of consistency is extremely important for search engines in associating that word or phrase with that specific URL. Tied in with that, there's usually only one top-level header per page: the name of the page is contained within the only <h1> tag on the page, which is another thing that helps to establish the page's subject for search engines.

There is at least one active MediaWiki extension that can potentially help further with search-engine rankings: the extension WikiSEO, which adds to the <meta> and <title> tags of a wiki page's HTML source code. It defines a parser function, appropriately named "#seo", which can be added anywhere to the page, and which is called in the following way:

```
{{#seo: title=... | titlemode=... | keywords=... |
description=... }}
```

The "title=" parameter either replaces, is appended or prepended to the contents of the HTML <title> tag, depending on the value of the "titlemode=" parame-

place, append or prepend. The "keywords=" and
rs get placed as the "name" and "content" attributes, re-
a> tag. If you don't know how best to set all of these tags,
ir meaning, and how they should be best used for SEO.
tion about WikiSEO here:

viki.org/wiki/Extension:WikiSEO

mplates on most pages, a good strategy is to place the
it you don't have to add it manually to each page; and
irameters from the infobox.

Running a wiki farm

It's not uncommon for organizations and corporations to want to run more than one
wiki; sometimes many more. A company that runs public wikis on different topics,
for advertising revenue or any other reason, may end up running a large number of
them. Internally, companies may want to host more than one wiki as well. Access
control to data is one reason, as noted on page 136: the most secure way to keep a
set of wiki data restricted to a defined group of users is to keep it in a separate wiki.
And different departments within an organization could each want their own wiki,
either to keep their data restricted or just because they have little need for sharing data
with other groups. In a very large company or other organization, the number of such
independent subdivisions that would want their own wiki could number even in the
hundreds.

Of course, each group that wanted their own wiki could simply set one up themselves; if they all use MediaWiki, installation is free and generally not too difficult.
(That, in fact, is how wikis have historically been introduced into organizations: small
groups setting them up themselves, in what's known as "skunkworks" projects). But
that kind of setup can quickly become unwieldy: if a different person needs to become
a wiki expert for each wiki to be created and maintained, that's too much work being
expended. Even if all the wikis are managed centrally by a single IT person or department, that can become a tedious amount of work when it's time to upgrade the
software.

In such a situation, what you should be using is what's known as a "wiki farm", or
sometimes "wiki family": a group of wikis that are managed from a single place, and

to which it's easy to add additional wikis. In MediaWiki, there are a variety of ways to create a wiki farm. The best reference for reading about the different approaches, and how to set up each one of them, is here:

https://www.mediawiki.org/wiki/Manual:Wiki_family

There are many approaches listed on this page: single vs. multiple code bases, single vs. multiple databases, single vs. multiple instances of LocalSettings.php, etc. However, there's only one approach we really recommend, which is to use a single code base, multiple databases and multiple settings files. This essentially corresponds to the "Drupal-style sites" approach described in that page.

We won't get into the full technical details here, but the basic idea is this: you have a separate database for each wiki, as well as a separate settings file. Each per-wiki settings file gets included from within LocalSettings.php. The individual settings files set the database name for each wiki, and let you customize the wiki's settings, including standard features like the wiki name, logo, skin and permission; in addition to allowing for extensions that are only included for some wikis.

The "Wiki family" manual includes a simple combination of a PHP and shell script for this approach, that together let you create and update the database for each wiki.

You also need to decide on a URL structure for the different wikis: the two standard approaches are to use subdomains, like "wiki1.mycompany.com", or subdirectories, like "mycompany.com/wiki1". This structure has to be handled by a combination of LocalSettings.php (which has to figure out which settings file to use, based on the URL), and the server configuration, which, if Apache is being used, is usually the file httpd.conf. The specific settings for both are covered within the "Wiki family" manual.

If you know ahead of time that you'll have multiple wikis, it may be helpful to have shared user accounts across all of them, so that users don't have to create a new account on every wiki that they want to edit. Wikipedia does this in a complex way, using the "CentralAuth" extension, but for other wikis, this can be done in a much simpler way, by just having the various databases share a single set of tables on user information. You just have to decide on which database will hold the information, and then add the following to LocalSettings.php:

$wgSharedDB = "*main-database-name*";

Though "shared DB" sounds like a big deal, by default only tables that have to do with user information are shared.

Multi-language wikis

Of all the things that wiki administrators typically want to do, possibly the most conceptually tricky is to have their wiki support multiple languages. That's because there's a tradeoff in place: you want the text each person reads in their language to be as precise as possible, but at the same time you want to avoid redundancy, because redundancy means more work to try to ensure that the contents in different languages all match each other.

First, some good news: the text of the interface itself – like the text in the "Edit" and "View history" tabs, or the text in special pages – is usually not an issue, because if a user sets their own language under "User preferences", chances are good that all of that text has been translated into their language, thanks to MediaWiki's top-notch translation setup.

That just leaves the contents of the wiki. For that, the right approach depends mostly on whether the content is meant to be created only by users who speak one language, but read in multiple languages; or whether content is meant to be generated by users speaking multiple languages.

There are essentially three approaches. In order from most difficult to least difficult, they are:

- **Separate wiki for each language.** This is the Wikipedia approach. You can have a different wiki for each language, ideally identified by each one's two-letter language code. Pages can then refer to their other-language counterparts via interwiki links (see page 31), as is done on Wikipedia. This approach is ideal when the content is truly independent for each language, or when you want to ensure that every user experiences the wiki entirely in their language. See "Running a wiki farm", above, for how to set up such a thing.

- **Multiple translations for each page.** You can have one wiki, where each page has multiple translations. The standard approach is to have a main language (such as English), and then allow users to create translation pages for each one, while linking each page to all its other translations via a navigation template at the top or bottom. The standard way to name such pages is via language codes; so, for instance, for a page called "Equipment", its Amharic translation would be at a page called "Equipment/am". This approach offers a pragmatic compromise, and it's fairly popular. The Translate extension makes it easy to go with this approach, by providing a framework for creating and displaying all the translations. Once you have Translate set up, it's mostly just a matter of adding the right tags to each page that's meant to be translated: `<translate>` around blocks of text that should be translated, and `<languages />`, usually at the top or bottom of the page, to display a bar linking to all the versions of that page in other languages. You can read more about it here:

https://www.mediawiki.org/wiki/Extension:Translate

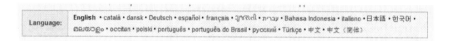

Figure 15.4: A bar with links to different translations of a page, provided by the Translate extension

- **Machine translation of content.** With this approach, you keep all content in one language, and then just have a mechanism for people to translate the contents via a machine-translation service. The Live Translate extension is the recommended approach for this: it provides an easy-to-use interface, some nice additional features, and it allows for using both the Google and Microsoft translation services. This is by far the easiest approach to multiple languages. You can read about it here:

https://www.mediawiki.org/wiki/Extension:Live_Translate

Chapter 16

Semantic MediaWiki

Semantic MediaWiki is an extremely important extension to MediaWiki. It defines a framework for storing data in the wiki, and then querying it – which has the effect of turning a wiki, which is often considered to be just a storage system for text and images, into something more like a database. SMW, as it's abbreviated, is great by itself, but it's when it is used together with spinoff extensions that it starts to become (dare I say) magical. SMW has over 50 spinoff extensions, that cover all aspects from entry of data, to browsing and search, to visualization, to enhanced storage, etc. Some extensions are more popular than others, and we'll cover the extensions that are most essential in this book.

In conjunction with its extensions, SMW can transform a regular wiki into a kind of collaborative database. It's much more collaborative than a regular database because the version history stored by the wiki means that you can open up editing of all your data to any number of people – something that is very rarely possible with a standard database-backed application.

Why is it called "Semantic MediaWiki"? "Semantic" is a word that, in its most general form, indicates meaning – not the display or exact phrasing of text (i.e., the "syntax"), but rather its underlying meaning. In modern context, the term "Semantic Web" has gained a lot of buzz since the early-to-mid-2000s. Ironically, the meaning of the phrase "Semantic Web" is itself ambiguous (see page 177), but the main idea behind it is to get at an underlying meaning of the text that readers see online – a meaning that that can then be reused and processed, by humans as well as machines. And that is the main idea behind Semantic MediaWiki as well.

Semantic MediaWiki may not be the single most important MediaWiki extension (ParserFunctions probably holds that title), but it is clearly the one that has taken on the greatest life of its own. Besides the 50+ extensions that make use of it, it also has a thriving community of users and developers, at least some of whom would consider themselves SMW users first and MediaWiki users second. As of 2014, SMW is in use on most likely over 1,000 active wikis. SMW has its own website (semantic-mediawiki.org), its own mailing lists and IRC channel, and its own conference (the twice-yearly SMWCon). There's no other MediaWiki extension that has anything comparable.

Semantic MediaWiki was created in 2005 by Markus Krötzsch and Denny Vrandečić. It was originally conceived as functionality for Wikipedia – a way to store data in order to make the hundreds of thousands of manually-generated lists and categories on Wikipedia less necessary. Its use on regular MediaWiki was, at least at the beginning, only of secondary importance to its creators. That quickly changed, as regular wiki users started to discover its benefits and embrace the technology, while the Wikimedia Foundation adopted a "wait and see" attitude on SMW.

The original dream is now coming to fruition, with the Wikidata project, which started in mid-2012, and was originally headed by Vrandečić. Wikidata is an extremely exciting project that aims to create a single data repository for all the different language Wikipedias, so that they can all populate their structured data, like infoboxes, automatically. One type of data, links to the same article in other languages, is already handled exclusively via Wikidata. Some of Semantic MediaWiki's code to handle back-end storage was spun off into separate libraries, now used by both SMW and Wikidata (or, more specifically, Wikibase, the software powering Wikidata) to store their data.

The current structure of Wikidata is quite a bit different from how SMW was originally proposed for use on Wikipedia. Most notably, Wikidata is meant to support hundreds of languages at the same time. And the current syntax for storing and querying data via Wikidata is almost completely different from the standard SMW syntax. So it's possible to make too much of the fact that Wikidata's storage component will be code that originated in SMW. Still, if Wikidata is successful, it could end up raising Semantic MediaWiki's profile considerably. This would be a nice side effect to Wikidata's main goal, which is to create the largest structured database of general-knowledge information in the history of the world.

But enough about Wikidata: for the rest of this chapter, we'll focus on Semantic MediaWiki as it is used in regular wikis, and explain the many benefits it can provide.

If you got this book only to read about core MediaWiki, hopefully you'll still read the following chapters, because in my opinion SMW can provide benefits to nearly every wiki.

How SMW works: an example

Let's say you have a wiki about wines. Now, you want to be able to see a list of all the Chardonnay wines grown in the South of France. On a typical wiki, whether it's Wikipedia or anything else (even, for the most part, non-MediaWiki wikis), there are essentially two options: you can compile such a list manually on some wiki page, or you can tag all such pages (assuming there's a page about every wine) with a category like "Chardonnay wines from the South of France".

Both types of actions are done on Wikipedia all the time, and on many other wikis as well. However, they both have problems: the first option, manually compiling a list, takes a lot of work, and requires modifying each time a new wine page is added that would go that list, or when some error is discovered. In the second case, the list (on the category page) is generated automatically, but the information has to be added painstakingly to each page. And if you're expecting users to do it, they need to be given precise instructions on how to add categories and what the categories should be named (should it be "the South of" or "Southern"?), and in general, what the ideal data structure should be. Should there be a "Chardonnay" category for each country covered in the wiki, even those with only one or two wines to their name? And, conversely, should countries, or regions, with many wines to their name be further split up, say by year? Or should the year be tagged with a separate category?

Semantic MediaWiki offers a solution to this problem. Instead of compiling lists, or having an overload of categories, you can define a single infobox template meant to be put on wine pages, that both displays the relevant information (region, variety, year, etc.) for each wine, and stores that information in a way that can be queried. So instead of having to manage a large and probably somewhat chaotic set of categories, you can keep the data structure simple, and move the complexity (such as there is) to the queries that display the data.

What about the infoboxes - isn't it still difficult for users to learn how to add and populate those? For that, there's the Semantic Forms extension, covered in the next chapter, that provides forms so that users don't need to see the underlying wikitext syntax in order to create and change data.

Finally, SMW, in conjunction with some other SMW-based extensions, allows you to go one better than simply displaying information in lists or categories - for our example, you can show the information in tables, you can display wines on a map, you can aggregate wines by country, year, etc. to show their breakdown, and you can allow users to do faceted searches on all of those fields in order to find the wine(s) that interest them.

Downloading and installing

The first step in using Semantic MediaWiki is of course to install it. General instructions for downloading and installing Semantic MediaWiki can be found here:

> https://semantic-mediawiki.org/wiki/Help:Download
> https://semantic-mediawiki.org/wiki/Help:Installation

If you're using SMW 1.9 or later, following these instructions is crucial – SMW now requires many more extensions than it used to, though thankfully the setup is fairly easy, thanks to SMW's use of the Composer utility.

SMW adds its own tables to the database. Since version 1.8, you can add these tables in the same way as other extensions' tables get added, by calling the MediaWiki script "update.php". But you can instead (and, if you're using an earlier SMW version, you have to) go to the page Special:SMWAdmin, and click on the button "Initialise or upgrade tables". A database update should also be done if you update your version of Semantic MediaWiki – its database schema has been modified a few times during its history, and will likely be modified again.

The page Special:SMWAdmin can also be used to do refreshes of the data in those tables, and to register one's wiki on semantic-mediawiki.org. The latter is not a very important task, but you can see more about it here:

> https://semantic-mediawiki.org/wiki/Registry

The database upgrade needs to be done before other SMW-based extensions are installed, since some of them expect those tables to be in place already.

Semantic triples and properties

Semantic MediaWiki is built around data, and in Semantic MediaWiki every piece of data is represented as a "triple" – a semantic-web concept that indicates a three-part structure: a subject, a predicate and an object. An example of a triple would be:

Canada Has capital Ottawa

"Canada" is the subject; "Has capital" is the predicate, or relationship between the two concepts; and "Ottawa" is the object.

In Semantic MediaWiki, the predicate is known as the "property". And the subject is always the page on which the value is stored.

The easiest way to encode this specific triple would be to go to the page on the wiki named "Canada", click on "edit", and write the following:

```
[[Has capital::Ottawa]]
```

This looks similar to the MediaWiki syntax for encoding links, and for storing category information. The difference here compared to both of those is that there are two colons instead of one. "Has capital" here represents the predicate, or middle value, or property, of the triple.

What gets displayed on the page? It depends on the "type" of the property. If the property is defined as being of type "Page", i.e. a link, then "Ottawa" shows up as a link. If it's defined as being of type "String" or "Text", then it shows up on the page as simply a string. (There are other property types, but they wouldn't make sense for this case.) We'll get to property types in the next section.

Semantic MediaWiki offers another way to store data, and that's the #set parser function. Here's how it would be called for this case:

```
{{#set:Has capital=Ottawa}}
```

In the case of #set, nothing is shown on the screen: #set works "silently", and stores data without displaying anything. There are various cases in which you may want to store a value without displaying it, and #set is ideal for those cases.

Defining properties

Every property in Semantic MediaWiki has a type. The type of a property dictates how that property's values are displayed on the page, how its values are displayed and handled elsewhere, and what kind of values are allowed for that property. By default, properties are of type Page, though it's good to always define the type explicitly.

How is a property's type defined? With yet more semantic annotation. Every property has its own page on the wiki, in the "Property" namespace (or whatever the corresponding name is in the wiki's language). So the page for the "Has capital" property would be named "Property:Has capital". In that page, you could add the following:

```
[[Has type::Page]]
```

This would define the "Has capital" property to be of type Page. "Has type" is what's known as a "special property": a property that's pre-defined in SMW with special meaning.

You could also define the property to be a simple string of characters, by adding the following instead:

```
[[Has type::String]]
```

There are various other standard types defined in SMW. The current full set is: Page, Text, Number, Boolean, Date, URL, Email, Telephone number, Code, Quantity and Temperature. Most of these are (hopefully) obvious from their name:

- "Page", as noted before, holds the name of a wiki page.

- "Text" holds text values. Until version 1.9 of SMW, text values were stored using two different property types, "String" and "Text": "String" could hold only up to 255 characters, while "Text" could hold an unlimited number, but could not be queried on (though they can both be displayed in queries). Since SMW 1.9, "Text" can hold an unlimited number of characters and can also be queried on; although for now it's only the first 40 characters of the string that are searched by queries.

- "Number" can hold any integer or decimal number.

- "Boolean" can take in any of a number of values meaning "true" and "false": "yes" and "no" are allowed, as well as values specific to the language of the wiki.

- "Date", "URL", "Email" and "Telephone number" hold the information that you'd expect them to hold, and are displayed (and linked) appropriately.

- "Code" is a minor type that's basically the same as "Text", but meant to be displayed in a pre-formatted way.

"Temperature" and "Quantity" are covered in an upcoming section, "Custom units". There's another property type, "Record", but it's obsolete, and is best ignored.

Setting allowed values

There are also properties for which you may want to predefine a set of allowed values; in programming terms, these are usually known as "enumerations". These can be defined in SMW as well, though not with a special type: rather, each allowed value is specified on the property's page, using the "Allows value" special property. For instance, if we wanted to define a property called "Has day of week", we might add the following to its page:

```
The allowed values for this property are:
* [[Allows value::Sunday]]
* [[Allows value::Monday]]
* [[Allows value::Tuesday]]
* [[Allows value::Wednesday]]
* [[Allows value::Thursday]]
* [[Allows value::Friday]]
* [[Allows value::Saturday]]
```

Enumerations can be of any type, although in practice, they're almost always either of type Page or Text (String before version 1.9).

Creating property pages

You can of course hand-create any property page. The easiest way to create properties, though, is via the extension Semantic Forms (see page 188). If you have Semantic Forms installed, then going to any uncreated property page should show a "create with form" tab near the "create" tab, which brings you to a form that just needs to be filled out and saved. You can also use either the Special:CreateProperty or the Special:CreateClass pages, both defined by Semantic Forms as well.

Custom units

You can also define properties that are stored in units – for weight, distance, energy and so on. These can let you convert between different units: the special property "Corresponds to" lets you define the conversion between one and another.

For example, to define a property called "Has distance" that by default is displayed in miles, you would put the following in the page "Property:Has distance":

```
[[Has type::Quantity]]
[[Corresponds to::1 mile, miles]]
[[Corresponds to::1.609 km, kilometers, kilometres]]
```

If a value is stored using the property "Has distance", it will then always be displayed in miles when it's queried, or exported via RDF (page 177).

The "Temperature" type is the one type with units that's pre-defined in Semantic MediaWiki – it's the exception because conversion between temperature types can't be done through simple multiplication.

Special properties

In addition to user-defined properties, there are also properties that can be defined by the code, i.e. by Semantic MediaWiki and other extensions. These are called "special properties". We've already looked at two of them: "Has type" and "Allows value". There are also special properties defined by other extensions, like "Has default form" defined by Semantic Forms; we'll get to those later.

Special properties should never be used for a purpose other than their intended one. This occasionally happens with "Has type", because it has such a generic name. But this will result in strange behavior; if you're thinking of creating a property called "Has type", you should use a name like "Is of type", "Has car type", etc. instead.

Wikis in languages other than English will have their own translations for such special properties, although the English-language version should always work as well.

There are also special properties that are not meant to be set by the user, but rather are stored automatically. Two such special properties are "Modification date" and "Has improper value for". The first is stored, by default, for every page – it holds the date on which the page was last modified, and is useful for showing lists of recently-edited pages. The second, "Has improper value for", shows, for every page, each of the properties it holds that has a value that's not allowed.

The set of special properties stored for pages can be changed – in addition to showing the last modified date, you can also show the creation date, the username of the last editor, etc. The values that are stored can be set via the $smwgPageSpecialProperties setting, described here:

http://semantic-mediawiki.org/wiki/Help:$smwgPageSpecialProperties

Another extension, Semantic Extra Special Properties, lets you store additional meta-data, such as the full set of users who edited a page; see page 243.

Queries

What can we do with the data once it's stored? Most obviously, we can query it. Queries in SMW are done using a parser function called #ask. Here is a simple call to get the list of countries in a wiki, and their capitals:

```
{{#ask:[[Category:Countries]]|?Has capital}}
```

Let's go through the components of this query. The first, "[[Category:Countries]]", is the "filter" – it defines which pages get queried; in this case, all pages in the "Countries" category. The second is the "printouts" section – it lists the property or properties (in this case, just "Has capital") that is or are printed out in the output generated. Each property to be printed out is placed after a question mark. By default, this information would be shown in a table, which would look something like the following:

	Has capital
Afghanistan	Kabul
Albania	Tirana

And so on. In this example, the values are all links, because, "Has capital" is a property of type Page, and thus every string in the table happens to have its own wiki page.

The top row is the header row. By default it's rather cryptic-looking, displaying a property name for each printout column, and blank for the page name column. The following query would have a nicer display for the top row:

```
{{#ask:[[Category:Countries]] |?Has capital=Capital
|mainlabel=Country}}
```

"mainlabel" is just one of the many parameters that #ask queries can take – we'll get to the full set later.

By far the most common usage for queries is to display page sets – to list either an entire set of pages that match the general conditions, or the set of pages that match a particular "parent" page. For instance, if a particular wiki is a location directory that holds information about each specific location, there will probably be a separate page for any area, such as a city or country; so we could then add to each such page a query listing all its "children", i.e. all the places of interest that are listed as being in that area. In a wiki that holds information about museums, for example, we could, add to a page called "Santiago" a query like the following:

```
{{#ask:[[Category:Museums]][[Has city::Santiago]]}}
```

This makes it easy for users to see aggregated data without having to create queries or otherwise run a search: by simply going to the page called "Santiago", they can see the full list of museums there, formatted in a way that makes sense for this particular wiki (in addition to any specific information presented about Santiago).

If there's any more than one or two cities, countries etc. in the wiki, it probably makes sense to create templates called "Country", "City", etc. to be used in those pages; and then to have each such template hold an aggregating query (in addition to any data we might want specifically about those places). Here's a query that could go into a template called "City":

```
{{#ask:[[Category:Museums]][[Has city::{{PAGENAME}}]]}}
```

Adding a call to the "City" template will then display, for any city, the set of museums in that city.

You can also perform what are called inverse queries, where you query on a property in its reverse direction (this can only be done for properties of type Page). Inverse queries are done by adding a "-" before the property name. They are usually not that useful, but in certain cases it can be. Some countries have more than one capital – South Africa has three, for instance – so you could do an inverse query on "Has capital" to list all of a country's capitals, and information about each one. Here is a query to display all of the capitals of South Africa, and the total area of each of them:

```
{{#ask:[[-Has capital::South Africa]] |?Has total
area}}
```

In addition to just querying on specific values, you can also do "greater than" or "less than" queries, using the operators "::>" and "::<" (though by default, these actually test for "greater than or equal" and "less than or equal"). Here's how to get a list of countries, and their populations, for only countries with a population of greater than or equal to 10 million:

```
{{#ask:[[Category:Countries]][[Has
population::>10000000]] |?Has population=Population
|mainlabel=Country}}
```

And for String and Page properties, you can also use the "::~" operator to find partial string matches. Here's how to get the set of countries with "New" in the name of their capital:

```
{{#ask:[[Category:Countries]][[Has capital::~*New*]]
|?Has capital=Capital |mainlabel=Country}}
```

The "::~" check may or may not be case-sensitive, depending on the configuration of your database server.

There are various other standard parameters that you can add to #ask queries, to modify the set of results and their display:

- `format=` - sets the display format for the result (this is covered in depth in the next main section, "Display formats").

- `limit=` - sets the number of pages to return (the default is usually 20).

- `sort=` - the property name, or names, on which to sort.

- `order=` - the order in which to sort values, if they're sorted; should be `ascending` (which is the default), `descending`, or `random`.

- `headers=` - whether the headers (by default, the property names) should be shown; the options are `show` (the default), `hide`, or `plain`, which shows headers but not as links.

- `mainlabel=` - the header given to the page names themselves; if this is set to "-", the page names are not displayed.

- `link=` - sets what parts of results should be links – the options are `all` (the default), `none`, or `subject`, where only page names are links but printouts are not.

- `default=` - the default text printed if there are no results.

- `intro=` - introductory text printed, if there are results.

- `outro=` - concluding text printed, if there are results.

- `searchlabel=` - text for the "further results" link; by default, it's "«... further results»".

- `offset=` - the result number at which to start displaying (this is used for pagination, and is rarely included explicitly in queries).

Displaying individual values

#ask is geared for showing lists, tables and other aggregated displays. But what if you want to show just a single value? For that, there's the #show parser function, which has a similar syntax to #ask, but a simpler one. The following call would simply display the text "Brasilia", for example:

```
{{#show:Brazil |?Has capital |link=none}}
```

Linked properties and subqueries

It's usually a good idea to avoid data redundancy. For every museum, you could store both its city and country, but if every city page already has its country stored, then that's unnecessary: you could just store the city, and query on the rest.

Let's take a practical example: say your museum wiki only stores the city for each museum, with the property "Has city"; and the country for each city is then stored on pages for each city, with the property "Has country". (We'll ignore for now the problem of different cities with the same name in different countries, and assume that a museum tagged as being in, say, "Moscow" is always in the one in Russia, as opposed to in another city with the same name.) With such a structure, how can you find all the museums in a certain country? You could do it with a query like:

```
{{#ask:[[Category:Museums]][[Has city.Has
country::Nepal]]}}
```

Here, "Has city" and "Has country" are what's known as linked properties – the period between the names defines the linking. The query looks for pages that have the property "Has city" pointing to a page that in turn has the property "Has country" with the value "Nepal".

You can even do more complex queries using subqueries, which are queries contained within a <q> tag. Here's one example:

```
{{#ask:[[Category:Museums]][[Has city::<q>[[Has
population::>100000]][[Has country::Argentina]]</q>]]}}
```

This query will find all museums in any city with 100,000 or more people in Argentina.

Unfortunately, both linked properties and subqueries work only on the "filter" part of the query, and not on the "display" part – so your query can't contain a property printout like "? Has city.Has country". That limitation is there for performance reasons, but it has definitely caused problems.

Display formats

Display formats, also known as result formats and query formats, are extremely important: they're a way to set the display of the data returned by queries, if you want to show it in a way more interesting than just lists or tables. To set the display format, you just need to add the parameter "format=..." to the #ask query.

There's a whole extension devoted to just holding various display formats, Semantic Result Formats, and another one, Semantic Maps, which holds formats related to mapping; both are described in Chapter 18. But there are various basic formats that are defined within Semantic MediaWiki itself:

- **list** - displays results as a simple list, separated by default by commas. This is the default display when only page names are queried.

- **ul** - a bulleted list.

- **ol** - a numbered list ("ul" and "ol" are both the names of the relevant HTML tags used – they stand for "unordered list" and "ordered list", respectively).

- **table** - a table of data. This is the default display when there are additional printouts in the query.

- **broadtable** - a broadtable. This is identical to the "table" format, except that the width of the table is 100% of the page.

- **category** - displays results in the format that pages appear in on category pages, with a separate header for each new starting letter.

- **template** - applies a template to set the display of each query result; see below.

- **csv**, **dsv**, **json**, **rss**, **rdf** - machine-readable data formats; these are discussed on page 258.

- **count** - simply displays the number of pages that match the query criteria.

- **embedded** - displays each page that matches the query criteria, in full, one after the other. (This format unfortunately causes each of those pages' categories to be applied to the page that holds the query.)

- **debug** - displays a printout of the database queries used for this query; useful only for debugging.

Some of these formats have their own custom parameters that can be used, in addition to all the standard parameters. The "category" format, for instance, allows for a "columns=" parameter, which sets the number of columns into which to split results. The best way to see the entire set of parameters for each format is to go to the page Special:Ask on the wiki, which shows the name and a brief description for each one. Special:Ask is described in the upcoming section, "Semantic search page".

Query templates

Using templates to display query results is a very versatile approach, which lets you apply custom formatting and text around the set of properties displayed for each query result. It's of course available for the "template" format, but it's also available for many other formats, including "list", "ol", "ul", "category" and various formats defined in the extensions Semantic Result Formats and Semantic Maps, like "calendar" and "maps". (We'll get to these extensions and formats in Chapter 18.) To apply a template, you need to create a template on the wiki that takes in values and applies some formatting to them, then add "|template=*template name*" to the #ask query.

The template needs to have numbered parameters for each value, starting with 1, where the first parameter is passed in the page name. Here's an example of the contents a template that could be used to display information about music albums, if the additional query printouts are for the artist, year and genre:

```
''{{{1|}}}'', {{{2|}}} ({{{3||}}}) - genre:   {{{4|}}}
```

Here's what a query that called that template could look like, if that template were named "Album display":

```
{{#ask:[[Category:Albums]]|format=ul|template=Album
display|?Has artist|?Released in year|?Has genre}}
```

Notice that the format here is "ul", not "template" – that's so each row will appear as a nice bulleted item. The output would be a series of lines that looked like this:

- *Computer World*, Kraftwerk (1981) - genre: Electronic

- *Crescent*, John Coltrane (1964) - genre: Jazz

Here, you can see that even simple formatting can serve to make the display of data much more legible and reader-friendly.

Concepts

Categories (page 43) are the basic building block, within both MediaWiki and Semantic MediaWiki, for defining a collection of pages, but they're not the only way to do it. Semantic MediaWiki also provides for "concepts", which are essentially the set of pages that correspond to a particular query: you can think of a concept as a query that can be referred to.

Let's take a simple case: you have a category called "Cars", and each page for a car has, among other fields, one indicating the car's country of origin: Germany, England, etc. You could indicate the country using a category, e.g. "German cars" etc., but by now you know that using SMW's semantic properties is the much better way to go. So you instead go with a property like "Has nationality". But what if you have a lot of queries on your wiki that refer to, say, Japanese cars, and you're tired of typing "[[Category:Cars]][[Has nationality::Japan]]" every time, and you long for the simplicity of "[[Category:Japanese cars]]"? In that case, concepts are the answer.

Concepts are defined within their own namespace, which in English is "Concept:", and they use the parser function #concept. So you could create a page called "Concept:Japanese cars", which just contains the following text:

```
{{#concept:[[Category:Cars]][[Has nationality::Japan]]}}
```

A #concept function call looks just like a call to #ask, but with no display-related parameters: the call contains only the filtering for the set of pages. After it's defined, you could add "[[Concept:Japanese cars]]" into any query, and it would work just like a category tag. For example, you could have the following query:

```
{{#ask:[[Concept:Japanese cars]][[Has
layout::Front-wheel drive]]|?Has size |?Has
manufacturer}}
```

The concept page itself will list all the pages it "contains", i.e. those that match its query, just like a category page does; and the display of a concept page mimics that of a category page (see page 45).

Concepts are also useful with at least two other extensions: Semantic Forms and Semantic Watchlist. With Semantic Forms, you can have either autocompletion or a dropdown in a form based on the pages in a concept, just as you could with the pages in a category. And with Semantic Watchlist, you can watch for changes in the set of pages contained within a concept. Both extensions are covered later in the book.

Semantic search page

Semantic MediaWiki provides a special page, at Special:Ask, that has an interface for constructing queries. It has separate fields for the query filters, the query printouts, and all additional parameters, like the query format. Special:Ask has four purposes:

- It can be used to query the data on the wiki.

- It can be used as a "wizard" – a helpful interface to generate a query that is then placed somewhere in the wiki. Once a query is created, Special:Ask lets you view the corresponding #ask call, which you can then copy and paste into any page.

- It is also used by regular queries – if a query has more than a certain number of results, only some will be displayed (usually 20), and then there will be a link below that says "View more results". This link takes you to the Special:Ask page, where the first set of results are displayed. Special:Ask has pagination, so you can scroll through all the results, no matter how many there are.

- Special:Ask is also used to display the export query formats like CSV and JSON; in this way, Special:Ask can function as an API for SMW data (though not the most recommended one – that would be the "smwask" API action; see page 151).

Storing compound data

Not all data can be stored using simple properties. Specifically, "two-dimensional" data – data that is usually displayed in a table – cannot be stored using regular Semantic MediaWiki properties.

Let's take as an example the set of ingredients for a recipe – which you can think of as a table of data, with each row for an ingredient corresponding to a row in a table. One of the recipe's rows calls for 3 tomatoes. How would you store that information? You could add the tag "`[[Has ingredient::tomatoes]]`", but a tag like "`[[Has quantity::3]]`" wouldn't work – it wouldn't be clear which ingredient that applies to. So you could create a separate page for each row; but this would lead to a large number of pages – 10 or more for each recipe – that could easily become overwhelming. (To take one example, if you wanted to delete a recipe, you would have to delete all the ingredient pages for it.) Nearly as bad, there's no obvious naming system to use for each ingredient page – you would have to go with something along the lines of "Lasagna recipe tomatoes row", or, even more cryptically, "Recipe row 73411". In any case, maintaining all these pages could become a nightmare.

Instead, the recommended solution is to store all this information (in this example, the entire recipe) in a single page. There are two approaches that allow this: the #subobject parser function, and the Semantic Internal Objects extension. The two have a slightly different syntax, but are otherwise essentially the same.

Subobjects

#subobject is a parser function defined by Semantic MediaWiki, that lets you store compound data of this sort. A call to #subobject is defined as:

```
{{#subobject:subobject name |property 1=value 1
|property 2=value 2 |...}}
```

For the original example, in a page called "Greek salad", you could have a call to #subobject that looks like:

```
{{#subobject:- |Has ingredient=tomatoes |Has
quantity=3 |Is row in recipe={{PAGENAME}} }}
```

It's recommended to always include a property pointing back to the main page (using {{PAGENAME}}), to make querying easier.

To display all the rows in this recipe from another page, you could run a query like this one:

```
{{#ask:[[Is row in recipe::Greek salad]] |?Has
ingredient |?Has quantity |mainlabel=-}}
```

Why is "`mainlabel=-`" in there? Because here, as in many cases, there's no reason to display the name of each row - which were

To show all the recipe pages that call for at least two tomatoes, you could run this query:

```
{{#ask:[[-Is row in recipe::<q>[[Has
ingredient:tomatoes]][[Has quantity::>2]]</q>}}
```

Note the inverse query.

Why is the first value passed to #subobject a "-"? (It could also be blank.) It's because that parameter can take in a subobject name, if you want to pass in a pre-set name – like "Tomatoes row". In practice, this is very rarely done.

Semantic Internal Objects

The Semantic Internal Objects extension provides a very similar approach to storing compound data. It defines a parser function, #set_internal, that holds what it calls an "internal object" within the page that has semantic properties of its own, as well as a property that links the object back to the page. Any number of internal objects can be defined for a single page. A call to #set_internal is defined as:

```
{{#set_internal:  object-to-page property |property
1=value 1 |property 2=value 2 |...}}
```

With #set_internal, objects are never given a name – a name is always automatically assigned to each one. And there's a specific parameter for setting the property pointing from the object to the page.

Let's see how this works in action. For the original example, in the page called "Greek salad" you could have a call to #set_internal that looks like:

```
{{#set_internal:Is row in recipe |Has
ingredient=tomatoes |Has quantity=3}}
```

The query to get all the rows in a single recipe is then identical to the last one we saw for #subobject:

```
{{#ask:[[Is row in recipe::Greek salad]] |?Has
ingredient |?Has quantity |mainlabel=-}}
```

Why use SIO instead of subobjects? In most cases, the only reason to go with #set_internal is the slightly nicer syntax.

Recurring events

There's one case within Semantic MediaWiki where you can store values via a formula, instead of just manually entering them, and that's for recurring events. A recurring event is any event that happens on a regular basis: a birthday, a weekly meeting, a once-a-month deadline, etc. The standard way to store a recurring event is to use the #set_recurring_event parser function. Let's take an example: let's say you plan to have a weekly sales meeting every Monday, for a year and a half. To complicate things, let's also say that, for scheduling reasons, on two of those weeks the event should instead be held on Tuesday. On a page called "Weekly sales meeting", you could accomplish that with the following call:

```
{{#set_recurring_event:Is instance of
|property=Has date
|start=January 7, 2013
|end=June 9, 2014
|unit=week
|period=1
|include=March 19, 2013;March 26, 2013
|exclude=March 18, 2013;March 25, 2013
}}
```

This defines a weekly event, that is composed of a group of subobjects (see previous section) in the "Weekly sales meeting", each of which points to its parent page using the property "Is instance of". Each of these subobjects also has a property called "Has date" – that property is set by the "property" parameter, and it has to be of type "Date". The parameters "unit" and "period" together define the frequency of the event. "unit" can be any of the values 'year', 'month', 'week' and 'day', while "period" is an integer. If this were an event that happened every two weeks, the unit would be 'week', and the period value would be 2.

The "include" and "exclude" parameters let you manually change the set of date values, if necessary.

What if this event happened on, say, the 3rd Wednesday of every month? For that, there's an additional parameter, "week number". If you have "unit=month", and add "week number=3" to the call, then, if the start date falls on a Wednesday, every automatically-generated date will fall on the 3rd Wednesday of the month.

There is one notable limitation to #set_recurring_event: it doesn't allow for defining a duration of the event, so that you can, for instance, specify that your weekly meeting always runs one hour, between 12 and 1 PM. This is a weakness that will hopefully get addressed in upcoming versions.

To display a list of the four next weekly sales meetings, you could have a query like the following:

```
{{#ask:[[Is instance of::Weekly sales meeting]]
[[Has date::>{{CURRENTYEAR}}-{{CURRENTMONTH}}-{{CURRENTDAY}}]]
|mainlabel=-
|?Has date
|format=ul
}}
```

("CURRENTYEAR", "CURRENTMONTH" and "CURRENTDAY" are all pre-defined variables within MediaWiki. There are various ways to encode the current date within queries, but this is the most standard one.)

Refreshing data

On rare occasions, it can be helpful to refresh all of Semantic MediaWiki's data. Usually, the data stored accurately reflects the contents of the wiki's pages; and when a template is re-saved, all the pages that call that template automatically get their semantic data refreshed, so changes to the data structure don't require any additional action. However, there are times when a mass refresh is useful. One case is when some of the semantic values are calculated, instead of being retrieved directly from the page, like if values are themselves the results of queries. Another case is if something went wrong during the initial storage.

There are two ways to do a mass refresh of a wiki's SMW data. The first is to press the button "Start updating data" in the page Special:SMWAdmin.

The second is to call the script "SMW_refreshData.php", located in SMW's /maintenance directory. There are various parameters for this script; you can see the full list of options here:

> https://semantic-mediawiki.org/wiki/Help:Repairing_SMW%27s_data

Tooltips

You may want to have "tooltips", i.e. little icons that a user can click on to see a popup with additional information. These are useful in both regular pages and in forms (Chapter 17). For no strong reason, the best way to display these is defined within Semantic MediaWiki: the #info parser function. To display a tooltip, just place a call like the following anywhere on a page, template or form:

```
{{#info:Here is some additional information!}}
```

This will produce an icon where the #info tag was placed, which, when clicked on (and, for more recent versions of SMW, hovered over), brings up a tooltip balloon.

Here is an example screenshot of the result of #info, from a hypothetical chemistry wiki:

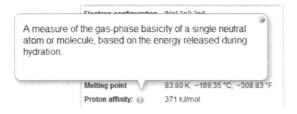

RDF and SPARQL

Although the extension is named Semantic MediaWiki, this chapter has for the most part not covered anything related to the so-called Semantic Web.

What is the Semantic Web? The term has been used, arguably to the point of breaking, to refer to at least four mostly-unrelated things: technologies like RDF and SPARQL; publishing data online in any sort of structured way; computers trying to read and understand text on the web (which can include analysis of both facts and opinion); and computers trying to understand and answer natural-language questions.

We'll just look at the first one, because it's the one that Semantic MediaWiki can in fact make use of.

RDF, which stands for Resource Description Framework, is a framework for storing data in the form of triples (of the kind that SMW itself uses). In some cases, what are called "triples" are actually "quads", with the fourth element holding information about the context of the triple. There are RDF triplestores (sometimes they're quadstores), which are essentially databases that are geared specifically to hold and query on data in RDF form. Just like MySQL and Oracle are examples of relational database systems, there are a variety of RDF triplestore systems: some of the best-known ones are Virtuoso, Jena and 4store.

SPARQL, which stands for SPARQL Protocol and RDF Query Language (it's a recursive acronym), is a query language specifically for querying and modifying RDF data. It works like SQL (a language that does the same thing for relational databases), and its syntax is somewhat similar.

You can set up SMW to store its data in a triplestore, and then to use that triplestore when running #ask queries. If you do that configuration, SMW will still store its data in the regular relational database as well – there are a few cases, like special properties, where SMW queries the relational database even if a triplestore exists. Still, it can be helpful to store data in an RDF triplestore. The main advantage is that it lets outside systems query that data directly, using SPARQL. Then, in theory, data from the wiki can be queried at the same time as RDF data from other systems and websites. That's because one very nice thing about SPARQL, which makes it different from SQL, is that you can construct queries that access any number of RDF sources at the same time. There are also some other potential advantages: in theory, the performance should be faster, since RDF triplestores are optimized for the querying of triples; though no comparative study has been done for SMW. Another advantage is that querying of the semantic data is now on a different system than the normal operation of MediaWiki, so if one of the two becomes bogged down, the other should still work fine.

Setting up SMW to work with an RDF triplestore isn't that hard, once you have the actual triplestore set up. You can read more about the process and configuration options here:

> https://semantic-mediawiki.org/wiki/Help:Using_SPARQL_and_RDF_
> stores

Additional resources

There are several resources available if you need help with Semantic MediaWiki, or any of its related extensions. Two mailing lists exist: semediawiki-user and semediawiki-devel; the first for users, and the second for developers. And if you're on IRC, the SMW IRC channel can also be a helpful resource. You can find links and instructions for these at this page:

> https://semantic-mediawiki.org/wiki/Help:Getting_support

Additionally, Semantic MediaWiki has a two-page quick reference, or "cheat sheet", available here:

> https://semantic-mediawiki.org/wiki/File:SMW_quick_reference.pdf

It covers not just SMW, but related extensions like Semantic Result Formats, Semantic Forms and Semantic Drilldown – all of which we'll get to in the following chapters. If you're planning to do any substantial work with these extensions, it's worth printing out.

Chapter 17

Semantic Forms

Though there are many extensions that make use of Semantic MediaWiki, Semantic Forms is the most widely-used. It provides a way to edit both template calls and sections within a page, where the templates are expected to in turn use Semantic MediaWiki to store their values. It thus complements SMW, by providing a structure for SMW's storage capabilities.

This chapter begins with an explanation of how (and why) SMW and templates are used in conjunction, and then gives an in-depth listing of Semantic Forms' syntax and features.

A template-based approach to SMW

We covered templates on page 33, and Semantic MediaWiki in the previous chapter. Both are quite useful on their own; but it's when the two are used together that the full power of both emerges. Templates without a storage system like SMW can provide structure to pages, and a nice standard display, but all that data stored within their fields just goes to waste: you can't use or display it anywhere outside that page. Meanwhile, Semantic MediaWiki, when used by itself and outside of a structure like templates, is interesting but not very practical.

This is the naive approach to using SMW tags – to intersperse them among free text, like:

```
Bob works in [[Has department::Accounting]].
```

But there are a number of problems with this approach. Most obviously, it requires people to learn and understand a new syntax. The tag syntax is another bit of wikitext that users have to understand, even when they don't plan to edit anything related to semantic properties. But more importantly, there's lots of ambiguity about the actual data in question. What if Bob moves to a different department – is it enough to change the department name, or should there also be a property like "Had department", pointing to the old value? And is there specific naming that should be used for each department? You could have software that provides autocompletion for semantic properties and their values, but it still won't resolve all of the ambiguity. The main confusion springs from the fact that users can't inherently know what the correct "data structure" should be for each page – the ideal set of semantic properties, and the expected value or values there should be for each. A template implicitly defines these things. Without a template, there is no easy way to define, or to clarify to users, which properties should be used and which shouldn't. But a template serves as both the definition and the container for a data structure.

There's another benefit to using templates: they can also set the relevant category or categories for a page. For MediaWiki installations that don't use Semantic MediaWiki, categories can end up getting used for a large variety of purposes (see page 43). In SMW, the number of categories tends to be much smaller, but categories are still used to define a page's type: whether a page represents a person, department, movie, fish, etc. A template can add such a category tag automatically, so that users don't have to add it separately.

In short, Semantic MediaWiki provides meaning to templates, while templates provide structure to Semantic MediaWiki; it's a combination that works very well together.

Let's see how it works in practice. We'll start with a simple example: a template that defines data for a page about an employee. We want this template to hold, for every employee, their phone number, email address and current position. Let's say the template is called "Employee". A call to this template could look like:

```
{{Employee
|Phone number=x1234
|Email address=bob@acme.com
|Position=Senior accountant
}}
```

(The employee's name is not included in the template because it will be the name of the page.) Here's how the relevant part of the template definition would look:

```
{|
!  Phone number
|  [[Has phone number::{{{Phone number|}}}]]
|-
!  Email address
|  [[Has email address::{{{Email address|}}}]]
|-
!  Position
|  [[Has position::{{{Position|}}}]]
|}
[[Category:Employees]]
```

This code defines an infobox-style table, with one row for each parameter; and it stores each parameter, using a semantic property, at the same time that it displays that parameter. And note also that the template sets a category tag for the page – every page that includes this template gets automatically added to the "Employees" category.

So now, adding the simple template call above to any page, with the relevant data filled out, will display the data, store it semantically for querying elsewhere, and add the page to the right category – all without any extra work needed on the user's part.

What if we want to allow a field to hold more than one value? Of course, there's nothing stopping users from just entering a comma-separated list of values for a template parameter, but then the semantic property won't be set correctly, as we'll see in a moment. For such a case, there's the #arraymap function. #arraymap is actually defined by the Semantic Forms extension, which is covered in the next section. (It's somewhat of an accident of history that it's defined in Semantic Forms, since there's nothing semantic or form-based about #arraymap, but nevertheless that's where it is.) We'll get to the full syntax of #arraymap (and its sibling, #arraymaptemplate) later in this chapter – for now, let's just look at an example of how it's used.

Say you want to add to the Employee template a new parameter, "Previous positions", that holds a comma-separated list of all the positions the person previously held at the company. In other words, you want a template call to look like:

```
{{Employee
...
|Previous positions=Junior accountant, Accountant
}}
```

In the template, you could of course just attach a semantic property like "Has previous positions" to the "Previous positions" field – but it's much preferable to separate out the values in the list, so that each is its own property value. (Someone at some point might want to query on anyone who has had the previous position "Accountant", for example.) To do that, we use the #arraymap function. Here is how the relevant lines of the template would look:

```
!   Previous positions
|  {{#arraymap:{{{Previous positions|}}}|,|x|[[Has
previous position::x]]}}
```

#arraymap splits up the value by the specified delimiter (in this case, a comma), and applies the same "mapping" (in this case, assigning a semantic property) to each resulting element.

Now, there may be more information you want displayed about each of those previous positions – the start and end date for each, for instance. If you want to store this kind of compound information semantically, you'll need to use special syntax (see page 173). But in terms of simply placing these elements on the page, the template system can handle it quite well. To have such compound data, you just need to create a template that holds a single "row" of information, and then have repeated instances of it on the page. In this case, a good solution would be to have a template called "Position". It would eliminate the need for both the "Position" and "Previous positions" fields in the "Employee" template, and it could be called like the following:

```
{{Position
|Title=Senior Accountant
|Start date=January 1, 2009
|End date=
}}
```

Each employee page would then have an instance of this template for every position that the employee has had, past or present.

There are two standard ways in which calls to such templates can be added to a page. The first is to place the calls to the template after the main template, in this way:

```
{{Employee
...
}}
```

```
{{Position
...
}}
{{Position
...
}}
...
```

And the second is to place calls to the multiple-instance template within the call to the main template, like this:

```
{{Employee
...
|Positions={{Position|...}}{{Position|...}}
...
}}
```

We'll see later in this chapter how Semantic Forms lets you create and edit pages with either of these structures.

In theory, you could keep going down multiple "levels" of data – if you have embedded template calls, they could themselves have template calls embedded within them, etc. For instance, for each position you could then store the set of bosses the employee worked for at the time, with a start and end date for each. This is not recommended, though – one level of additional data is usually all that works in practice, mostly because Semantic Forms doesn't support having more than one level of embedding, but also because that's just too much complexity for most users to deal with.

There's one exception to that, though: if you just want to have a list of values for a field in one of those multiple-instance templates – for instance, if you just want to have a list of bosses for every position – that's possible. Again, see page 173 for a full explanation of handling compound data.

Introduction to Semantic Forms

So far we've covered the usage of Semantic MediaWiki and templates together, and why they're such an important combination. Semantic Forms fills in the missing piece of the puzzle: an easy way to create and edit such pages. It lets you define forms for all your wiki's different page structures, to let users then easily create and edit pages that contain template calls. The beauty of Semantic Forms is that users don't have to know the syntax for template calls, and they don't have to know the names of the templates to use, or the names of their fields. Really, they don't even have to know that what they're editing is a wiki page. All they have to do is fill out a form.

Semantic Forms, or SF as it's abbreviated, makes use of the data structure defined via SMW to display more intelligent forms. The form input that is displayed for each template field is by default based on the SMW property, if one exists, that corresponds to that field. So, for instance, if a certain template field is stored using a property of type Date, then SF displays a date input to edit that field. And if the property is an enumeration, i.e. it has a pre-defined set of allowed values using "Allows value", then the form displays a dropdown for that field, with that set of values. The form can be set to override these default input type options, but at its core, SF uses SMW to understand and thus enforce the desired data structure for the wiki.

On a deeper level, SF and SMW complement each other in an important way, which is that together they can be used to simulate a standard database-backed website of the kind one sees all over the web. We're used to seeing data in terms of a structured set of fields, used to editing such data with forms, and used to then seeing that data be aggregated and displayed in various ways. That's true for product-review sites, self-publishing sites like Flickr, YouTube or blogs, or any of a wide variety of content-management systems that people use for their jobs. SF and SMW together let you mimic that kind of interface. The user, importantly, just sees the interface: they don't have to think about the wikitext or semantic markup, and are freed to think about the important stuff, which is the data itself. There are in fact many cases where users of an SMW/SF-backed system aren't aware that the system they're dealing with is semantic, or even a wiki.

This brings up an obvious question: if it's a great success for a wiki to mimic non-wiki software, why not just use that other software in the first place? That's because using a wiki has a number of big advantages. The primary one is that the system keeps a version history of every change – which means that you don't have to fear random users going in and modifying your data, because any bad changes can always be reverted. That in turn means that suddenly you can open up your data to editing by everyone, which is actually a revolutionary change. In most database-backed systems, tight controls are placed over editing – regular users can usually only edit information that pertains to them, while the editing of general-use information is restricted to a very small group of people who can be trusted to not delete important data, either accidentally or on purpose. And if mistakes happen, they may require a concerted effort to fix – like going through old database backups. On the other hand, with a wiki, having everything editable by everyone is no problem at all – in fact, it's the default state. So if you're trying to create a set of general data, you've just seen your potential base of editors jump up from a handful of people to, theoretically, billions – or, more realistically, hundreds.

Even if you only want a small group of people to edit the data, though – for example, you run an internal knowledge base for a small team of people within a company – having the data stored in a wiki is helpful. Let's say that, on a page for a project, there's a detail that you disagree with. On a wiki, a quick check of the history page would let you see who added it, and when – or whether you in fact added it yourself and then forgot. With a non-wiki system, the only real option is to send out an email to the group and hope that someone remembers; which becomes more difficult the larger the size of the data set, and the larger the number of editors, and the longer it's been in place.

There are two other advantages that an SMW/SF-based system has over non-wiki software. The first is the flexibility of the data structure; and it springs from the fact that the data, and the data structure, in the wiki are all stored as text, and not in a relational database. Text is a very flexible medium, and changes to the data structure can be both easily done and easily undone. You can thus open up editing of the pages that define the data structure – forms, templates and the like – to everyone, without the fear of having drastic, irreversible changes made. In a conventional database-backed system, the editing of the data structure, i.e. the set of database tables and their fields, has to be restricted to a very small group of technical experts.

(To be fair, there's a new wave of "document-oriented database" systems, like MongoDB, also referred to as "NoSQL" systems, that offer this same advantage of flexibility, though without the built-in interface tools.)

Getting started with Semantic Forms

The rest of this chapter provides a breakdown of the syntax and workflows you can use with Semantic Forms. But if you're just getting started, the best approach is to use Semantic Forms' helper pages to quickly create pages. There are essentially five good options:

1. Use the page Special:CreateClass to create everything at once – categories, prop-

erties, templates and forms.

2. Use the individual pages Special:CreateProperty, Special:CreateCategory, Special:CreateTemplate and Special:CreateForm to create the entire data structure. This is a more hands-on approach, which is less ideal for starting out, but it's quite useful if you already have templates and categories in place (and possibly properties as well), and only want to create what is still missing.

3. Similar to the previous option, you can go to any specific uncreated property, category, template or form page, and click on the "create with form" tab, which displays a form that matches the form found in the relevant one of those four special pages.

4. Copy from an existing installation or package. If you see a data structure setup that you like elsewhere, you can copy and paste all the necessary files to your wiki. (Though it's usually a good idea to get their permission first, even if legally it probably isn't necessary.) And there may be a package of such pages, created with a generic purpose like project management in mind, that you want to copy onto your wiki. At the moment, the company semantic::apps offers such packages, though not for free - see page 100.

5. Use the Page Schemas extension. See page 244 for an introduction to this extension; it lets you create a set of "schemas" for your data structure, from which forms, templates etc. can be automatically generated.

First, let's look at Special:CreateClass. Figure 17.1 shows the interface that appears on that page.

Using this interface, you can define an entire "class" – a data structure to represent a single page type, which is composed of a template, a form, a category, and properties. Not every page type can be defined in this way – some pages will contain more than one standard template, for instance – but in many cases it's a good starting point. The set of fields at the bottom is used to create the template, the form, and the properties.

Why bother creating the category? Because, in Semantic Forms, the category is where the connection between pages and their forms is defined, so that an "edit with form" tab shows up at the top of each page. This is done via the "Has default form" special property, which we'll get to later.

Another option is to use the special pages Special:CreateProperty, Special:CreateCategory, Special:CreateTemplate and Special:CreateForm, all defined by

Create a class

Enter all the data here to create the properties, template, form and category for a single class. For more options, use the pages Create a property, Create a template, Create a form and Create a category instead.

Template name: _____

    Output format: ● Table ○ Side infobox ○ Plain text ○ Sections

    ☐ This template can be included multiple times on the page.

Form name: _____

Category name: _____

Field name:	List of values?	Property name:	Type:	Allowed values:
1. _____	☐	_____	Page ▾	_____
2. _____	☐	_____	Page ▾	_____
3. _____	☐	_____	Page ▾	_____

Figure 17.1: Special:CreateClass page

Semantic Forms. These have the advantage of granularity – you can create, or regenerate, any specific pages – and they also have the advantage of additional fields that Special:CreateClass doesn't offer.

For example, in Figure 17.2 you can see part of the helper form at Special:CreateForm – it lets you set all the allowed parameters for each form field, with the group of parameters based on the selected input type. We'll get to all of these specific parameters in the next section.

Field: 'City'

This field defines the property Has city, of type String.

Form label: City   Input type: text with autocomplete ▾

☐ Other parameters

mandatory: ☐	restricted: ☐	class: _____
A value must be entered for this input	Only administrators can edit this input	The HTML "class" attribute for this input
property: _____	default: _____	size: _____
A semantic property that this field corresponds to	The default value for this input	The size of this text field, in characters
maxlength: _____	placeholder: _____	uploadable: ☐
The maximum allowed length of the text in this field	Help text that appears in the input until the user clicks on it	Place an "Upload file" link next to this input
default filename: _____	values: _____	values from property: _____
The default filename for uploaded files	The set of values for this input, separated by commas	A property whose values in the wiki should be this input's set of values
values from category: _____	values from namespace: _____	values from concept: _____
A category whose pages should be this input's set of values	A namespace whose pages should be this input's set of values	A Semantic MediaWiki "concept" page whose pages should be this input's set of values

Figure 17.2: Special:CreateForm page

By the way, you may find it odd that the pages Special:CreateProperty and Special:CreateTemplate are contained in Semantic Forms, since they have nothing to do with forms (other than the fact that they provide a helper form to generate pages – which is not the same thing). And the same argument could actually be made for Special:Templates, which Semantic Forms also provides. For the case of CreateTemplate and Templates, they are part of Semantic Forms because Semantic Forms is based around templates in a way that almost nothing else is among core MediaWiki and its extensions. For Special:CreateProperty, though, it's really just an accident of history that it's part of Semantic Forms and not Semantic MediaWiki, which would be the obvious home for it. It could be that in the future Special:CreateProperty will move to SMW.

Form definitions

Semantic Forms provides an entire syntax for defining forms, that makes use of special tags contained within triple curly brackets. Pages that define forms should always go in the "Form:" namespace (or, for non-English-language wikis, its equivalent in another language). Such pages are not called forms, but rather "form-definition pages", to distinguish them from the actual corresponding forms that users see.

Before we define the syntax, here's an example of the full contents of a form-definition page, for a "Project" form:

```
<noinclude>
This is the 'Project' form.
To add a site with this form, enter its name below;
if a page with that name already exists, you will be
sent to a form to edit that page.

{{#forminput:form=Project|autocomplete on
category=Projects}}
</noinclude><includeonly>
<div id="wikiPreview" style="display:  none;
padding-bottom:  25px; margin-bottom:  25px;
border-bottom:  1px solid #AAAAAA;"></div>

{{{for template|Project}}}
```

```
{| class="wikitable"
! Client
| {{{field|Client|autocomplete on category=Clients}}}
|-
! Start date
| {{{field|Start date}}}
|-
! End date
| {{{field|Start date}}}
|-
! Status
| {{{field|Status}}}
|}
{{{end template}}}
{{{for template|Task|multiple|label=Tasks}}}
{| class="wikitable"
! Task name
| {{{field|Task name}}}
|-
! Deadline
| {{{field|Deadline}}}
|-
! Status
| {{{field|Status}}}
|}
{{{end template}}}
</includeonly>
```

Already, without getting into any of the specifics of the syntax, you can notice a few things:

- The form-definition page serves a dual purpose: within the <includeonly> tag it holds the *form definition*, while within the <noinclude> tag it holds a brief explanation of that form, and an input to get to the actual form. (These two tags, <includeonly> and <noinclude>, serve the same purpose that they do in templates – see page 33.)

- Form definitions hold a mix of regular wikitext and special syntax, the latter of which is defined within three curly brackets.

- A form can specify more than one template within a page – in this case, there are two.

- Form fields, for the most part, can be simple, although they can also take in parameters. (Form field tags tend to be simple because Semantic Forms can already get a lot of information about the nature of each field from the template(s), and the semantic properties they use.)

We'll get to a full explanation later of almost all the elements of this definition, but one thing that won't be covered later is the `<div id="wikiPreview">` element. That is there so that, when the user hits the "Show preview" button, the Semantic Forms code can display both the form and the previewed page on the screen at the same time. It's an optional element.

You can see what this form page looks like when a user goes there in Figure 17.3. Only the top part of the page's contents, within the <noinclude> tag, is displayed.

Figure 17.3: A form definition page's display

When they reach the input on the form definition page, the user has to enter a page name. Let's say that they enter the text "Planting flower garden" and press "Create or edit". Figure 17.4 shows what the resulting form page, defined by the "Project" form definition, would look like in action (after the user also presses the "Add another" button once).

It's very important to note that this form can be used to both create new pages and edit existing ones; the form will look the same in both cases, other than having its values pre-populated for existing pages.

Now, let's go through the form-definition syntax.

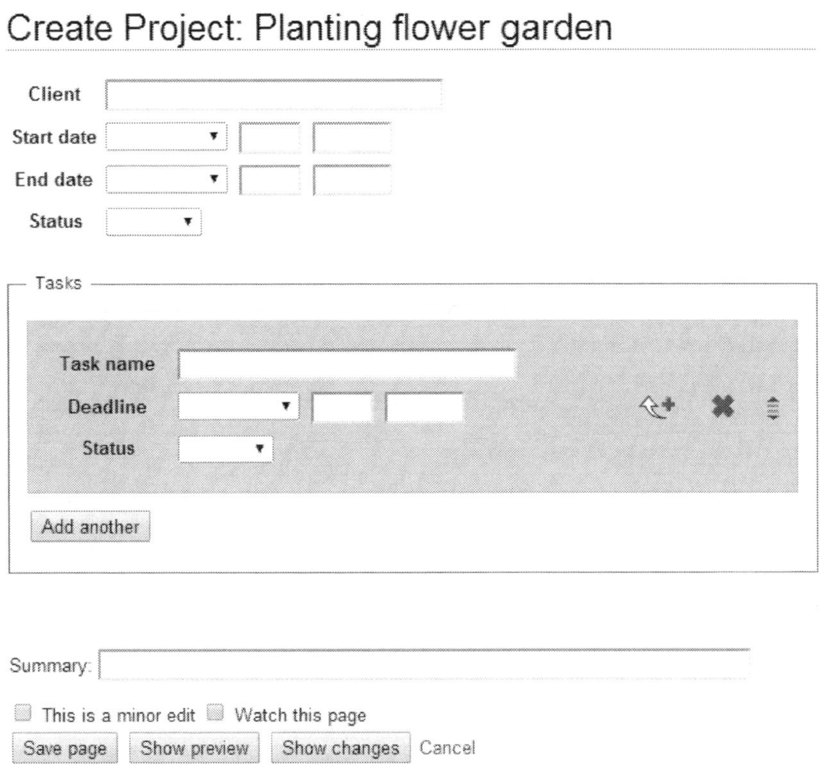

Create Project: Planting flower garden

Client	
Start date	▾		
End date	▾		
Status	▾

Tasks

Task name

Deadline ▾

Status ▾

Add another

Summary:

☐ This is a minor edit ☐ Watch this page

Save page | Show preview | Show changes | Cancel

Figure 17.4: A Semantic Forms-based form

Form markup language

Forms are defined using a set of tags that specify templates and fields within those templates. Wikitext, and some HTML, can be freely embedded anywhere outside of the tags. Semantic Forms tags are always surrounded by three curly braces, have pipes to separate their "parameters", and usually contain at least one extra parameter, to define the name. The text "`{{{field|Start date}}}`" from the previously-shown form definition is an SF tag, for instance. They differ from template calls because they have three curly brackets instead of two. And they differ from parameters within template definitions, which have three curly brackets, because those can only be used in the "Template:" namespace, whereas SF tags can only be used within the "Form:" namespace.

Below is a listing of the allowed tags in form definitions, and the allowed parameters for each. It may be helpful to refer back to the sample form definition on page 190, to see how these tags can fit in context.

'info' tag

The 'info' tag holds special information about the form. This tag is optional, but should be placed at the top of the form if it is present. Allowed parameters of this tag are:

- `create title=`*`title`* - Sets the title for the 'FormEdit' page, if the form is being used to create a new page.

- `edit title=`*`title`* - Sets the title for the 'FormEdit' page, if the form is being used to edit an existing page.

- `query title=`*`title`* - Sets the title for the 'RunQuery' page.

- `page name=`*`formula`* - Sets a formula for automatic setting of the name of the page being added; see "The one-step process".

- `query form at top` - Places the form at the top, instead of the bottom, for the 'RunQuery' page.

- `onlyinclude free text` - Indicates that the free text in the page generated by the form should be placed within an "<onlyinclude>" tag, so that pages created by the form can be transcluded in other pages without affecting those other pages' semantic properties.

- `partial form` - Indicates that this form is a partial form; partial forms are not recommended, though, and may become deprecated in the future.

'for template' tag

The 'for template' tag specifies a template name, and declares that all of the following fields (until 'end template' is reached) will be those of this template. The text immediately following the 'for template' declaration is the name of the template. Allowed parameters of this tag are:

- `label=`*`label text`* - Specifies a label to be placed in a square around the entire set of this template's fields in the form. This is especially useful if the template can have multiple instances.

- `multiple` - Specifies that the user can change the number of instances of this template in the form, allowing multiple (or zero) occurrences; see "Multiple-instance templates", on page 204.

- `minimum instances=`*number* - For multiple-instance templates, sets the minimum number of allowed instances.

- `maximum instances=`*number* - For multiple-instance templates, sets the maximum number of allowed instances.

- `add button text=` - For multiple-instance templates, sets the text in the "Add another" button.

- `strict` - Specifies that only fields in the form that correspond to fields used by the template should get turned into form elements.

- `embed in field=`*template name*[*field name*] - Specifies that the call(s) to this template within the generated pages will get embedded within a field of another template (i.e., "{{main template | some field={{embedded template | ...its fields...}} ... }}"). It is used in conjunction with the "holds template" parameter for the 'field' tag (see below). Note that the template to be embedded must appear after the template in which it will be embedded.

'end template' tag

The 'end template' tag ends the range of a template. There are no parameters for this tag.

'field' tag

The 'field' tag specifies a field to be placed in a form, corresponding to a template field. The text immediately following the field declaration is the name of the template field. There are a large variety of possible parameters to this tag, some of which can only be used for certain input types. Parameters that can be applied to any field are:

- `input type=`*input type* - Specifies the type of input this field will have in the form. If a field corresponds to a semantic property, the form will usually have the correct input type by default; otherwise the default is text. If the corresponding semantic property cannot be automatically determined (e.g. if it's in a template being called indirectly), you can use the parameter "property" to manually specify it (see below). The allowed set of input types is different for every semantic property type; see page 200 for the full list of options.

- `hidden` - Specifies that this field will be hidden in the form; used to preserve values in edited pages.

- `mandatory` - Specifies that this field must be filled in by the user. Note: `mandatory` should not be used in conjunction with `hidden`. Use of both in the same field will cause the mandatory check on any field to fail when the form is saved.

- `restricted` - Specifies that this field will be editable only by admins/sysops and disabled for all other users. This parameter can also be called as "`restricted=group name`", which restricts editing of the field to the specified user group.

- `default=default value` - Specifies a default value for this field. For date-related fields, default=now will set the value to the current date and possibly time. For text fields, `default=current user` will set the value to the username of the user adding this page. For the checkbox input type, `default=yes` will check the checkbox by default. (The "checkboxes" input type, on the other hand, like the "listbox" type, requires specifying the actual values, like `default=Value A, Value C`.) You can also include templates, parser functions, and magic words within the "default=" value.

- `class=class name` - Specifies a CSS class that the input for this field should have.

- `property=property name` - Specifies that the field corresponds to a certain semantic property, and should thus get the appropriate input type, autocompletion, etc.

- `list` - Specifies that this field contains a list of values.

- `delimiter=delimiter` - Specifies the delimiter character or string this field should use, if it represents a list of values; the default is ",".

- `holds template` - Specifies that this field is meant to hold a multiple-instance template, and does not have its own form input. It is used in conjunction with the "embed in field" parameter for the 'for template' tag (see above).

Parameters that can only be applied to fields that hold a list of uploaded files are:

- `uploadable` - Specifies that a link should be placed next to this field, that opens a popup window to let the user upload a file; see "Uploading files", below.

- `image preview` - Specifies that a thumbnail of the uploaded image should be placed under the field in the form.

- `default filename=`*filename* - Specifies the default filename for files uploaded with this field.

Parameters that can only be applied to fields of type 'textarea' are:

- `rows=`*num rows* - Specifies the number of rows.

- `cols=`*num cols* - Specifies the number of columns.

- `autogrow` - Sets the textarea to "auto-grow" its height to match that of its contents, so that a scrollbar won't be needed.

- `editor=`*editor type* - Adds a JavaScript-based editor to the textarea to make editing its contents more user-friendly. Currently only one value is allowed: "wikieditor", for the WikiEditor extension (which must be installed for this to work). If you want to add any additional custom toolbars to WikiEditor, you will need to add them in the JavaScript to ('#free_text').wikiEditor, just as they exist for ('#wpTextbox1').wikiEditor.

Parameters that can only be applied to inputs that have a set of pre-defined values, either that the user must select from (like the "dropdown" input) or that are suggested (the "autocomplete" and "combobox" inputs):

- `values=`*possible values* - Specifies a set of either possible values or auto-completion values (depending on the input type) that this field can have, over-riding whatever set of values may have been set from the semantic property. This set of values is separated by commas by default, but the delimiter can be modified using the `delimiter=` parameter.

- `values from property=`*property name* - Similar to `values=`, but gets its values from the set of all values that a certain property points to.

- `values from category=`*category name* - Similar to `values=`, but gets its values from the names of all pages belonging to a specific category.

- `values from concept=`*`concept name`* - Similar to `values=`, but gets its values from the names of all pages belonging to a specific concept.

- `values from namespace=`*`namespace name`* - Similar to `values=`, but gets its values from the names of all pages belonging to a specific namespace. (To get values from the main namespace, use "Main" for the namespace name, or just leave it blank.)

- `values from url=`*`URL identifier`* - Used only for autocompletion. Specifies that autocompletion should be based on the values retrieved from an outside URL; see page 203 for how to do this.

- `remote autocompletion` - Specifies that autocompletion values should be retrieved dynamically from the server, instead of directly from a list of values hidden in the page's HTML.

- `existing values only` - Set a combo box to only allow the autocomplete values, and not any arbitrary values, thus having it function even more like a dropdown.

- `show on select=`*`value 1=>element ID 1`*`;`*`value 2=>element ID 2`*`;`*`etc.`* - Can be used for inputs of type 'checkbox', 'checkboxes', 'radiobutton', 'dropdown' and 'listbox' to specify that one or more tags with a certain ID should only be displayed to the user if a certain value (or values) is selected within that input. For inputs of type 'checkbox', simply "`show on select=`*`element ID`*" should be used.

- `values dependent on=`*`template name[field name]`* - Can be used for inputs of type 'combobox', 'text with autocomplete' and 'textarea with autocomplete'. Specifies that the current set of allowed values for this field depends on the values a user selected, or will select, for another field in the form. For example, if a template is called "Restaurant" and it has template fields (not properties) named "Country" and "City", and you want the set of cities that are autocompletion values to be only those cities *in the country that the user selected*, then the field tag for the City field should look something like: `{{{field|City|input type=combobox|values dependent on=Restaurant[Country]}}}`.

Other parameters that can be added for certain input types:

- `size=size` - Used for text entries, combobox and listbox. Specifies the width of a text entry or combobox, or the height of a listbox.

- `placeholder=`*placeholder text* - Used for text and textarea fields. Specifies help text that is displayed in the input before the user clicks on it.

- `maxlength=`*maximum length* - Used for text and textarea fields. Specifies the maximum allowed length of the input.

- `include timezone` - Used for inputs of type 'datetime'; specifies that a time zone field should be included.

'section' tag

The 'section' tag specifies a textarea to be placed in a form, that corresponds to a page section. The name immediately following "`section|`" is the name of the section. For the most part, this tag takes in all the same parameters that the textarea input type can take in - see above. The one additional parameter is "`level=`", which can take in a number from 1 to 6, specifying the level of the section heading.

'standard input' tag

The 'standard input' tag is used for nine different inputs that usually appear at the bottom of every form. The text immediately after "`standard input|`" is the name of each input. The most notable of these inputs is 'free text', which is a textarea that holds all the non-template text in a page. The other seven are form elements such as the "Save" and "Preview" buttons; see page 204 for the full list. The 'free text' input has more elaborate handling than the other standard inputs; see "The free text input" for its allowed parameters.

For the other standard input types, the allowed parameters are:

- `label=`*label name* - Specifies the text associated with this input on the form.

- `class=`*label name* - Specifies the CSS class for this input.

- `style=`*label name* - Specifies the CSS style for this input.

In addition, the 'watch' input type can take in the parameter 'checked', which checks the "Watch this page" checkbox by default.

Allowed input types for data types

Each defined Semantic MediaWiki data type has a default input type, and, when applicable, a default input size as well. Additionally, some data types have special handling if the field holds a delimited list of values, instead of just a single value.

Here are the defaults and the other allowed input types for each data type, for single values:

Date type	Default input type	Default size	Other allowed input types
Page	text with autocomplete	35	text, combobox, textarea, textarea with autocomplete, tree
String (SMW < 1.9), Text (SMW ≥ 1.9)	text	35	text with autocomplete, combobox, textarea, textarea with autocomplete
Text (SMW < 1.9)	textarea	5 x 30	text
Code	textarea	5 x 30	text
URL	text	100	textarea
Number	text	10	textarea
Date	date		datetime (holds additional fields for the time), year (simply a text input)
Enumeration	dropdown		radiobutton
Boolean	checkbox		dropdown, radiobutton

And here are the default and other allowed input types for *delimited lists* of a certain data type, enabled by the use of the "#arraymap" function in the template:

Data type	Default input type	Default size	Other allowed input types

Page	text with autocomplete	100	text, textarea, textarea with autocomplete, tree, checkboxes
String	text	100	text with autocomplete, textarea, textarea with autocomplete
Enumeration	checkboxes		listbox

In addition, several other extensions define additional form input types, most notably Semantic Maps and Semantic Forms Inputs. We'll get to those in subsequent chapters.

Autocompletion

One of the big strengths of Semantic Forms is that it supports autocompletion – you can enable a field to show a dropdown list of possible completions when the user starts typing.

If a field represents a semantic property of type "Page", autocompletion will be enabled by default – the field will autocomplete on the names of all pages that are already pointed to by that property. For fields representing a semantic property of type "String", there is no default autocompletion, but you can achieve this same effect simply by adding "input type=text with autocomplete" or "input type=textarea with autocomplete" to the field's definition. You can also autocomplete on other sets of values:

- to autocomplete on all the values of a specific property, add "values from property=*property-name*" to the field definition

- to autocomplete on the names of all pages in a category, add "values from category=*category-name*"

- to autocomplete on the names of all pages in a namespace (like "File"), add "values from namespace=*namespace-name*" (if you want to autocomplete on the main namespace, use "values from namespace=Main", or just "values from namespace=").

- finally, you can autocomplete based on the values in an external URL; which lets
  you get autocompletion values from essentially any outside system. See "Autocompleting on outside values", below, for how to do this.

If a field is specified to hold multiple values (see below), autocompletion will, by
default, support multiple values: after a value is entered, and a delimiter placed, a
new autocompletion will start for the next value. You can manually specify that a
field should have multiple-value autocompletion, by adding the "list" parameter to the
field's definition. You can also specify the delimiter for this list of values, using the
"delimiter=..." parameter (the default is a comma).

The set of a field's possible values for autocompletion is, by default, contained right
within the form's HTML page, in a JavaScript declaration. For performance reasons,
there is a limit to how many values can be placed in the page; this number is defined
by the variable $sfgMaxAutocompleteValues, which by default is set to 1000. If you
have more than this number of possible values for a field, you should probably use
remote autocompletion instead, where autocompletion happens through an Ajax call
to the server, based on what the user has typed. This type of autocompletion is slower,
but always returns a comprehensive set of results. You can enable this by adding the
"remote autocompletion" parameter to the field's definition.

By default, Semantic Forms autocompletion matches on the beginning of every
word in the set of possible values. However, you can change autocompletion to instead match on every character, by adding the following line to LocalSettings.php:

```
$sfgAutocompleteOnAllChars = true;
```

This feature is especially important for wikis that have values with non-ASCII characters, such as wikis in languages with non-Roman alphabets; since the default, word-
based autocompletion doesn't yet work with non-ASCII characters.

Finally, you can disable autocompletion, if it's enabled by default for a field, by
setting the input type to be simply "text" or "textarea".

Combo box input

For any input that holds a single value, you can set the input to be a combo box by setting "input type=combobox" in the field definition. This input functions like a regular
autocomplete field, but has an additional down-arrow icon, like that of a dropdown, to
let the user see all the available values at once. You can also set the combo box to only
allow the autocomplete values, and not any arbitrary values, thus having it function

even more like a dropdown, by adding the additional parameter "existing values only" to the field tag.

Autocompleting on outside values

Autocompleting on values from outside the wiki is currently a rather intensive process, because you have to massage the outside data to get it into exactly the right format. Ideally this will change in the future, so that arbitrary lists of values can be used within forms. Until then, to have a field autocomplete on outside values, you have to take the following steps:

1. Create a page/web service that takes in a substring via the query string, and displays a set of autocompletion values; the values should be in JSON format, and look like the JSON returned by the MediaWiki API (see page 151). This also makes it easy to autocomplete on the values from another wiki.

2. Decide on a short string to represent this URL.

3. Add a line to LocalSettings.php that looks like this:

   $sfgAutocompletionURLs['*URL-identifier-string*'] = '*URL*';

   The URL in this line should look like a call to that web service, but with the substring replaced by the string "<substr>".

4. Add the parameter "`values from url=`*URL-identifier-string*" to the relevant field in the form definition.

Multiple values for the same field

Semantic Forms supports having multiple values within a given field, and some form input types – like "checkboxes" and "listbox" – are specifically geared for fields that contain multiple values. Text and textarea fields can also support autocompletion for multiple values. If a form field is meant to hold multiple values, the corresponding template field should most likely contain a call to either #arraymap or #arraymaptemplate – see page 205. Regardless of what is contained in the template, though, the fact that a field is meant to hold multiple values can be hard-coded in the form definition by adding the parameter "list" to the {{{field}}} tag. The parameter "delimiter=" can also be helpful, if the delimiter between values is meant to be something other than the default (a comma).

Multiple-instance templates

If you add the 'multiple' parameter to a template, it will allow for multiple (or no) instances of this template in the form, and therefore in the generated page. The sample form on page 190 is a good example of a form with multiple-instance templates. There's a button labeled "Add another"; clicking on it will create a new instance of that template and its fields. Instances can be removed, by clicking on the "Remove" button, and they can also be rearranged, by clicking on the "ribbed arrow" icon on the right-hand side and dragging the instance up or down within the set.

You can rename the "Add another" button to any other text, using the `"add button text="` parameter. For instance, to change the button to read "Add another occupation" for a template called "Occupation", you could have:

```
{{{for template|Occupation|multiple|add button
text=Add another occupation}}}
```

If you want to semantically store all the data contained in these multiple-instance templates, it is recommended to use the Semantic Internal Objects extension – see page 174.

Uploading files

If a field in the form is meant to hold the name of an uploaded file (say, an image), you can allow users to upload this file directly through the form. This is done simply by adding the parameter "uploadable" to that field's declaration in the form definition. This will add a link reading "Upload file" next to this field in the form; if the user clicks on this link, it will pop up a "lightbox"-style window that lets the user upload a file. Once the user has done so, the window will close, and the field will contain the name of the uploaded file. (For more on uploading files, see page 63.)

If the field is configured to contain a list of values, the new file name will be appended to whatever was there before; otherwise, the file name will overwrite whatever the field contained before.

Defining the bottom of the form

The user inputs at the bottom of the form can be customized using the "standard input" tag. The layout, inclusion and text of each input can be modified. Each user input is defined as a "standard input" tag with its own value; the allowed values are:

- `save` (for the "Save page" button)

- `preview` (for the "Show preview" button)

- `save and continue` (for the "Save and continue" button – this lets users save the page without leaving the form)

- `changes` (for the "Show changes" button)

- `summary` (for the "Summary" text field)

- `minor edit` (for the "This is a minor edit" checkbox)

- `watch` (for the "Watch this page" checkbox)

- `cancel` (for the "Cancel" link)

- `run query` (for the "Run query" button in query forms)

So, for example, the button for "Save page" could be specified with "`{{{standard input|save|label=Save this page}}}`", which would place the button where it was defined, with the text on the button reading "Save this page". If no standard input tags are included in the form definition, the basic seven inputs (all except for "save and continue" and "run") will appear at the bottom of the form, just as they do for regular "Edit" pages. However, if even one such tag is included, then only those inputs which have been included will be displayed, in the order, and with the wikitext, that they appear in in the form definition.

Enabling multiple field values

There are two parser functions defined by Semantic Forms, #arraymap and #arraymaptemplate, that enable holding multiple values within the same field, by applying the same semantic property to each element of a comma- (or otherwise-) delimited list (a comma-delimited list is a piece of text in which distinct values are separated by commas). There is nothing form-specific, or even semantic-specific, about these functions; but they seem to have not been necessary until Semantic Forms was created, which is why they're stored there. Of these, #arraymap is the more important: it's used much more frequently, and it's the one applied automatically within templates by both Special:CreateClass and Special:CreateTemplate when a field is specified to hold a list of values. #arraymaptemplate is useful when the mapping required is too complex for #arraymap.

#arraymap

The generic call for this function is:

```
{{#arraymap:value            |delimiter |var |formula |new
delimiter}}
```

The function splits the 'value' by the 'delimiter', and then, for each one, applies the same mapping that 'formula' does to 'var', and finally joins all the values again using the 'new delimiter'. For example, if you have a form that populates the field 'author', and you want that field to be able to hold multiple values, separated by commas; and you want each value to also be stored with the semantic property "Has author", you could add the following to the template code, instead of a regular semantic tag:

```
{{#arraymap:{{{author|}}}|,|x|[[Has author::x]]}}
```

Essentially this function "maps" the property tag onto each comma-delimited value in the field. (The 'delimiter' parameter defaults to "," and 'new delimiter' defaults to ", " (note the extra space) if they are not set.) The user can thus enter all the values on the same line, with or without spaces around the commas. (Note, by the way, that the "x" is used here as an internal variable: if the property name itself contains the letter "x", that will lead to problems, and you should replace the letter "x" with some character or string that does not appear in the property name, like "@@@@".)

The 'new delimiter' parameter sets the text that's placed between values in the resulting output. It is optional, and is usually not set, because its default value – a comma plus a space – is generally what's needed. However, this parameter is useful in certain cases. It's especially helpful if none of the resulting values are actually displayed, because in that case you wouldn't want the output to be a string of commas. A common example of that is if the original value holds a list of category names, and each name gets turned into a category tag, but is not actually displayed. To avoid displaying commas in that case, you should set the 'new delimiter' value equal to a space, using something like " ", the HTML encoding for a space. (Using just "| " at the end won't work, because the MediaWiki parser will ignore it.) Here is how such a thing would be called:

```
{{#arraymap:{{{categories|}}}|,|x|[[Category:x]]|&#32;}}
```

If you use the 'CreateTemplate' or 'CreateClass' pages to create a template, and you specify that a field that can take more than one value, then an #arraymap call will be automatically added to the generated template.

#arraymaptemplate

There are some kinds of mapping that are complex enough that they cannot be placed in the #arraymap function. For this purpose, you can instead use the similar #arraymaptemplate function. To use this function, create a template that takes in a single field and applies the mapping you would like to that field. Then apply #arraymaptemplate onto the main template field just as you would with #arraymap, using the following format:

```
{{#arraymaptemplate:value |template |delimiter |new
delimiter}}
```

...where 'template' is the name of the mapping template in question.

\n delimiter

For both #arraymap and #arraymaptemplate, the string "\n" in the value of either `delimiter` or `new delimiter` will get converted into a newline. If you want an actual line break to appear between values, you should have two newlines (i.e, "\n\n") as the delimiter, since MediaWiki requires two newlines in order to display a line break.

The "edit with form" tab

If a user is not allowed to edit a page that is form-editable, the tab will show up for them as "view form" instead; clicking on the tab will show the disabled form.

Getting "edit with form" to appear

There are three ways to get the 'edit with form' tab to appear for specific pages:

Based on category

The first, and recommended, way, is to use categories. To enable a page to have a tab in this way, you must do the following two steps:

1. First define that page as belonging to a specific category – categories are the standard Semantic MediaWiki approach to defining a page's type. The best way to

match pages with a category is to place a 'Category' tag inside the main template that defines this page type; that way, every page that uses this template will become part of this category.

2. Once you have done that, you should place the semantic property 'Has default form' in the page for that category; the tag should look like `[[Has default form::`*form-name*`]]`. You can do this automatically if you create the category using the 'CreateCategory' page.

Based on namespace

The second possible way is to match the pages' namespace to a form. You can do that by placing a 'Has default form' property in the page defining that namespace. If, for instance, your wiki is called 'MyWiki', and the namespace you want to associate with a form is 'User', the page in which you need to add the property will probably be called 'MyWiki:User' (you will probably need to create this page). If the namespace you want a default form for is the main one (i.e., the one with no name), you will need to create and add this property to the page called 'MyWiki:Main', or whatever the main namespace is called in the language of this wiki.

Once you've added this property, every page within that namespace will have that form associated with it, unless it already belongs to a category that has an associated form (categories take precedence over namespaces).

Within the page

With the special property "Page has default form", any page can set its own form. This is especially useful when the category and namespace options aren't possible, such as when pages belong to multiple categories that have different default forms; or for editing category pages themselves. To apply it, place this property either directly within the page, or in a template that the page calls, using syntax like this:

```
[[Page has default form::form-name]]
```

Configuring the editing tabs

For pages that have an "edit with form" tab, you may want the regular "edit" tab to be renamed or even removed altogether. There are flags you can set in "LocalSettings.php" to change the appearance of the editing tabs:

- $sfgRenameEditTabs - if set to true, renames the "edit with form" tab to "edit", and the "edit" tab to "edit source" (in whatever language the wiki is being viewed in)

- $sfgRenameMainEditTab - if set to true, renames only the "edit" tab to "edit source" (in whatever language the wiki is being viewed in)

- $wgGroupPermissions[...]['viewedittab'] - can be set, for different types of viewers, to toggle whether each type will see the regular edit tab. One common modification is to set it to false normally (i.e. for viewer type '*'), and to true for 'sysop' viewers:

    - $wgGroupPermissions['*']['viewedittab'] = false;
    - $wgGroupPermissions['sysop']['viewedittab'] = true;

If these settings are added to LocalSettings.php, they should be placed in the file after the inclusion of Semantic Forms.

Linking to forms

How do you get users to forms to create the pages in the first place? The standard way is via the #forminput parser function call, which displays a single input for users to enter the name of a page; if they enter such a name and click the button, they are sent to a form to create that page – unless a page with that name already exists, in which case they are sent to a form for editing the existing page. This is what is known as the "two-step process". The reason for the initial step, of having the user first enter the page name, is to ensure that users don't accidentally overwrite existing pages. This process is so standard that it is built into the default forms produced by Semantic Forms' Special:CreateForm and Special:CreateClass helper pages: any form-definition page created by Semantic Forms includes, at the top, a call to #forminput, so that users who go to that form page can automatically start to use the form.

However, it's also possible to skip the first step, of entering the page name – that's what you should do if the form contains a formula for setting the page name based on the user input. That's the "one-step process", and it uses the parser function #formlink instead of #forminput.

Query forms, which use Special:RunQuery, have their own linking method, using the parser function #queryformlink – we'll get to those on page 215.

The two-step process

The two-step process, i.e. the standard way to get users to forms, is done using the #forminput parser function.

Using #forminput

Here is the syntax of the #forminput parser function:

```
{{#forminput:form= |size= |default value= |button
text= |query string= |query string parameters
|autocomplete on category= |autocomplete on namespace=
|remote autocompletion |placeholder= |popup}}
```

All arguments are optional. An explanation of the parameters:

- `form=` - the name of the SF form to be used; if it is left empty, a dropdown will appear, letting the user choose among all existing forms.

- `size=` - the size of the text input (default is 25).

- `default value=` - the starting value of the input (default is blank).

- `button text=` - the text that will appear on the "submit" button (default is "Create or edit page").

- `query string=` - you can use this option to pass information to the form; this information generally takes the form of *templateName[fieldName]=value*. It should look like a typical URL query string; an example would be `"query string=namespace=User&User[Is_employee]=yes"`. Additionally, any query string values can be passed directly in as parameters – so the values above could instead be passed in as `"|namespace=User|User[Is_employee]=yes"`.

- `autocomplete on category=` - adds autocompletion to the input, using the names of all pages in a specific category.

- `autocomplete on namespace=` - adds autocompletion to the input, using the names of all pages in a specific namespace (only one of these two can be used).

- `remote autocompletion` - specifies that autocompletion values should be retrieved dynamically from the server, instead of directly from a list of values hidden in the page's HTML (thus allowing many more values).

- `placeholder=` - "placeholder" text that appears in the form input before the user types anything.

- `popup` - opens the form in a popup window.

Adding pages of a specific namespace

You can have a page-input form create pages within a specific namespace (like 'User:') by default, without forcing users to type in that namespace every time. To do that, add "`namespace=namespace-name`" to the `query string=` parameter.

Adding subpages

In MediaWiki, you can create subpages by including a slash in the page name (see page 52). To have the page that's added automatically be a subpage, you can add a value for "`super_page=`" in the query string. To make it a subpage of the current page, you can set this value to "`super_page={{PAGENAME}}`". This will prepend a *"current-page-name/"* onto the beginning of the page name that the user types in.

The one-step process

You can have the name of the page created by the form be set automatically, by adding a "page name" parameter within the form definition's "info" tag. There are two types of "variables" one can include in the value for this parameter:

- `<TemplateName[FieldName]>` - gets replaced with the value for the specified field *FieldName* in the specified template *TemplateName*.

- `<unique number>` - by default, gets replaced by the lowest number for which the page title that's generated is unique. Normally, this value starts out as blank, then goes to 2, then 3, etc. However, one can manually set the starting number for this value, by adding a "`start=`" parameter; this number must be 0 or higher. For instance, to have the number start at 1 and go upward, you should set the tag to be `<unique number;start=1>`. You can also instead set it to be a random six-digit number, by adding the "random" parameter, so that the tag looks like "`<unique number;random>`". Note that the parameter in either case is delimited by a semicolon.

Note that the "`page name=`" value cannot start with "`<unique number>`", due to a bug in Semantic Forms; there has to be some text before that. And it cannot contain the character "#", because MediaWiki does not allow pound signs in page titles.

As an example, imagine a form for storing notable quotes. Its `{{{info}}}` tag could have a parameter of "`page name=<Quote[Author name]> quote <unique number;start=1>`". This would include the author's name in the name of every quote page, as well as a number to guarantee the uniqueness of every opinion-item page added. A user could then go to the URL "http://mywiki.com/wiki/Special:FormEdit/Quote" and fill out the form; if they set the author to be "Ernest Hemingway", and no other quotes in the wiki had him as an author, then hitting the "Save page" button would result in a new page called "Ernest Hemingway quote 1".

The "start" value can have leading zeroes; a value of "001", for instance, would lead to pages that had the value "001", then "002", etc.

The "page name=" value gets parsed by the MediaWiki parser, so you can also add parser functions, pre-defined variables, etc. into the value.

Note that users must be sent to the page "Special:FormEdit/*form-name*" for this automatic page-setting to work; if they somehow end up at a #forminput call and are prompted for a page name, that name will override whatever the automatic page name would be.

Using #formlink

If you want, you can generate a link to a "one-step process" form using the "#formlink" parser function, instead of creating the URL directly. This function is called as:

```
{{#formlink:form= |link text= |link type= |query
string= |query string parameters |target= |tooltip=
|popup}}
```

The "form=", query string and "popup" arguments work much the same way that their equivalents in #forminput work, and "link text=" works like #forminput's "button text=". The "link type=" argument sets the display of the link: if it's set to "button", the link will show up as a button; if it's set to "post button", it will be a button that sends the query-string value(s) using "POST" instead of via the URL – this is helpful when a lot of data has to be preloaded, and it is more robust with special characters like line breaks in the query string; if it's set to blank or anything else, it will show up as a regular link. The "target=" parameter shouldn't usually be used, but it sets the target page to be edited, if you want to link to the editing of a specific page. The "tooltip=" parameter displays a "tooltip", displayed if a user hovers the link.

An example call to #formlink would be:

```
{{#formlink:form=Quote |link text=Add a quote
for this author |link type=button |query
string=Quote[Author]={{PAGENAME}} }}
```

This will link from the page, via a button, to a form for adding a quote, with the "Author" field filled in with the current page name.

You may want to have the link to the form be an image, instead of text or a button. For that, you could call something like:

```
{{#formlink:form=Quote
|link text= [[File:edit.png|link=]]}}
```

Pointing red links to a form

In MediaWiki, links to nonexistent pages are called 'red links', because they are usually colored red. By default, these links go to a page for adding the article to the wiki using the standard edit interface. However, if that nonexistent page is being pointed to by a semantic property, the red link can instead take the user to the correct SF form to add the page.

The standard way to point red links defined by a property to a certain form is to simply add the special property "Has default form" to the page for that property. For instance, in a property page like "Property:Has employee", you could have the following:

```
This property uses the form [[Has default
form::Employee]].
```

Setting the default form can be done directly within the 'CreateProperty' page.

In addition, or instead, you can add one or more 'Has alternate form' special properties to the property page, so that the user gets other possibilities when they click on the red link. This is useful when a single property can point to pages that use different forms.

Note also that, if you've defined a *namespace* as having a default form, red-links that go to a page within that namespace will also go to the right form, without any extra work needed.

By default, Semantic Forms checks, for every red link, for the existence of properties across the wiki pointing to that page in order to find default forms. However, for pages with a large number of red links, this can slow down page loading. If that's an issue for you, you can change the behavior so that SF only checks properties on the page in question, instead of throughout the whole wiki. To do that, add the following to LocalSettings.php, after the inclusion of Semantic Forms:

```
$sfgRedLinksCheckOnlyLocalProps = true;
```

Populating red-linked pages automatically

It's nice to have red links point to the right form for creating the page, but this still calls for work on the part of users – they have to click to the form, fill out the fields and save the page. This is especially bothersome when the form contains few or no fields, and/or if there are many such pages to be created. You can instead have such red-linked pages get automatically created by the system.

To do this, instead of using "Has default form" (or "Has alternate form"), you should add the special property "Creates pages with form" to the property that you want pointing to those automatically-created pages. For instance, if you have pages that point with the property "Has country" to other pages, and you want those other pages to automatically be created using a form called "Country", you just need to add the following to the page at "Property:Has country":

```
[[Creates pages with form::Country]]
```

It should be noted that it may take a while for each page to be created, since page creation is done through MediaWiki "jobs", which can take anywhere from a few seconds to several hours or more to run, depending on the length of the job queue.

Preloading data

You may want a form to already contain some data when the user goes to it. (Note that this only applies to adding new data, or to query forms; for editing an existing page, there is no way to set the contents of the form to anything other than the current contents of that page.) There are various ways to do this:

- Specify a "default" value for whatever fields you want to have a value for in the form.

- Specify a "preload" page for the "free text" input, which will preload the free text field with the contents of that page.

- Add 'preload=*preload-page-name*' to the query string value in the 'forminput' call; this will preload the entire form with the contents of that page.

- Similarly, you can add a "preload=..." value to the query string for a 'FormStart' or 'FormEdit' URL.

- Add "*template-name[field-name]=field-value*" to the query string value in the 'forminput' call, to set the value for a specific field. To preload values for more than one field, use "&": "template1[field1]=val1&template1[field2]=val2".

- Similarly, you can add a value for a specific field to the URL query string for 'FormStart' or 'FormEdit'.

- Finally, you can create your own custom handling, using the 'sfEditFormPreload-Text' hook. If another extension calls this hook, it can preload data however it wants. The function registered with this hook should have a header like:

   function-name(&$page_contents, $page_title, $form_title)

Creating query forms

Forms can also be used for querying, as opposed to adding or editing data. In other words, you can create a form that will not modify any pages, but will instead be used for searching existing data – in which a user enters values in different fields and then sees some set of pages that match those fields.

To have query forms, you need to use the Special:RunQuery page, which displays a form in a manner similar to Special:FormEdit, but with no associated target page. Instead, when the user submits the form by hitting the "Run query" button, the user stays on the Special:RunQuery page, but now the page shows what the template looks like when displayed with the values they entered. The template that the form uses should most likely contain one or more Semantic MediaWiki inline queries, to query data using values the user entered.

The "Run query" button

By default, a button called "Run query" shows up at the bottom of forms if they are accessed via Special:RunQuery. You can change the location and text of this button, using the tag "`{{{standard input|run query}}}`" (or "`{{{standard input|run query|label=...}}}`", etc.) within the form definition.

Query form at top

If you add the parameter "`query form at top`" to the `{{{info}}}` tag, the query input field will show up at the top of the results page, instead of the bottom.

Creating links to query forms

Once a query form has been created, you can link to it using syntax that looks like this:

```
[[Special:RunQuery/<query form name>]]
```

However, the preferred solution, because it's easier and more powerful, is to use the #queryformlink parser function. A basic call to that function would look like:

```
{{#queryformlink:form=<query form name>}}
```

Here's the complete syntax of #queryformlink:

```
{{#queryformlink:form= |link text= |link type= |query
string= |query string parameters |tooltip= |popup}}
```

These parameters are almost identical to the ones used by #formlink (page 212).

Embedding query forms

You can also embed a query form within another page. To do that, add the following in a page where you want the query form to appear:

```
{{Special:RunQuery/<query form name>}}
```

Modifying pages automatically

You can create links that, when clicked on, create or edit pages automatically in the background, with a preloaded set of values, using the #autoedit parser function. This function is called, and is displayed, in a very similar manner to #formlink – the difference is that the link only performs an action in the background, instead of bringing the user to a form. The syntax for #autoedit is

```
{{#autoedit:form= |target= |link text= |link type=
|query string= |query string parameters |reload }}
```

All these parameters but 'reload' work in the same way as they do in #formlink; 'reload', if added to the call, reloads the current page after the link is clicked.

As an example, let's say you want to create a simple voting scheme, letting users vote between "Vanilla", "Chocolate" and "Strawberry". You have a page for each, and each one contains a template called "Flavor", with a field called "Num votes" – that field, in turn, sets a semantic property called "Has number of votes". And there is a form, also called "Flavor", to edit such pages. To create a link that, when clicked, increments the number of votes in the "Vanilla" page by one, you could place the following call on the page:

```
{{#autoedit:form=Flavor |target=Vanilla |link
text=Vote for Vanilla |query string=Flavor[Num
votes]={{#expr:{{#show:Vanilla|?Has number of votes}}
+ 1}} }}
```

What happens when a user clicks on such a link? They'll stay on that page, but the link will turn into text that reads "Successfully modified *target page* using form *form name.*" If the user refreshes the page, or goes to that page later, they'll see the original link again – and they can click on it; there's no limit to the number of times a user can click on an #autoedit link. (Though you can embed an #autoedit call within an #if call, if you have ParserFunctions installed, to only display it for certain users, or in certain situations.)

This functionality is also available via the MediaWiki API (page 151), as the "sfautoedit" action – this enables outside scripts, and bots, to modify template calls within wiki pages. You can find the full documentation on this by searching for "sfautoedit" on your wiki's api.php file; essentially the parameters are the same as for #autoedit.

Semantic Forms Inputs

Semantic Forms Inputs (SFI) is a helper extension for Semantic Forms: it serves as a container for additional input types that are less essential, though still useful. The current input types defined in SFI are:

- **datepicker** – provides a JavaScript-based input for picking dates using a mini-calendar, of the kind seen often on the web. It looks like this:

- **datetimepicker** – like datepicker, but includes a time input.

- **regex** – a regular text input that can include custom validation rules, using a "regular expression" – useful for, for instance, a phone number input (a regular expression is a piece of syntax that is used to find matches in strings).

- **datecheck** – similar to "regex", but intended only for date values.

- **menuselect** – displays a set of text values as a hierarchical menu of options. Users can choose any element in the hierarchy. Here is an example, for a clothing item field:

- **two listboxes** – a multi-select tool that lets uses move items between a "selected" and an "unselected" listbox.

Chapter 18

Displaying data

This chapter covers the ways in which data can be displayed and visualized within MediaWiki. With the exception of the Maps and DynamicPageList extensions, all the options in this chapter depend on Semantic MediaWiki. There are non-SMW-based data display tools for MediaWiki – there are a number of calendar extensions, for instance – but these are almost always hacks to some degree, since they don't rely on data in any kind of standardized format. If you want calendars, charts and maps on your wiki, the Semantic MediaWiki approach is the most flexible, and the easiest one to maintain.

Semantic Result Formats

Semantic Result Formats (SRF) is an extension that contains a wide variety of result formats, or query formats, for Semantic MediaWiki – essentially all of the important visualizations for SMW data, other than mapping, are contained in Semantic Result Formats. You can read more about it here:

> https://www.mediawiki.org/wiki/Extension:Semantic_Result_Formats

The next few sections will cover formats defined by this extension. However, this book does not provide a comprehensive reference to all the parameters and customizations that each format can take (which in some cases is a lot). For that, there are two main options: use the page Special:Ask on your wiki (page 172), assuming you have a wiki and SRF is installed on it, to see all the allowed parameters for each format and try them out on real data; or read the documentation on each format.

Not every format in SRF is enabled by default when it's installed; most are, but five – 'googlebar', 'googlepie', 'exhibit', 'filtered' and 'excel' – are not, for various reasons. To enable any of these formats, you just need to add it to the $srfgFormats global array. For example, to enable the 'googlebar' format, add the following to LocalSettings.php, after the inclusion of SRF:

```
$srfgFormats[] = 'googlebar';
```

Calendars

Figure 18.1: Calendar created with the 'calendar' format

After maps, calendars may be the second-most-common form of data visualization. The 'calendar' format for SMW queries, defined in Semantic Result Formats, lets you display date-based data in a monthly calendar. Here's an example of a call to display a calendar:

```
{{#ask:[[Category:Meetings]]
```

```
|?  Has date
|format=calendar
}}
```

This will display a calendar that could look like the one in Figure 18.1.

The navigation at the top lets the user move to other months; the current month being displayed is set in the URL's query string.

There's an inefficiency at the heart of the Calendar format: unlike other formats, it doesn't stop querying after it gets a certain number of results. Instead, it goes through every result, in order to get all the ones that apply to the current month. If there are thousands of dates, or more, this could potentially slow down the system. Unfortunately, the Calendar format can't query on only the dates within the specified month, because of how SMW works: all the querying is done before the format code kicks in. But there's a workaround you can do – just change the query to look like the following:

```
{{#ask:[[Category:Meetings]]
[[Has date::>{{#calendarstartdate:}}]] [[Has
date::<{{#calendarenddate:}}]]
|?  Has date
|format=calendar
}}
```

#calendarstartdate and #calendarenddate are parser functions, defined by the Calendar format, that simply display the first and last dates of the month that the user is currently looking at. This can dramatically reduce the amount of querying work that needs to be done. (Note the colon contained in both calls – this is necessary so that the parser function will actually be called.)

You can display additional data for each calendar entry, just by adding more print-outs to the query (like "?Has attendees"). And you can display all of that data via a template, using the "template=" parameter – see page 170.

And you can set the color that each entry is displayed with, using the parameter "color=". This isn't very interesting for a simple query, where every event would be displayed as the same color, but it can become quite useful when calendars are displayed using Semantic Compound Queries – see page 232.

There are more customizations possible for the calendar – you can see them all here:

https://semantic-mediawiki.org/wiki/Help:Calendar_format

Charts and graphs

There are various formats defined in SRF that do a chart- or graph-style display:

- **jqplotchart** – supports a number of different standard charting options – bar, pie, line and donut – using the jqPlot JavaScript library.

- **jqplotseries** – similar to jqplotchart, but intended for multiple sets of data; adds additional "bubble" and "scatter" charting options.

- **googlebar, googlepie** – bar and pie charts created via the Google Charts API (behind the scenes, the code sends the numbers to Google, and gets back an image).

- **d3chart** – allows for more unconventional chart types (treemap, bubble, etc.) using the D3 JavaScript library.

- **dygraphs** – meant for very large data sets. It gets its main data from a CSV file, but allows for adding annotations to specific points using semantic properties. It uses the dygraphs library.

- **sparkline** – creates "sparklines", small inline charts meant to just show a general trend, using the jquery.sparkline library.

- **timeseries** – aggregates pages by a date property value, using the flot library.

- **graph** – shows pages and the properties between them as a unordered "graph", displayed with an image generated by the GraphViz application.

- **process** – like the graph format, but shows a "process graph", a specific type of graph used in workflow modeling.

Many of these charting and graphing formats are configurable – they can take parameters to set attributes such as the height and width, the chart title, the color scheme used, etc.

The default usage for formats like the jqPlot-based ones is to display a set of page names and a number for each, using a property of type "Number". For instance, you could have the following:

```
{{#ask:[[Category:Departments]] |?Has number of
employees |format=jqplotbar}}
```

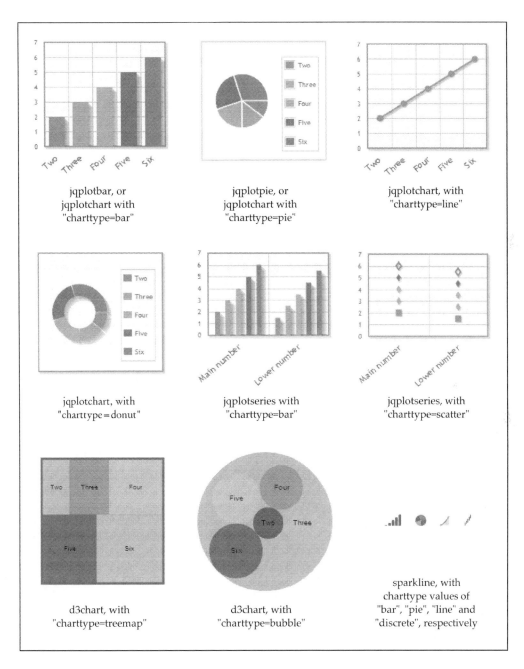

Figure 18.2: Various charting formats from the Semantic Result Formats extension, using (rather pointless) sample data

However, the jqPlot-based formats, and other charting formats, can also display a "distribution" instead – and this is ultimately the more important usage. For the case above, what are the chances that you'll have a semantic property that holds an exact count of employees in each department? It's more likely that what you'll have semantically stored is just pages for the employees themselves, and you'll have to count them "manually" for each department. Adding "`distribution=yes`" to the query makes it display a count of the number of pages for each value – instead of just listing the pages and their values. So you could instead have a query like:

```
{{#ask:[[Category:Employees]] |?Has department
|format=jqplotbar |distribution=yes}}
```

Though the two queries look very different, they will actually produce the same result, assuming both work.

Mapping

Two MediaWiki extensions – Maps and Semantic Maps – provide the best mechanism for displaying coordinate-based data, and related functionality like geocoding of addresses. These two extensions were created together, and are meant to be used together – Maps can be used by itself, but Semantic Maps requires Maps. They support two mapping services at the moment: Google Maps and OpenLayers. (Another service, Yahoo! Maps, was supported at one time, but was dropped after Yahoo! itself abandoned the service.) More mapping services may eventually get added.

Google Maps probably needs no explanation – it's the dominant mapping service on the web, and rightly so, since it's extremely well done. (We are talking here about the Google Maps service, not the Google Maps website located at maps.google.com.)

OpenLayers is interesting, because it's an open-source, generic framework for displaying any mapping data – in theory, even Google Maps can be displayed within OpenLayers. Usually, though, when OpenLayers is used, it's used to display mapping data from OpenStreetMap. OpenStreetMap is a very exciting mapping service, which is completely open-source, and is generated collaboratively by users via a wiki interface (not MediaWiki – it uses its own custom software). Google Maps is free to most users, but with exceptions – non-public websites need to pay to use it, as do public websites that make massive use of it (the exact amount of traffic before Google requires payment seems to be in flux at the moment). For those cases, and others, the combination of OpenLayers and OpenStreetMap is an increasingly viable alternative.

This book, by necessity, skips over a lot of smaller details, and that's certainly true of the sections about the Maps and Semantic Maps extensions – these two extensions have a variety of parameters and administrative settings that won't be mentioned here. To see a complete overview (and a lot of interesting demos), please go to the extension homepages:

> https://www.mediawiki.org/wiki/Extension:Maps
> https://www.mediawiki.org/wiki/Extension:Semantic_Maps

The Maps extension

Maps allows for the display of maps, with or without points on them, in various, non-semantic ways. Maps defines six main functions, each of which are available as both a parser function and a tag function. One does the actual display of maps: display_map. The other five are utility functions, which do a variety of tasks related to coordinates: coordinates, distance, finddestination, geocode, and geodistance.

Let's go over display_map first. Like all the others, it can be called as either #display_map or <display map>. It can take the following parameters:

- `points=` , or an unnamed parameter – the set of points to be displayed, separated by semicolons, taking the form of either addresses or coordinates. There is an entire syntax for these points (see below).

- `center=` (or `centre=`) – sets the center of the map. This can take in either coordinates or an actual address.

- `service=` – sets the mapping service to be used; the current possible options are `googlemaps`, `openlayers` and `osm` (for the combination of OpenLayers and OpenStreetMap).

- `geoservice=` – sets the geocoding service to be used, if any geocoding is to be done; the current possible options are `geonames` and `google`.

- `width=` – sets the width of the map – can be in "px", "em" or a percentage (if no unit is specified, pixels are assumed). The default is "100%".

- `height=` – sets the height of the map; works like the `width` parameter. The default is 350 pixels.

- `zoom=` – sets the zoom level of the map. This is an integer, whose range of settings depends on the mapping service being used.

- `icon=` – an image to show for all markers (this, like most parameters, is optional).

- `lines=` – sets the group of points between which to draw lines, with groups separated by semicolons, and then points within groups separated by colons.

- `polygons=` – same syntax as the "lines" parameter, but sets filled-in polygons.

The syntax for defining the parameter for the points, which can either be unnamed or named as `points=`, depends on whether "display_map" is called as a parser function or a tag. In both cases, if you simply want to display one point (the most common usage), and don't want any specific formatting, this value can just be coordinates (like "43.9° N, 103.5° W"), or an address or descriptor (like "Eiffel Tower"). If you want to show more than one point, or have extra formatting, the full syntax is as follows:

For #display_map:

```
point 1~title 1~caption 1~marker 1;point 2~title
2~caption 2~marker 2
```

For <display_map>:

```
point 1|title 1|caption 1|marker 1
point 2|title 2|caption 2|marker 2
```

Here's an example of a call to <display_map>:

```
<display_map zoom=11 width=475 height=350>
Nairobi National Park|Nairobi National Park|Kenya's
first national park.|Green marker.png
</display_map>
```

And the equivalent call to #display_map would be:

```
{{#display_map:Nairobi National Park~Nairobi National
Park~Kenya's first national park.~Green marker.png
|zoom=11 |width=475 |height=350}}
```

Either call would produce the output seen in Figure 18.3. This image shows the map if the marker is clicked on, and then hovered over – the "title" field serves as both the title of the caption, and the hover text.

Figure 18.3: Map created using #display_map, from the Maps extension

In addition, Maps defines the following functions (all available as both tags and parser functions), which are helpful when dealing with geographical data:

- **coordinates** – converts coordinates from one format to another (such as converting from degrees-minutes-seconds to a decimal number)

- **distance** – converts a distance from one unit to another (such as miles to kilometers)

- **finddestination** – displays the coordinates of a location, given an initial location, a bearing (an angle) and a distance

- **geocode** – displays the coordinates of a location, given an address or place name

- **geodistance** – displays the distance between two coordinates or place names

Semantic Maps

The Semantic Maps extension requires the extensions Semantic MediaWiki and Maps (it also requires Validator, which is also required by those other extensions). It defines a new SMW property type, "Geographic coordinate", that is used for coordinates. It provides a way to display coordinate data from multiple pages on one map, through various query formats. And it also lets you use a map to enter coordinates in a Semantic Forms-based form.

Here's an example of a simple query that displays a map:

```
{{#ask:[[Category:Parks]] |?Has coordinates
|format=googlemaps}}
```

In order for this query to work, one or more pages in the category "Parks" need to have the property "Has coordinates" set for them, with valid coordinates; and the property "Has coordinates" needs to be defined as having type "Geographic coordinate".

Queries with Semantic Maps can take in most of the same additional parameters that the display_map function from Maps can. Its set of allowed parameters is: `center/centre`, `width`, `height`, `zoom`, `geoservice`, `template`, `icon`, `forceshow` and `showtitle`. The last four parameters are new to Semantic Maps. The "template" parameter lets you set the layout of the caption for each point; see page 170 for how it can be used. The "icon" parameter sets the icon/marker image to be used for the points. The "forceshow" parameter shows a map even if there are no results to display; by default it's set to "yes". And the "showtitle" parameter dictates whether page titles are shown for each point on the map; by default it's set to "yes" as well.

There are various other parameters, that are specific to each mapping format.

Here's an example of a more complicated query:

```
{{#ask:  [[Category:Locations]]
|  ?Has coordinates
|  ?Has location type
|  ?Located in
|  format=map
|  template=Location Popup
|  showtitle=no
|  icon=Blue_marker.png
}}
```

This query uses a template, "Location Popup", that formats the set of values for each point – there are three values for each point, but the page title is not one of them, because "showtitle" is set to "no" as well. And every point is shown with a custom icon – the uploaded image "Blue marker.png".

The query formats that Semantic Maps supports are "maps", "googlemaps", "openlayers" and "kml". The first three are hopefully self-explanatory; they are identical to the "service" parameter values for the Maps extension. The last one, "kml", exports the data in KML (Keyhole Markup Language), a standard file format for coordinate data.

Map form inputs

The other very useful feature of Semantic Maps is that it provides form inputs for map-based entry of coordinates within Semantic Forms forms. Since it's usually unlikely that users will know the geographical coordinates of a place, a map lets users easily find the point, and automatically determine the coordinates.

Figure 18.4 shows how a map form input looks. Here, the user has entered "causeway bay, hong kong" into the address lookup field, and clicked on "Look up coordinates". The map now shows a location on the map, and the coordinates field (which is the field whose value actually ends up on the resulting page) is set to match that location. Assuming the real location the user is looking for is somewhere around there, the user now has three options to try to pinpoint it: zoom in and click on the exact point on the map (the standard, and easiest, option); enter a more specific address in the address lookup field, and look it up again; or manually set the coordinates in the coordinates field (which would be an unlikely option).

It's worth noting that the address lookup field, below the coordinates, exists only for lookup purposes, and does not show up on the page that's generated. So if you have a form where both the address and the coordinates are meant to be entered, the user may end up typing in the address twice.

The SF form input types that Semantic Maps defines are "map" (which displays whatever the default mapping service is), "googlemaps" and "openlayers".

Other visualizations and displays

There are various other visualizations provided by Semantic Result Formats. Here are the relevant format names, and a description of each:

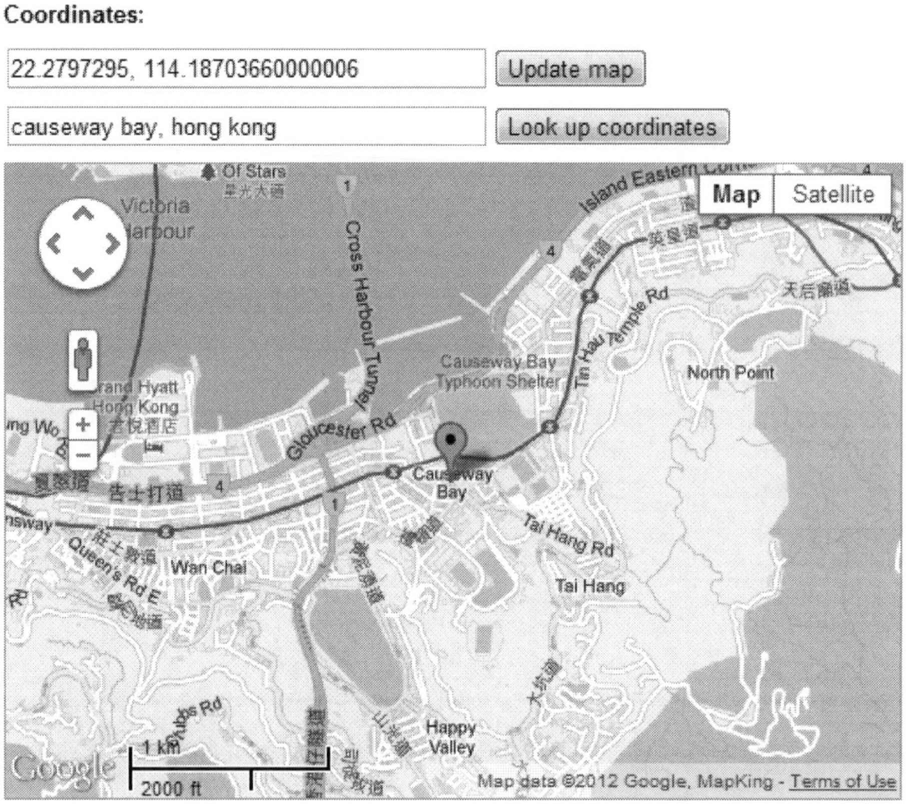

Coordinates:

Figure 18.4: Semantic Maps form input for Semantic Forms, using Google Maps

- **timeline** – displays the values for a "Date" property of the queried set of pages on a scrollable, JavaScript-based horizontal timeline.

- **eventline** – similar to the "timeline" format, but displays multiple points if any page has multiple values for the Date property.

- **gallery** – displays a gallery of images, similar to the display of the `<gallery>` tag (see page 69), where the images are either the actual pages being queried, or a property of the pages being queried. Instead of displaying the images as a gallery, it can also be used to display images one after another, in either an automated "slideshow" (if you add `widget=slideshow`) or a manually-scrolling "carousel" (if you add `widget=carousel`).

- **outline** – splits up the set of queried pages by a set of properties that they have, grouping them so that the result resembles an outline.

- **tree** – shows an outline of pages that have a hierarchical relationship with one another. The usefulness of this format is currently somewhat limited, because it requires all pages to have the same property pointing to one another; which only works for fairly generic properties, like "Located in".

- **array** – has a display similar to the "list" format defined in Semantic MediaWiki, but allows for more customization of the separators used between page names, and between values.

- **hash** – similar to the "array" format, but outputs display in a format that can be directly used by the MediaWiki extension HashTables (https://www.mediawiki. org/wiki/Extension:HashTables).

- **tagcloud** – shows a set of property values and their frequency, via a "tag cloud" display, where values with a higher frequency show up in a larger font. (This is similar in concept to the "distribution" option for the chart result formats, described previously.)

- **valuerank** – similar to "tagcloud", but simply shows the number of instances of each value, instead of changing the font size.

Semantic Result Formats also provides some formats that are just mathematical functions, that display a single number based on some "Number" property that all the queried pages hold. The mathematical formats in SRF are **min**, **max**, **average**, **median**, **sum** and **product**. You can probably guess what each of these do, based on their names.

There are a variety of other result formats defined in Semantic Result Formats. Here is the current list, and their descriptions:

- **eventcalendar** – similar to the "calendar" format, but uses the FullCalendar JavaScript library to display a calendar, instead of HTML, which can make for a slicker user experience.

- **filtered** – shows "filters" for one or more of the printed-out properties, where a filter is a set of checkboxes for all the possible values for that property, letting the user filter the results. It's similar in basic concept to the Semantic Drilldown extension (page 237), but it uses JavaScript instead of PHP to display results –

which means that it runs faster, though it may not be able to deal as well with a large number of pages.

- **listwidget** – splits up results into pages, with a clickable table of contents at the top – the most common use is to split up results by alphabetically, by the first letter of their name.

- **pagewidget** – intended to be a generic format for breaking up results into pages of display. It currently only supports one interface: "carousel", which lets users use buttons to scroll back and forth through the different pages.

- **incoming** – shows the incoming properties pointing to each page in the results.

Semantic Compound Queries

One thing the #ask parser function can't do is display the results of more than one query at the same time. There are various circumstances when it makes sense to do that, but the most common is to display multiple sets of points on the same map, with a different marker for each set. For that, you'd need to use the Semantic Compound Queries extension, and the parser function it defines, #compound_query.

As an example, let's say you want to show a map of all hospitals and banks in a city. Displaying a map requires the Semantic Maps extension (see page 227). In our map, hospitals will get a red-cross icon, while banks get a dollar sign (we'll say that the city is in some country that uses dollars). To complicate things, on the wiki, pages for hospitals have their own category, "Hospitals", while pages for banks are part of the general category "Businesses", with a value of "Bank" for the property "Has business type". Figure 18.5 shows an example of how such a map could appear.

The first thing you would need to do is upload images for the icons you want to display. Let's say you upload images for the two icons shown in Figure 18.5, and name them "Red cross.png" and "Dollar sign.png".

The call to #compound_query would then look like:

```
{{#compound_query:
[[Category:Hospitals]] ;?Has coordinates ;icon=Red
cross.png
|[[Category:Businesses]][[Has business type::Bank]]
;?Has coordinates ;icon=Dollar sign.png
```

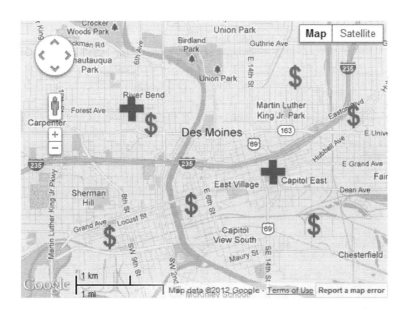

Figure 18.5: Map created using Semantic Compound Queries and the 'googlemaps' format

```
|format=googlemaps
|height=200
|width=400
}}
```

The syntax for #compound_query consists of, essentially, combining several #ask queries into one call. The parameters of each #ask query are turned into sub-parameters instead, separated by semicolons instead of pipes. Parameters relating to the display are kept as full parameters, since they're only called once.

The two geographical-coordinates properties being displayed in the query are in this both called "Has coordinates" here, but they could theoretically have different names.

What if we want to add to our map a third set of points, for all businesses that aren't banks, each point represented with a picture of a building? Thankfully, #compound_query makes it easy to do that: pages that are covered by more than one of the sub-queries are only displayed by the first sub-query that they apply to. So as long as the more specific queries are included before the general ones, the last query or queries can serve as a catch-all for everything that didn't fit previously. Here's how you could do it:

```
{{#compound_query:
[[Category:Hospitals]] ;?Has coordinates ;icon=Red
cross.png
|[[Category:Businesses]][[Has business type::Bank]]
;?Has coordinates ;icon=Dollar sign.png
|[[Category:Businesses]] ;?Has coordinates
;icon=Office building.png
|format=googlemaps
|height=200
|width=400
}}
```

Besides maps, the other somewhat common application of Semantic Compound Queries is to display multiple types of events on calendars, each of which can be differently color-coded. As an example, to display meetings and task deadlines on the same calendar, with meetings in blue and deadlines in orange, you could call the following:

```
{{#compound_query:
[[Category:Meetings]]
[[Has date::>{{#calendarstartdate:}}]]
[[Has date::<{{#calendarenddate:}}]]
;?Has date ;color=blue
|[[Category:Tasks]]
[[Has deadline::>{{#calendarstartdate:}}]]
[[Has deadline::<{{#calendarenddate:}}]]
;?Has deadline ;color=orange
|format=calendar
|height=200
|width=400
}}
```

Figure 18.6 shows what such a query could generate.

Compound queries can also be used for more basic formats like tables and lists, though in practice that's rarely done.

You can read more about Semantic Compound Queries here:

Figure 18.6: A calendar created using Semantic Compound Queries and the 'calendar' format

https://www.mediawiki.org/wiki/Extension:Semantic_Compound_
Queries

DynamicPageList

There are actually two extensions named DynamicPageList, or DPL for short. They originated in the same code, but the code was then forked into two versions when the decision was made to use the code on the Wikinews site. This required removing some of the DPL functionality, for both security and performance reasons, which then led to the spinoff into two separate extensions. The version intended for use by Wikimedia sites gained the alternate name "Intersection", while the other version got the alternate name "DPL2", but both are still known officially as "DynamicPageList". For several years, only the Wikimedia version was recommended, due to security issues with the other one, but now the security problems seem to have been fixed in DPL2, so both can be used. Here are the homepages for the two:

> https://www.mediawiki.org/wiki/Extension:DynamicPageList_ (Wikimedia)
> https://www.mediawiki.org/wiki/Extension:DynamicPageList_ (third-party)

The two are fairly similar in their functionality. The Wikimedia version is the safer choice. For wikis where performance is not paramount, the "third-party" version is the more powerful, and seemingly more popular, choice.

In theory, DynamicPageList (both versions) works somewhat similarly to Semantic MediaWiki, in that they both let you query pages and display the results in different ways. The difference is that DPL doesn't store any data of its own; it uses existing data like categories, namespaces, and – if the FlaggedRevs extension is installed – various FlaggedRevs metrics of page quality, to generate lists and galleries of pages.

Most notably, DPL is used to find intersections of categories, as well as to display all the pages in one category. For instance, to show a sorted list of pages about 18th-century composers, you might have the following:

```
<DynamicPageList>
category = Composers
category = 18th century births
order = ascending
</DynamicPageList>
```

(This specific call would work with both versions of DPL. The third-party version, i.e. DPL2, also supports the <DPL> and #dpl functions, which have some additional features that the <DynamicPageList> tag does not support.)

A regular user of Semantic MediaWiki might say that this is an overuse of categories in the first place, and that such information is better stored as properties. Nevertheless, many wikis don't use SMW, in which case DPL can certainly be helpful. DPL is in use on some Wikimedia sites, including Wikinews and Wikibooks.

Chapter 19

Additional Semantic MediaWiki functionality

There are over 50 extensions that make use of Semantic MediaWiki. Many are unmaintained or obsolete, so that number gives a false impression, but nevertheless there is a variety of interesting SMW-related functionality that hasn't been covered yet in this book. In this chapter we'll briefly go over some of it.

Semantic Drilldown

The Semantic Drilldown extension offers a drill-down interface to browse the data in each category, available at the special page Special:BrowseData. Each filter for a category corresponds to a single Semantic MediaWiki property. Figure 19.1 shows an example of the interface created by Semantic Drilldown, for a hypothetical wiki about astronomy.

The "BrowseData" page lets you browse one category at a time. Note the list of categories on the right-hand side: each of those is a link, to let you browse and drill down through that category's pages. The Semantic Drilldown interface shows, by default, the full set of top-level categories in the wiki (i.e., categories that do not have a parent category). Subcategories within each category are shown as additional filters.

Each defined filter lists the values that exist for that filter, along with the number of pages that match that value. Already, before even clicking on anything, the user is getting a lot of information:

Figure 19.1: Special:BrowseData page, from the Semantic Drilldown extension

- The number of pages in the wiki, in every main category.

- An alphabetical listing of the pages in the current category. (Though this isn't shown in the screenshots presented here.)

- The list of fields (or at least, a subset of them) that each page in the category holds.

- The breakdown of the data, including subcategories, in the current category.

- Any discrepancies, misspellings and gaps in the current data. The "None" values, for instance, indicate the number of pages that don't have a value for that field. There's no opportunity to see misspellings in the screenshots shown here, because all of the filters are either numbers or a combo box that has to be clicked on, but if there were a filter that showed a set of text values on the screen, then misspellings would easily jump out.

Figure 19.2 shows how that page from before would look, after the "2,000 - 3,500" value is clicked for the "Diameter, in miles" filter.

The header has been updated; and the other filters show their new values, for only the set of pages that fit the already-selected criteria. Clicking on additional values will further reduce the set of results.

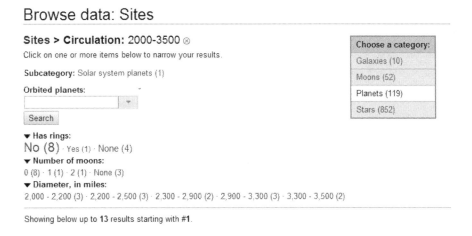

Figure 19.2: Special:BrowseData, after a filter click

Hopefully, this helps to demonstrate the usefulness of the Semantic Drilldown extension, and more generally, of the approach known variously as "drill-down", "faceted browsing" and "slice-and-dice".

Such an approach can certainly be found elsewhere on the web, though the more common approach is field-based search, where users just fill in values for different fields and then hit a big "Search" button at the bottom. Standard search may be more popular just because that sort of search is easier to implement. But a drill-down approach offers a number of big advantages, as we've seen.

If you do want a more search-like interface (what's sometimes known as "faceted search" in contrast with Semantic Drilldown's "faceted browsing"), you should instead use the "run query" option in Semantic Forms (see page 215).

Setting up filters

The interface available at Special:BrowseData is useful even if you don't create any filters, since it lets you view all of the wiki's categories and their pages in one place. However, it's even more useful if you do create filters. The easiest way to create a filter is via the filter-creation helper form, available at either the special page Special:CreateFilter or by directly going to a filter page that doesn't exist yet and clicking on the "Create with form" tab.

Figure 19.3 shows how the page Special:CreateFilter might appear for this astronomy wiki.

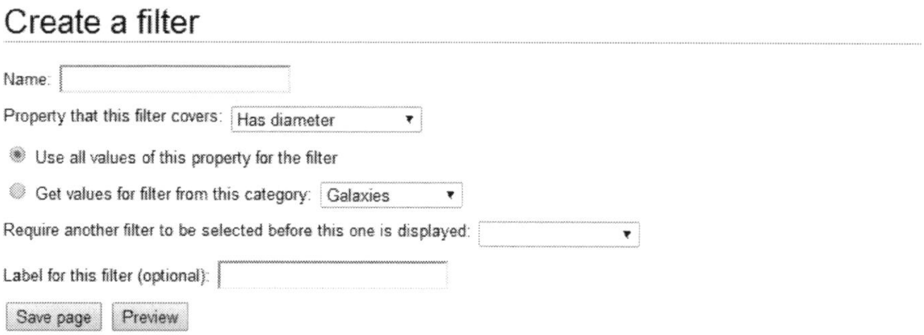

Create a filter

Name: [   ]

Property that this filter covers: [Has diameter   ▼]

  ◉ Use all values of this property for the filter

  ○ Get values for filter from this category: [Galaxies   ▼]

Require another filter to be selected before this one is displayed: [▼]

Label for this filter (optional): [   ]

[Save page] [Preview]

Figure 19.3: Special:CreateFilter page from Semantic Drilldown extension

Most likely, all you will need to fill out in this form is the top two fields – the name of the filter, and the property that it covers – before hitting "Save page". (And if you're reaching this form directly from a new filter page, you won't even see a "Name" field, since the page's name has already been set – you just need to set the property dropdown.)

Every filter corresponds to a single semantic property – it lets you filter pages based on those pages' values for that one property.

Regardless of how this helper form gets filled out, what ends up on the filter page is a set of wikitext, which is mostly comprised of Semantic MediaWiki property tags. Let's go through those now. (They're especially useful to know about if you're editing an existing filter, because the helper form only lets you create new filters, or overwrite the contents of existing filters – it doesn't help with editing existing contents.)

A filter is defined in a page in the "Filter" namespace. To use the example from before: let's say that those value for "Has rings" are set by a property also called "Has rings". (The filter and property don't have to have the same name.) To define a filter called "Has rings", that filters on the values for the "Has rings" property, you would need a page called "Filter:Has rings", that contains the following:

```
[[Covers property::Property:Has rings]]
```

You can change the display name, or "label", of each filter, using the "Has label" special property. For instance, maybe the "diameter" filter in the example is just at the page "Filter:Diameter", but you want the text to be "Diameter, in miles". This would be done with text like the following:

```
[[Has label::Diameter, in miles]]
```

So, you've created a filter. Now, how do you get it show up in Special:BrowseData for a certain category? To do that, you just need to link to the filter from the category page using the special "Has filter" property. For our example, in the page "Category:Planets", you would add something like the following:

```
[[Has filter::Filter:Diameter]]
```

There's an alternate way to create filters for categories, which is via the Page Schemas extension (page 244). This approach involves storing the filter data via XML and thus doesn't involve filter pages at all – which might be conceptually simpler.

Setting display of results

The tag-cloud-style display of results in the example shown, where the font size of a value is determined by how many pages it has, is not default behavior, but it can be done by setting the values of the variables $sdgFiltersSmallestFontSize and $sdgFiltersLargestFontSize in LocalSettings.php. Here were the settings used for this particular display:

```
$sdgFiltersSmallestFontSize = 12;
$sdgFiltersLargestFontSize = 21;
```

You can also change the display of the result pages, to show them in, say, a table or a map, instead of just as a list of page names. To show results in a table, you could add something like the following to the category page:

```
[[Has display parameters::?  Has coordinates;
format=googlemaps| ]]
```

There are various other features in Semantic Drilldown: you can manually set categories to appear or not appear in the list of categories (using the strings "__SHOWIN-DRILLDOWN__" and "__HIDEFROMDRILLDOWN__"), you can change the list of categories to show up as horizontal tabs instead of a vertical list, you can have certain filters only show up after other filters have been clicked on, etc. For more information and options, see the Semantic Drilldown homepage, at:

https://www.mediawiki.org/wiki/Extension:Semantic_Drilldown

Semantic Watchlist

The Semantic Watchlist extension lets users "watch" certain properties within certain groups of pages (i.e., categories, namespaces or concepts), in order to be notified by email any time one or more of those properties changes in any of those pages.

Figure 19.4 shows the interface, at the page Special:WatchlistConditions, that Semantic Watchlist provides for administrators in order to create watchlist groups for the wiki. Each watchlist group consists of a category, namespace or concept, a set of one or more properties to be watched, and then optionally some specific text that users get emailed with on certain combinations of property and value.

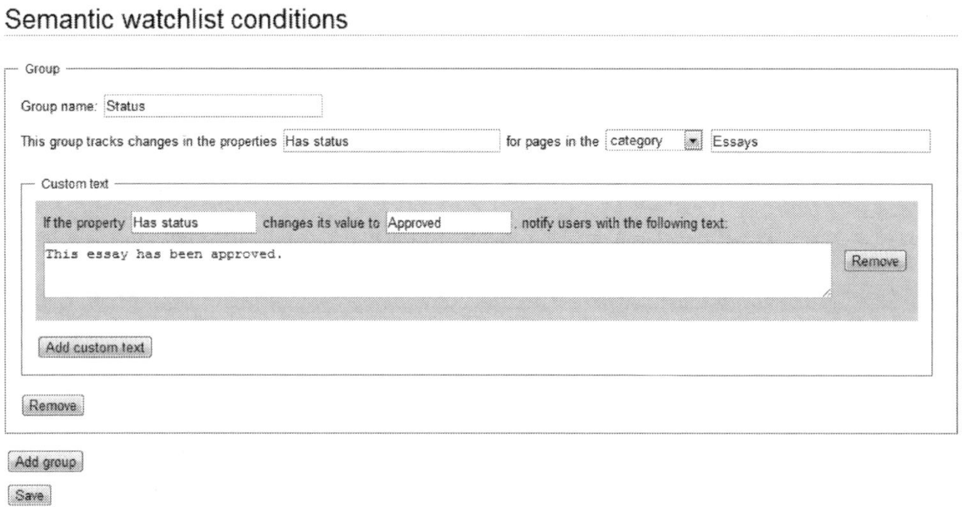

Figure 19.4: Special:WatchlistConditions, defined by the Semantic Watchlist extension

Users can then choose to "subscribe" to any such group. For performance reasons, only administrators can define watchlist groups; regular users can't (though of course they can request for new groups to be made).

You can read more about Semantic Watchlist here:

https://www.mediawiki.org/wiki/Extension:Semantic_Watchlist

Semantic Extra Special Properties

The Semantic Extra Special Properties extension lets you store additional wiki-specific metadata about each page, as semantic values that can be queried elsewhere. Among additional values that can be stored for a given page are: the user who created it, the set of all users who edited it, the number of page views it has, the number of revisions it has, and so on. (These special properties come in addition to the standard ones that Semantic MediaWiki offers for storing basic page metadata, such as the date a page was last modified - see page 164.) For uploaded files, you can also store some of the "Exif" data that came with the file, if there was any – for example, for photos taken with a digital camera, the date the photo was taken. You can then query on that metadata alongside true semantic data – to find, for instance, the most widely-viewed pages from a certain category. You can read more about this extension here:

> https://www.mediawiki.org/wiki/Extension:Semantic_Extra_Special_
> Properties

Semantic Tasks

The Semantic Tasks extension lets users receive an email when some date occurs, whether that's a holiday, a meeting or a deadline (not all of these are "tasks", of course). The emailing is entirely based on information stored via Semantic MediaWiki. To be part of the notification system, an event has to have its own wiki page, which should have dates stored with properties called "Reminder at" and/or "Target date" – these are both special properties. And the page should additionally have one or more values for the special properties "Assigned to" and "Carbon copy", which determine the email recipients. "Assigned to" and "Carbon copy" don't point to email addresses – instead, they point to user pages, and in turn each of those users needs to have an email address specified in order to receive the notifications.

You can read more about Semantic Tasks here:

> https://www.mediawiki.org/wiki/Extension:Semantic_Tasks

SMW+/DataWiki

SMW+ was a package of MediaWiki extensions, plus some peripheral elements, developed by the German company Ontoprise; it was first released in 2007. Ontoprise shut down in 2012; currently, some of its former developers are at a new company called DIQA-PM, where SMW+ is still maintained in some form, now under the name "DataWiki" (not to be confused with Wikidata).

If SMW+/DataWiki can be described in brief, the software takes a more standard Semantic Web-approach to data than the extensions we've covered so far, enabling free-form annotation of pages, ontology browsing, and the like. That's in contrast to the approach embodied by Semantic Forms, Semantic Drilldown, etc., where the details of properties and ontologies are hidden as much as possible from users. SMW+ also had two interesting additional extensions, one for WYSIWYG editing (which uses CKEditor) and one for access control. You can read more about DataWiki at http://diqa-pm.com/en/DataWiki.

Page Schemas

Page Schemas is an extension that aims to solve a general problem with Semantic MediaWiki and Semantic Forms, which is that long-term maintenance can be difficult. Semantic Forms offers various tools for automatically creating all of the data structure pages – the most popular being Special:CreateClass – but all of them create such pages from scratch; there's no way to edit an existing form or template to, say, add one field; other than manually editing the page source.

It's an alternate approach to data structure creation and maintenance that has started to gain more significant usage, as the software improves and as people learn about it.

With Page Schemas, you use a single "master" form to define the data structure; that form in turn creates a single piece of XML (stored on the category page), which can then be used to automatically generate all those other pages. You can then keep re-editing that schema, using a helper form, and re-generating all the corresponding pages. You can read more about it at:

https://www.mediawiki.org/wiki/Extension:Page_Schemas

Figure 19.5 shows an image of the interface provided by Page Schemas for editing a schema.

Edit schema

Figure 19.5: Page Schemas "Edit schema" screen

Chapter 20

External data and applications

External Data

We live in a world with an enormous and ever-growing amount of data, contained in lots of different sources: databases, spreadsheets, APIs, offline files and more. Sadly, most of it will never be entered into any wiki. But it can still be displayed and used within wikis, via the External Data extension. External Data provides an easy way to query data stored in various computerized formats. It can then be displayed on wiki pages or, via Semantic MediaWiki, stored for usage alongside the wiki's own data.

There are three basic data sources that External Data can query, handled by three different parser functions: #get_web_data, #get_db_data and #get_ldap_data. Let's go through each one in turn.

Getting data from the web

#get_web_data is used to retrieve data from any page on the web that holds structured data. It is usually used to retrieve data from a URL-based API, or what's sometimes known as a RESTful API (the "REST" here stands for "Representational State Transfer"); but it can also be used to get data from a standalone file. If it can read the contents of such a page, it can then retrieve some or all of the values that that page contains, and display them on the wiki.

#get_web_data is called in the following way:

```
{{#get_web_data:url=url|format=format
```

247

```
|data=local variable name 1=external variable name
1,local variable name 2=external variable name 2,...
|filters=external variable name 1=filter value
1,external variable name 2=filter value 2,...}}
```

The 'url' parameter is the URL being accessed. It does not have to be accessible to the user viewing the wiki, but it does have to be accessible to the wiki's own server.

The 'format' parameter holds the format that the data is in. The allowed values are 'CSV', 'CSV with header', 'GFF', 'JSON' and 'XML'. These represent, as you might guess, the data formats CSV, GFF, JSON and XML, respectively.

CSV, JSON and XML you may well have heard of: these are standard formats for representing data. CSV is an old, very simple format. It stands for "comma-separated values", and that's essentially all it is. The difference between 'CSV' and 'CSV with header' is that, for 'CSV', the data is assumed to start at the very first line, while for 'CSV with header', the first line holds the header information. JSON and XML are formats mostly associated with the web. GFF is used only for representing genomics data.

The "data" parameter defines a series of what could be called mappings. A mapping sets a local variable to have the value of a tag or field in the source document with the given name. So, for instance if the URL being accessed holds XML that contains a section like "`<dept>Accounting<dept>`", and the #get_web_data call has the parameter "`data=department=dept`", then a local variable, "department", will get set to the value "Accounting". This will similarly work, for XML, if the relevant value is a tag attribute (instead of tag contents), e.g. something like "`<employee dept="Accounting">`".

Handling XML documents can be tricky because their format can involve using the same generic tag or attribute name for different types of data. In the extreme case, you could imagine XML formatted like:

```
<employee name="Charles Coletti">

    <department name="Sales" />
    <position name="Head of sales" />

<employee>
```

In this case, each value is directly tied to an attribute called "name", so you can't just use the attribute name, as you normally would with #get_web_data. Instead, you would need to use the longer chain of tag and attribute names pointing to each value, using a simple query language known as XPath. You can do that in #get_web_data, by adding the parameter "use xpath". Here is how you could get the information from the previous example:

```
{{#get_web_data:url=http://example.com/employee_data.xml
|format=xml |use xpath |data=employee=/employee/@name,
department=/department/@name, position=/position/@name}}
```

This problem of disambiguation can also occur with JSON data, and in fact there's a syntax called JSONPath that does for JSON what XPath does for XML, but unfortunately External Data doesn't support it.

For CSV documents, the naming of fields depends on whether the file has a header row. If it does, i.e. it's of 'CSV with header' format, then each column gets the name assigned to it at the top; otherwise the names of the columns are just the sequential numbers 1, 2, 3 etc. For the basic 'CSV' format, a mapping parameter could look like "|data=department=4".

A #get_web_data call needs at least one value for the "data" parameter to be worthwhile; after all, some value needs to be set. By contrast, the "filters" parameter is optional. When used, the filters filter down the set of values in the accessed page by keeping only the row or rows of data that have the specified value(s) for the specified field name(s). For instance, if the file contains information about every employee, having a parameter like "filters=name=Irving Ivanov" will return only the row (if there is one) where the "name" field is set to "Irving Ivanov".

This filtering system leaves a lot to be desired – there's no way to match on substrings, for instance, or to use inequality operators for number fields. But in practice, that type of more complex filtering isn't often needed, because the URLs being accessed are often part of a web-based API, where necessary filtering can often be done via the URL itself. Here's an example of what such a call to an API could look like:

```
{{#get_web_data:
url=http://example.com/country_data_api?country=Morocco
|format=json |data=population=Population}}
```

Displaying and storing values

Once we have our local variables set, the next step is to display, or otherwise use them. How that's done depends on whether there is one, or more than one, value for each variable. In the simple case, we have one value that's been retrieved for each field. In that case, the parser function #external_value is used to display it on the screen. After the previous call to #get_web_data, for instance, the wikitext could contain the following:

```
The population of Morocco is {{#external_value:
population}}.
```

Assuming the "population" field was correctly retrieved before, this will insert a number into the text that's displayed.

If we want to also store the value as semantic data, so that it can be queried alongside the wiki's native semantic data, that's easy to do. If this call happens on a page called "Morocco", it's just a matter of adding a Semantic MediaWiki tag:

```
The population of Morocco is [[Has population::
{{#external_value:population}}]].
```

Storing external data via SMW should be done with caution, since if the data being retrieved gets changed, the SMW representation of it won't be updated until and unless it's manually refreshed in the wiki in some way.

Displaying and storing a table of data

If the data that was retrieved contains more one than row, i.e. it's a table of data, displaying it is slightly more complicated. For that, we use the function #for_external_table, which takes in a string that holds one or more variables, and loop through the values for them, printing out the string for each row. For example, let's say there's a web page holding information on books and their authors in CSV format, and we want to display the entire set of information in a wiki page. We can accomplish that using the following two calls:

```
{{#get_web_data:url=http://example.com/books_data.csv
|format=csv with header |data=book
name=title,author=author}}
{{#for_external_table:The book ''{{{book name}}}'' was
written by {{{author}}}.  }}
```

This will print out text in the form:

The book *Shadow of Paradise* was written by Vicente Aleixandre. The book *The Family Moskat* was written by Isaac Bashevis Singer. The book *The Sovereign Sun* was written by Odysseas Elytis.

Within #for_external_table, each field is displayed by putting its name in triple curly brackets; #for_external_table then loops all the way through the arrays of these values from start to finish, printing out the string for each.

Interestingly, there's no reference in the #for_external_table call to the #get_web_data query that created the arrays of these two values – they could have even come from two different #get_web_data calls. In general, though, it's assumed that a call to #for_external_table will handle the values retrieved from a single #get_web_data call, and that all the arrays will hold the same number of rows. If the two arrays are of different sizes – i.e. if there are more book rows than author rows, or vice versa – then you'll probably get some strangely-formatted results.

Chances are good that you wouldn't want to print out a table of data as a long series of sentences – instead, you'll probably want to display them as a table. That can be done via a minor hack. First, you'll need to create the "!" template to hold a " | ", as described on page 38. Then, you can have a call that looks like the following:

```
{| class="wikitable"
!  Book
!  Author {{#for_external_table:<nowiki/>
{{!}}-
{{!}} {{{book name}}}
{{!}} {{{author}}}
|}
```

This will print out the correct wikitext for a table, including header rows.

There's one other interesting feature of #for_external_table, which is that it lets you URL-encode specific values, by calling them with {{{field-name.urlencode}}} instead of just {{{field-name}}}. For instance, if you wanted to show links to Google searches on a set of terms retrieved, you could call:

```
{{#for_external_table:  http://google.com/search?q={{{
term.urlencode}}} }}
```

It's also possible to store the table of data semantically, if you have the Semantic Media-Wiki extension (chapter 16) installed. Instead of using #for_external_table, you would use a separate parser function, #store_external_table. It functions like a cross between #for_external_table and SMW's #subobject (though its syntax is closer to that of the parser function #set_internal, defined in the Semantic Internal Objects extension (page 174). Here's how a call for the previous set of data would look:

```
{{#store_external_table:Is book in list |Has
title=book name |Has author=author}}
```

If you're familiar with #set_internal, this should look familiar. "Is book in list" is a property that points from each internal object to the main page, while "Has title" and "Has author" are additional properties for each subobject. A new subobject is created for each row of original data. Just as with #subobject (and #set_internal), #store_external_table doesn't display anything to the screen; so to display the data, you would have to make another call – presumably either a call to #for_external_table or simply a query of the data, using #ask. In fact, this presents another way to display a table of data on the screen – instead of using #for_external_table and the table-display hack, you could use the #store_external_table call above and then call the following, on the same page:

```
{{#ask:[[Is book in list::{{PAGENAME}}]] |?Has
title=Book |?Has author=Author |format=table}}
```

Secret keys and whitelists

Some APIs require a "key", placed within the URL, which serves as an identifier in order to prevent public abuse of the API. In some cases, this key is meant to be a secret; when that happens, it wouldn't work to place the full URL of the API directly within the wiki page. For that reason, External Data also allows the use of secret strings, whose real value is defined within LocalSettings.php. So if you want to access an API whose URLs are in the form "http://worlddata.com/api?country=Guatemala&key=123abc", you can add the following to your LocalSettings.php file, after the inclusion of External Data:

```
$edgStringReplacements['WORLDDATA_KEY'] = '123abc';
```

After that, you can instead place within the wiki URLs like:

```
http://worlddata.com/api?country=Guatemala&key=WORLDDATA_KEY
```

...and the replacement will happen behind the scenes.

If you're a security-minded individual, you may have already thought ahead to a possible counterattack that a malicious user could do to find out the value of a secret string: put somewhere in the wiki a call to #get_web_data, pointing to a URL in a domain that that user controls, that also contains the replacement string. Then the user just has to check that domain's server logs to find out the true value. Thankfully, a defense exists for this: you can create a "whitelist" of domains for External Data, so that only URLs contained within that list can get accessed by External Data.

To create a whitelist with multiple domains, you should add something like the following to LocalSettings.php, after the inclusion of External Data:

```
$edgAllowExternalDataFrom        =        array('http://example.org',
'http://example2.com');
```

And if the whitelist has only one domain, you can just have something like this:

```
$edgAllowExternalDataFrom = 'http://example.org';
```

Getting data from a database

Data can also be retrieved from databases, using the call #get_db_data. #get_db_data can access most major database systems, including MySQL, PostgreSQL, Microsoft SQLServer, Oracle, SQLite and the non-SQL MongoDB. The process for each of them is the same. First, the login information to access any particular database has to be added to LocalSettings.php (after the inclusion of External Data), in a format like this one:

```
$edgDBServer['database ID'] = "server name";
$edgDBServerType['database ID'] = "DB type";
$edgDBName['database ID'] = "DB name";
$edgDBUser['database ID'] = "username";
$edgDBPass['database ID'] = "password";
```

Here the string "database ID" is an arbitrary ID for the database; it can be any string. You can set information for as many databases as you want to in LocalSettings.php, with a different ID for each.

For the database systems SQLite and MongoDB, the group of settings is slightly different, and for SQLServer, some additional software may be required; see the extension homepage for details.

The call to #get_db_data then takes the following form:

```
{{#get_db_data:db=database ID |from=table name
|where=filters |data=mappings}}
```

The idea is the same as for #get_web_data, though the parameters are different. The db parameter holds the database ID, which is defined in LocalSettings.php. The next two parameters are based on elements of the "SELECT" statement in SQL, if you're familiar with that. The `from` parameter holds the database table name, or a join of tables if there's more than one; it's the equivalent of a SELECT statement's FROM clause. The `where` parameter holds the filters, or the set of conditions that we are restricting results on, with each filter separated by " AND "; this is equivalent to the SELECT statement's WHERE clause. Just as with #get_web_data, the `data` parameter holds the set of fields we want to retrieve, along with the mapping of a local variable for each field. It's similar to a SELECT statement's SELECT clause, though not identical.

Here's an example of a #get_db_data call – this one retrieves some information about a room in a building whose name is the same as the current page name:

```
{{#get_db_data:db=myDB
|from=rooms r JOIN room_status rs ON r.room_status_id
= rs.id
|where=r.name={{PAGENAME}}
|data=capacity=r.capacity, building name=r.building,
status=rs.name
}}
```

Note that table aliases (here, "r" and "rs") can be used, just as with a SQL statement.

There are some additional parameters that can be passed in to #get_db_data:

- `limit=` – adds a "LIMIT" clause to the SELECT statement, setting the number of values to be returned.

- `order by=` – adds an "ORDER BY" clause to the SELECT statement, setting the order of results.

- `group by=` – adds a "GROUP BY" clause to the SELECT statement, grouping results by the values for a field.

If you're accessing MongoDB, the syntax could be different: there are some restrictions, like that you can't include "OR" in the "where=" parameter, and you can set queries directly using the parameter "find query=", in place of "from=" and "where=". See the documentation for more details.

Once the data is retrieved, it can be displayed and stored using #external_value, or, if the data is an array, using #for_external_table and #store_external_table – once the data is set to local variables, it's indistinguishable from data retrieved by #get_web_data.

Getting data from an LDAP server

You can also get data from an LDAP server, if your organization has one, in a similar manner to how data is extracted from databases. As with getting data from a database, you first need to set the connection details in LocalSettings.php, then query the data using #get_ldap_data. We won't get into the details here, since it's a less frequently-used feature, but you can see the full syntax and examples on the External Data homepage.

As you would expect, #external_value, #for_external_table and #store_external_table can then all be called on the local values that have been set as a result.

Accessing offline data

What about offline data – data that's not available via the network, or perhaps is not even on a computer? The External Data extension doesn't have any special power to bend the laws of physics, but it does offer a utility that makes it possible to put such data online with a minimum of fuss: the page "Special:GetData". To use it, you first need to get this data into CSV format, i.e. rows of comma-separated values, with a single header row defining the name of each "column". This may or may not be a challenge, depending on the nature of the data and what form it's currently in, but CSV is, at the very least, a data format that's easy to create.

Once the CSV is created, it should be put into a page in the wiki – any name will work for the page. As an example, you could have a collection of information about a company's employees, and put it into a wiki page called 'Employee CSV data'. The page's contents might look like this:

```
<noinclude>
This page holds information about Acme Corp's
employees.
</noinclude><includeonly>
```

```
Employee name,Department,Position,Phone Number
Alice Adams,Accounting,Accountant,5-1234
Bob Benson,Sales,IT administrator,5-2345
...
</includeonly>
```

The "<noinclude>" and "<includeonly>" tags are optional – they let you set a nice explanatory display when users view the page. If those tags aren't included, the entire page will be parsed as CSV, while if they are included, the "<noinclude>" sections will get ignored.

The page Special:GetData then serves as a wrapper around that data, providing a sort of "mini-API" for accessing its content. A typical URL for 'GetData' would look like this:

> http://example.com/wiki/Special:GetData/Employee_CSV_data?Employee
> %20name=Alice%20Adams

The name of the page with the CSV data is placed after "Special:GetData", with a slash between them. Then, in the URL's query string (i.e., after the '?'), values can be set for different column names to filter down the set of values. In this case, Special:GetData will return all the rows of the page 'Employee CSV data' that have a value of 'Alice Adams' for the column named 'Employee name'.

That URL can then be passed in to a call to #get_web_data, just like any other API URL. Note that if you're using #get_web_data to query a 'GetData' page, you can apply filtering in either place: either within the API, or as a #get_web_data filter. Barring any reason to use one versus the other, it's recommended to do the filtering within the URL itself, since that's slightly faster.

Caching data

You can configure External Data to cache the data contained in the URLs that it accesses, both to speed up retrieval of values and to reduce the load on the system whose data is being accessed. To do this, run the SQL contained in the extension file "ExternalData.sql" in your database, which will create the table "ed_url_cache", then add the following to your LocalSettings.php file, after the inclusion of External Data:

```
$edgCacheTable = 'ed_url_cache';
```

You should also add a line like the following, to set the expiration time of the cache, in seconds; this example line will cache the data for a week:

$edgCacheExpireTime = 7 * 24 * 60 * 60;

Widgets

A wiki doesn't usually consist of text alone, and often it's helpful to embed outside media into the pages. MediaWiki itself doesn't allow for embedding HTML and JavaScript within pages, though (see page 32 for more information), which means that audio and video players, and other content like RSS viewers, can't be added by default into MediaWiki. To get around this problem, a staggering array of extensions have been created, tasked with embedding specific players and widgets. Of the around 1,000 extensions listed on mediawiki.org, 44 are in the "Video player extensions" category; and around 12 exist for YouTube alone. Each one embeds into the wiki page some variation of the required HTML and JavaScript. The need for all of these ended, however, in 2008, when the Widgets extension was released.

The Widgets extension is simple in concept: it allows for creating bits of custom HTML and JavaScript that can be embedded on a page. Each snippet of HTML and JavaScript, representing a single "widget", is stored directly within the wiki, in a page in the "Widget:" namespace.

Widgets can also store code, in the Smarty language – a PHP-based "template engine". This lets widgets modify the output with parameters, and use "if" calls and the like.

Due to the obvious security danger of allowing free HTML and JavaScript in pages, editing in the "Widget:" namespace is restricted to users in the 'mediawikiwidgets' group.

There is no need to "re-invent the wheel", and a large number of pre-defined widget pages already exist for the Widgets extension, and can be viewed at mediawikiwidgets.org. These represent video players, audio players, RSS readers, displays of information from individual websites like Facebook and Amazon, and others.

To display YouTube videos, for instance, you just have to go to this page:

http://mediawikiwidgets.org/Widget:YouTube

There, click on "View source", copy the entire contents, and paste it to the page "Widget:YouTube" on your wiki. After that, embedding a video in a page is just a matter of adding something like:

```
{{#widget:YouTube|id=video ID}}
```

...to the page, where "video ID" is YouTube's own ID for the video, viewable in the URL. Each widget can define as many parameters as it wants; the YouTube widget defines only one, for the ID. There are other parameters that this widget could have had, though: YouTube allows for settings for its embedded videos such as the color of a border rectangle, for example. Part of the beauty of the Widgets extension is that you can modify a widget yourself, once it's on your wiki, in order to, among other things, add more parameters to it.

Widgets don't necessarily have to involve embedded media of any kind – after all, they're simply a mechanism for creating text based on a set of parameters. One interesting widget, which is already pre-defined on mediawikiwidgets.org, is "Short link", which takes in a URL and produces a link showing only the domain of that URL. So passing in "http://123.com/abc" would display a link to that URL that read simply "123.com" – a convenient way of shortening long links.

Export-based SMW query formats

Some of the query formats defined by both Semantic MediaWiki and Semantic Result Formats are just standard data formats, that can be used to export data to other systems. SMW defines the 'csv' , 'dsv', 'json', 'rss' and 'rdf' formats, while Semantic Result Formats defines the 'icalendar', 'vcard', 'bibtex', 'excel' and 'feed' formats. CSV, DSV and JSON are generic file formats that can hold any sort of data, RSS is a syndication format for news and blog posts, and RDF is a framework/format used in the Semantic Web (see page 177). The iCalendar, vCard and BibTeX are standard file formats used for defining date-based, business-card-type and reference-related information, respectively; the 'excel' format exports directly into Microsoft Excel's .xls format; and the 'feed' result format supports both RSS and a competing standard, Atom (and will eventually replace the 'rss' format).

These query formats aren't used for displaying data inline within wiki pages: in fact, they can't be used for that purpose at all. When a query that has its 'format' parameter set to one of these values is placed within a wiki page, what's displayed on the page is just:

CSV

(or, instead of 'CSV', the name of the format in question.)

When a user clicks on that link, it takes them to the page Special:Ask, with parameters configured to that query. Special:Ask, in turn, displays not its usual interface but just the data, in that format; which will then either be displayed on the screen or downloaded as a file to the browser, depending on the server's configuration settings.

Via these export formats, then, the Special:Ask page can function as an API for reading the contents of the SMW data. An external system could use Special:Ask to directly access any specific information it wants, either for a set of pages or for any one page, without the need for any web scraping. The external system simply has to know how to format the Special:Ask URL to match the query it wants to run; and then of course it has to parse the results, although standard libraries exist to parse these data formats in many programming languages.

The outside system accessing the data can in fact be another wiki, and the External Data extension (see the start of this chapter) provides an easy way for a MediaWiki-based wiki, whether or not it uses SMW, to query and display the data from an SMW-using wiki.

For the CSV and JSON formats, you simply have to call a normal #ask query, and specify the format. For DSV, you should also specify the separator character, using the "sep=" parameter; by default it's ":". The iCalendar and vCard formats don't take in many special parameters, but they do require giving pre-specified names to a variety of query printouts, so that the code knows, for instance, which property corresponds to the person's work phone, for the case of vCard. Further information about all of these query formats can be found here:

https://semantic-mediawiki.org/wiki/Category:Result_formats

Chapter 21

Importing and exporting

There are two ways of using one system's data in another: you can either query system A's data in system B, or you can import the data from A into B. The right answer depends on where you want the data to "live" in the future. Ideally, any piece of data shouldn't be stored in more than one place, because data redundancy can quickly lead to inconsistent data, since the data can get modified anywhere it resides. So if you import data from one system to another, presumably the data will at the same time go away in the old one.

(There are exceptions to that rule, and one extension, "Push", lets you dynamically move content between two wikis; we'll get to that later.)

We covered both the querying of data within MediaWiki, and the querying of MediaWiki's data in other systems, in the last chapter. This chapter is instead focused on actually moving content into, out of or between wikis. There are essentially three kinds of possible moves: moving contents between two MediaWiki wikis; moving contents from another system, wiki or otherwise, into MediaWiki; and moving contents from MediaWiki into another system. Let's go through these one at a time.

Moving content between two MediaWiki systems

This is conceptually the simplest of the three kinds of moves. If you're just trying to move a wiki to a different location, then the best approach is to zip up all the Media-Wiki files, PHP and otherwise (going with the top directory will get them all), do a dump of the wiki's database, and then un-archive them both in the new location. Give or take a few modifications to LocalSettings.php, everything should just work.

If, however, you're trying to move contents from one wiki to an existing one (i.e., merging the two), it's more complicated. Thankfully, MediaWiki provides two great special pages that can be used for this purpose: Special:Export and Special:Import.

Special:Export (see Figure 21.1) lets you generate an XML file that holds the contents from any number of pages in the wiki. The XML is in a custom format defined by MediaWiki. Special:Export unfortunately doesn't provide an automatic way to export all pages at once. Instead, you assemble a list of pages to be exported; the page lets you add whole categories and namespaces to the list. Once you've assembled the full list, you can choose whether to export just the most recent revision of each page, or all of them. The latter is certainly recommended when exporting from one MediaWiki wiki to another.

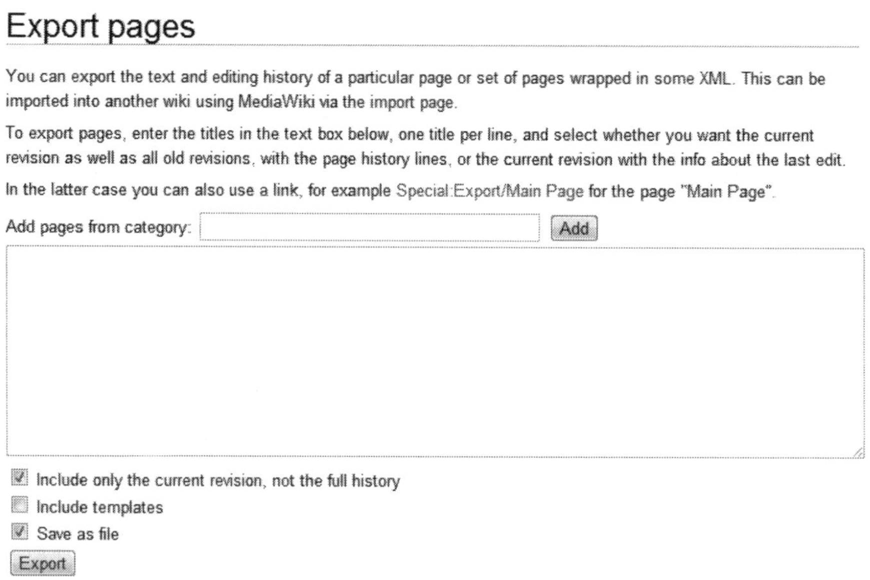

Export pages

You can export the text and editing history of a particular page or set of pages wrapped in some XML. This can be imported into another wiki using MediaWiki via the import page.

To export pages, enter the titles in the text box below, one title per line, and select whether you want the current revision as well as all old revisions, with the page history lines, or the current revision with the info about the last edit.

In the latter case you can also use a link, for example Special:Export/Main Page for the page "Main Page".

Add pages from category: [   ] [Add]

```
┌──────────────────────────────────────────────┐
│                                              │
│                                              │
│                                              │
│                                              │
│                                              │
│                                              │
│                                              │
└──────────────────────────────────────────────┘
```

☑ Include only the current revision, not the full history
☐ Include templates
☑ Save as file
[Export]

Figure 21.1: Special:Export page

Once you have the XML file generated and downloaded, it's time for the second step, which, as you might have guessed, is to use Special:Import in the other wiki. That page is simpler – there, you just upload an XML file, and it generates all the relevant pages. See Figure 21.2 for the Special:Import interface.

In order to access Special:Import, you need to have the 'import' permission, which

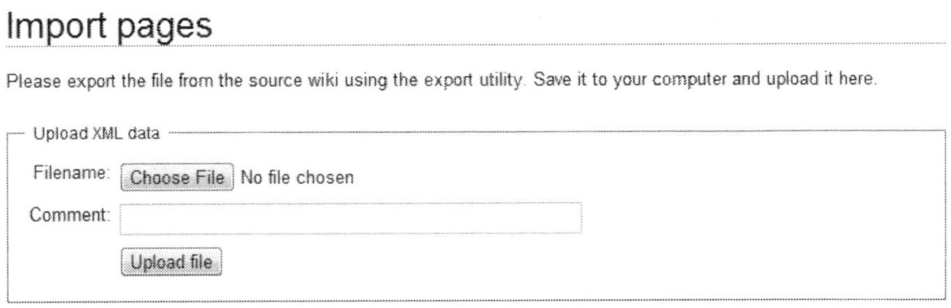

Import pages

Please export the file from the source wiki using the export utility. Save it to your computer and upload it here.

┌─ Upload XML data ──┐
│   │
│ Filename: [Choose File] No file chosen   │
│   │
│ Comment: [   ]   │
│   │
│   [Upload file]   │
│   │
└───┘

Figure 21.2: Special:Import page

by default is given to users in the "administrators/sysop" group.

For large sets of pages, using Special:Import might not work; the page might time out. In that case, you could use an import script to take in the XML file. There are a variety of scripts, all of which have their strengths and weaknesses; you can see the full list here:

http://meta.wikimedia.org/wiki/Data_dumps#Tools

There's the issue of what to do with pages that have the same name in both the source destination wikis; if both wikis are in English, then, for instance, there's a good chance that both will have a page called "Main Page". That's a question that has to be decided on a case-by-case basis; there's no mechanism for merging two wiki pages into one.

The use of Special:Export and Special:Import takes care of wiki pages; but that still leaves the transfer of uploaded files, the wiki's users, and the wiki's settings.

To import in uploaded files, there's a very helpful script in MediaWiki called "importImages.php", in the /maintenance directory, that takes in a folder containing images, and imports them into the wiki. You can use this script to import files (images and otherwise) from both another MediaWiki installation, and from other sources (which we'll get to in the next section). To import uploaded files from one MediaWiki instance to another, you just need to get the /images folder from the "source" wiki onto the same server as the "destination" wiki, if it's not there already. (It may help to archive the folder first, into a zip file or the like.) The script is then called in the following way:

php maintenance/importImages.php /path/to/images/directory png jpg gif bmp PNG JPG GIF BMP

The group of file extensions at the end is necessary because every type of file that you want imported has to be manually specified. There are various other settings you can call importImages.php with – you can see a full description here:

> https://www.mediawiki.org/wiki/Manual:ImportImages.php

Unfortunately, this script will not import old revisions of files – just the most recent ones.

Note that this is a separate process from importing the wiki pages for those files, i.e. pages in the "File:" namespace. If you have any special content in those pages, you should import them using the standard Special:Export/Special:Import process.

That leaves the issue of importing users – but that, unfortunately, seems to be impossible. You will simply have to ask users of the old wiki to re-register on the new one.

It should also be noted that the Special:Export/Special:Import approach can also be used to back up a wiki's contents, to prevent against data loss if something happens to the wiki. Archiving the database and files is the better approach, since it also includes user data and everything else, but using Special:Export is the lighter-weight solution, and one that can be used if you don't have access to the underlying database.

There can also be cases when you want to move content from one MediaWiki wiki into another, while keeping the "source" one around – this might happen if, for instance, your organization has two wikis with different levels of privacy, and you want some of the content generated in the more private wiki to also show up in the more public one. For that, you can use the "Push" extension, which lets you export content from one MediaWiki wiki to another, including regular pages, templates and images. You can read more about this extension here:

> https://www.mediawiki.org/wiki/Extension:Push

Importing contents from another system into MediaWiki

Importing content from outside MediaWiki into MediaWiki is probably the trickiest of the three types of content transfers, because the outside content can take any form whatsoever, and must be converted into MediaWiki's specific structure of pages and wikitext. There are various utilities you can use, depending on the nature of the source content.

If you have HTML content that needs to be converted to MediaWiki, there's a convenient online tool, the HTML2Wiki Converter, where you can paste in HTML and retrieve corresponding wikitext:

> https://toolserver.org/~magnus/html2wiki.php

There's also a MediaWiki extension to convert Microsoft Word documents to wiki pages, called Word2MediaWikiPlus – though its usefulness seems to depend on what exact versions you have of Word and MediaWiki:

> https://www.mediawiki.org/wiki/Extension:Word2MediaWikiPlus

If the type of information you're importing is structured, e.g. if it comes from a database; or if it consists of simple text that has already been assigned to page names, then the Data Transfer extension may be the right tool. This is an extension that allows both the import and export of structured data; for now, we'll just look at how you can import data with it.

To import data, Data Transfer provides two special pages: Special:ImportXML and Special:ImportCSV. These pages take in a file in XML or CSV format, respectively, and create a series of wiki pages based on their contents. You may be wondering what the purpose of Special:ImportXML is, given that turning XML into wiki page is already what Special:Import does. The difference is that Special:ImportXML takes in an entirely different XML format than Special:Import does. The XML format of Special:Import is wiki-based, holding the entire structure of a wiki page, while, the XML format of Special:ImportXML is data-based, holding each field of structured data separately; and the same is true for Special:ImportCSV. To put it briefly: Data Transfer supports the import (and, as we'll see later, the export) of structured data by translating that structured data into the individual parameters of template calls.

First, let's cover Special:ImportCSV, which is the simpler, and much more popular, of the two. CSV, which was already mentioned earlier in the book, is a standard format for storing a table of data; "CSV" stands for "comma-separated values". To use Special:ImportCSV, you must have a table of data that you want to import into the wiki, with one page per row. Special:ImportCSV requires a special format for the top, "header" row.

Here is a sample CSV file that could be imported via Special:ImportCSV:

```
Title,Superhero[Alias],Superhero[Special
powers],Free Text
Superman,Clark Kent,"Flying, Super strength",He's
from Krypton.
```

```
    Batman,Bruce Wayne,None,He just has a bunch of
gadgets.
    Wonder Woman,Diana Prince,"Flying (sometimes), Super
strength",She also has cool gadgets.
```

This page requires a specific syntax for the CSV files it imports. That syntax is:

- `Title` – sets the title of each page (required)

- *`Template name[Field name]`* – defines the value for a single field, within a template call

- `Free Text` – sets the "free", non-template part of each page.

And here is the resulting text for the page that would be created from the first row of data, i.e. the second row:

```
{{Superhero
|Alias=Clark Kent
|Special powers=Flying, Super strength
}}
He's from Krypton.
```

The strings "Title" and "Free Text" are in place for English-language wikis, but they can also be used in any other language. In addition, many (over 50) languages have their own counterpart for "Title" and "Free Text" – if your wiki is in a language other than English, you can see these values (and, if you want, even modify them) at the pages MediaWiki:dt_xml_title and MediaWiki:dt_xml_freetext.

"Title" is the only required column. If the data you want to import contains no structured fields, you can simply put all the text you want for each page in the "Free Text" column.

Any columns whose name doesn't conform to one of the standard structures will simply be ignored.

Before or after the import is done, you will of course need to create the template or templates used, if any, by the pages resulting from the import.

The page Special:ImportXML works in the same way, but takes in a file in XML format. See the next section for the XML format that Special:ImportXML would take.

The advantage of using XML over CSV is that it can hold more than one type of page in a single file – with CSV, you would need a different file for each combination of templates, whereas with XML you can put everything in one big file. The disadvantage of using XML, on the other hand, is that it's harder to create the file.

The homepage for the Data Transfer extension can be found here:

https://www.mediawiki.org/wiki/Extension:Data_Transfer

To import files, you can use the importImages.php script, described in the previous section.

You can also import users, if you put the user information from the other system into a CSV file first, via the ImportUsers extension:

https://www.mediawiki.org/wiki/Extension:ImportUsers

Exporting contents from MediaWiki to another system

Finally, we get to the third type of transfer: one where the source is MediaWiki and the destination isn't. This may be done for a variety of reasons: it could be because of an abandonment of MediaWiki (which of course we would never recommend). It could be done to get the wiki's data into an automated system, for some sort of analysis or display. (If that's the case, Semantic MediaWiki is actually the ideal way to do that – see Chapter 16 for more details.) Or it could be done in order to view the contents in a format like PDF or LaTeX.

If you want to export the entire contents in a structured format, the Data Transfer extension is the best approach. Unlike import, where Data Transfer supports two formats, CSV and XML, for export only one format is supported: XML, via the page Special:ViewXML.

Special:ViewXML lets you view structured XML for different sets of pages in the wiki, by selecting any number of different categories and namespaces. The XML is in the same template-based structure as the one used for Special:ImportXML, although it can also be displayed in a simplified format.

The page is called "ViewXML", not "ExportXML", because the XML is displayed directly on the screen instead of being downloaded, when accessed by a browser. Here is an example of XML that could show up on the screen:

```
<Pages>
    <Category Name="Local scripts">
        <Page ID="747" Title="A3J0TestSuite">
```

```
<Template Name="Local script">
  <Field Name="Author">Frode
  Fredriksen</Field>
  <Field Name="Status">In
  use</Field>
  <Field Name="Path">/home/fredriks/Utilities/
  A3J0TestSuite.pl</Field>
</Template>
<Free_Text id="1">A testing script
for performance of our A3J0 RAID
servers.</Free_Text>
</Page>
...
```

The exact appearance will depend on one's browser and/or relevant browser plugins.

There is also a "Simplified format" checkbox, that lets you do that same export but to a simpler XML format. Here is how that same data would appear, with the "Simplified format" option:

```
<Pages>

  <Local_scripts>

    <Page>

      <ID>747</ID>
      <Title>A3J0TestSuite</Title>
      <Local_script>
        <Author>Frode
        Fredriksen</Author>
        <Status>In use</Status>
        <Path>/home/fredriks/Utilities/A3J0TestSuite.pl
        </Path>
      </Local_script>
      <Free_Text id="1">A testing script
      for performance of our A3J0 RAID
      servers.</Free_Text>
```

```
</Page>

. . .
```

Instead of the `<Template>` and `<Field>` tags, the actual template and field names are used as tag names.

As you might expect, it's then up to the external system to parse this XML, in either form, and import it into its data structure.

Unlike with the wiki's text content, there's no standard mechanism for exporting either a wiki's uploaded files or its user data to a non-MediaWiki system.

PDF export

You can also save some or all of a wiki's pages into other file formats, for display purposes. There are several solutions for saving to PDF – the most popular one is the Collection extension:

https://www.mediawiki.org/wiki/Extension:Collection

Collection was developed in order to print Wikipedia articles in books, but it's used for a variety of purposes. With the extension, one can define "collections" of wiki pages, which then, in conjunction with other extensions, can be exported to PDF, .odt (the file format used by OpenOffice and LibreOffice), and the lesser-known DocBook and ZIM (a file format used by Kiwix – see next section).

PdfBook is another extension that can create PDF files from wiki pages:

https://www.mediawiki.org/wiki/Extension:PdfBook

PdfBook is easier to set up and run than Collection, although the display of the PDF files that PdfBook generates is not nearly as nice.

Another extension is Wiki2LaTeX, which can export wiki pages to LaTeX format, and then additionally from LaTeX to PDF:

https://www.mediawiki.org/wiki/Extension:Wiki2LaTeX

Offline viewing

In the context of the web, offline viewing means being able to do an initial download of some or all of a site's contents, then afterwards viewing it locally, whether it's on a mobile device or on a desktop or laptop. If your wiki's content is relatively small, a PDF file of everything (see above) may be the simplest solution. For larger wikis, and to have a more MediaWiki-like browsing interface, the Kiwix application (http://kiwix.org) is the way to go. It's an application that was mostly developed for offline viewing of Wikipedia, but can also handle other MediaWiki sites, as well as (in theory) any HTML site at all. You can use the Collection extension (see above) to generate the ZIM files used by Kiwix.

There's also the Miga Data Viewer, or Miga (http://migadv.com), which, like Kiwix, was developed with a specific focus on Wikipedia and MediaWiki but is in fact much more generic. Miga is intended more for structured data – of the kind, for instance, found in infoboxes – and offers automated ways to browse and drill down through that data, with an interface somewhat similar to that of the Semantic Drill-down extension (page 237).

Figure 21.3: A screenshot of Miga, used to drill down through structured data from Wikipedia

Chapter 22

Running a successful wiki

So you're planning your wiki, and you inevitably reach the question that almost everyone who creates a wiki asks: will anyone use this thing? It's a question common, of course, to nearly every website, and more broadly to nearly every new venture in the world, whether it's a company, product, or blog post. For wikis, though, it's in a sense double the uncertainty, because you're hoping your future users will not only read the content, but create it. Which is a classic chicken-and-egg problem: if there's little or no real content at the beginning, then people won't read it, but if you have no readers, then you can't expect anyone to start contributing. Thankfully, the situation is not as bleak as that might sound. There are two basic kinds of wikis: public, general-use ones; and private wikis, for internal use by companies and organizations. To this, we'll add one more group that's somewhere between these two: public wikis for loosely-affiliated organizations, where the content is meant to be edited mainly by members of, or people connected to, that organization. For all three of these cases, the dynamics of having a successful wiki are surprisingly similar. Still, there are important differences between the three, so, after some general thoughts on wikis, we'll discuss each case separately.

So, how do you convince people to start contributing to your wiki? This can be a challenge, even if, for the case of organizational wikis, contributing is now ostensibly part of their job. Most people have never edited a wiki. The situation today is of course different from 1995, when wikis were invented, or from 2001, when Wikipedia was created – many more people have experience editing wikis now, but compared to the overall population the number is still tiny. So, whatever set of people you want to contribute to your wiki, a sizable number of them, and most likely the vast majority, have never hit an "edit" tab before.

So you're facing an uphill battle. On the other hand, you have to your advantage the same thing that has driven the success of every other wiki, which can be summarized as a basic human need to improve things, to bring what's on the screen closer to complete accuracy. If people care about the subject matter, they will inherently want the wiki to be better.

Getting people to contribute to a wiki thus basically consists of two parts: finding people who care about the subject matter, and eliminating all of the obstacles that stand in the way of their natural inclination to improve things.

Finding people who care about the subject matter, or making sure that the relevant people in your organization care about it, is a challenge that depends on the type of wiki it is, so we'll cover that in additional sections.

Removing obstacles, then, is what we'll focus on. In our experience, the biggest thing that prevents people from editing content that they might naturally be inclined to is simply fear: people are afraid to edit wikis because they don't want to do the wrong thing. An incorrect edit could mess up the display of the page, or cause more work for others, or even bring complaints against them at some future time.

That's why the use of Semantic Forms (Chapter 17) is strongly recommended. Forms let people edit pages with much more confidence, and with a type of interface they're used to already. We really believe forms are a "game-changer", as far as getting new users to contribute.

Even the combination of MediaWiki and Semantic Forms isn't perfect, though: one big thing that's missing is a reliable WYSIWYG editor for the "free text" of a page. Editing-wise, that's the big advantage that some other wiki applications have over MediaWiki. The VisualEditor, a tool that's already in use on Wikipedia, will hopefully be the fix for this problem, and by the end of 2014 there may be a solution in place. (See page 104.)

Besides forms, it helps to have clear instructions. The front page is especially important, for explaining the purpose of the wiki, linking to the major sections, and pointing to where users can add additional data.

There's all sorts of other advice out there in books and websites for increasing wiki contributions, both in MediaWiki and otherwise. That advice includes contacting people after their first edit to the wiki (on their talk page, or, if the software doesn't include talk pages, via email) to welcome them; creating contests to reward people for the most or best edits; creating merchandise, like stickers, to promote the wiki (which can in theory be done for private wikis as well as public ones); etc. Other than the first one, we've never seen these done for a wiki, so we can't comment on how useful they are. But they all seem secondary compared to two things: having a clear rationale for why people should read and contribute to the wiki, and having an easy (and ideally form-based) way to edit the pages.

As to the first idea, though, of welcoming users with a message on their talk page: it's a popular approach, done on Wikipedia along with many other wikis, but there's some evidence to suggest that it's not effective: a study by the Wikimedia Foundation, presented at the Wikimania 2011 conference, found that Wikipedia users who got a welcome message when they first signed up actually had a lower editing rate than those who did not. Did some users feel patronized by the welcome message? Or was this just statistical randomness? In any case, the evidence is inconclusive that personalized welcomes are helpful.

Now, let's get to some specific tips for the different kinds of wikis.

Public wikis

The very successful public wikis tend to follow a standard model: other than the Wikimedia ones, plus wikiHow, WikiDoc and a few others, they tend to focus on pop culture themes. The average successful wiki focuses on (usually) one entertainment franchise and its manifestations in books, television, movies, video games etc., offering intricate detail that often can't be found elsewhere. This is by far the easiest way to start a successful wiki: find a popular entertainment franchise (ideally cross-media, and ideally having to do with science fiction or fantasy), that doesn't have a wiki for it yet, or at least doesn't have one in your language, and create it. That is the basic business model of the (MediaWiki-based) wiki farm Wikia, and it is the reason why Wikia is by far the most popular wiki farm, and currently among the top 200 websites in the world.

Let's say, though, that you have an idea for a wiki that doesn't involve a pop culture topic. Say, for example, that you want to create a wiki all about yoga (at the moment, there doesn't appear to be such a thing, though that could of course change). The idea would be to capture more detailed information than Wikipedia allows – information about all the aspects of yoga, plus all the notable teachers – and maybe even a full listing of every yoga venue in the world.

All the previous advice about creating user-friendly help text and the use of forms applies here. But beyond that, how can you get readers and editors?

Pre-seeding the wiki helps. Few people want to start editing a newly-empty wiki, because it seems like an endless task ahead. You can copy information from Wikipedia, since all its text is freely licensed for copying. But that's a potentially risky step, because then you have what's known as "forked" content. Any improvements to the Wikipedia article from that point on won't be reflected in your wiki, so unless you think your wiki's users will do a better job of uploading that content than Wikipedia's users, this is a risky thing to do.

On the other hand, if you plan to have more detailed information than Wikipedia does on those topics – if you can point to specific information about, say, Hatha Yoga that the Wikipedia article about it doesn't contain because it would have been too trivial for an encyclopedia – then copying over content seems like a fine starting approach.

And, for directory-style information like a listing of all yoga schools, there may be other sources that you can copy from; just make sure that you can copy and publish such information legally. If you're planning to use templates for such wiki pages (and possibly Semantic Forms as well), the Data Transfer extension might be useful for doing the data import – see page 265.

In addition, of course, you can start manually adding in information yourself.

What about marketing the wiki? Mailing lists related to the topic are a good place to advertise the wiki; chances are that if you're interested enough in a topic to create a wiki for it, you're already part of one or more online communities for it.

Beyond that, there are all the usual communication and self-advertising channels of the 2010s. Various wikis have their own blogs, mailing lists, Twitter accounts, Facebook pages, etc.

Private wikis

To get usage on a private wiki, like an internal wiki for a company, is of course different from for a public, general-user wiki, but not as different as you might think. On a private wiki you have a captive user base, and users who in some cases may be required by a company directive to contribute to the wiki; so getting people to edit the wiki might seem to be easier. On the other hand, if users find the interface confusing, or decide they prefer their old way of communication (which may involve emailing Word and Excel files back and forth, or putting such files on a shared network drive), then the wiki may just die quickly. We've certainly heard of that happening, company directives or no.

The previous advice on making the wiki user-friendly definitely applies here. Beyond that, it may help to arrange meetings for staff, to give demonstrations of the technology and to let people try it for themselves in a context where they can ask questions and get help.

At heart, though, getting the users to switch to using the wiki in place of whatever they were using before is just an example of the strange alchemy required to get people to adopt a new technology. It could be that tactics like handing out prizes, distributing stickers to advertise the wiki, and the like are helpful; we've never seen them in use, so we don't know.

Public, organizational wikis

Finally, there are the wikis that are public, but are specific to one organization: one example is a wiki meant to be used by the local chapters of a non-profit organization, and another is a wiki of documentation for the software produced by some company. Such wikis combine elements of both private and public wikis: like public wikis, the aim is to reach a large and distributed audience, but like with private wikis, people are using the wiki in furtherance of work-related goals, not as a goal in itself.

These sorts of public, organizational wikis might actually be the easiest to get readers and contributors for. That's because there's usually no alternative to it. For a standard public wiki, you're competing against every other relevant data source on the web, including Wikipedia. For a private wiki, you're competing against the previous methods people used to store and collaborate on information, most likely including email. But for a distributed community that needs to exchange information, there's likely no way to do it other than the centralized tool(s) that are given to people. So if a wiki is the available tool, and it's clearly explained how they should use it, chances are that they'll use it.

Still, setting up forms wouldn't hurt.

Chapter 23

MediaWiki development: a guide for the accidental developer

This book will not contain any direct guide to MediaWiki development. A really comprehensive guide unfortunately doesn't exist yet, though this page has links to a lot of good documentation:

> https://www.mediawiki.org/wiki/How_to_become_a_MediaWiki_
> hacker

This section will describe, in general terms, how we would recommend getting started with MediaWiki programming. Because it's general, a lot of this information holds true for dealing with any open-source software.

Most people who have done MediaWiki programming, that is, people who have modified MediaWiki code with the intent of changing or adding to its behavior, did not set out to become MediaWiki programmers, and probably still don't think of themselves as such. Rather, they just had certain requirements for their wiki that didn't seem possible with MediaWiki, or with the various extensions they looked at. So, armed with whatever PHP knowledge they had or could look up, they began to modify the core MediaWiki code, or modify some extension, or create a new extension, or modify some skin, or create a new skin. And then the resulting changes hopefully accomplished the task. In some cases, such people became hooked and kept writing

MediaWiki code, while in most cases, such people moved on to other work, staying with the development only long enough to maintain the code and add some features over the years. Whichever group you fall into, we would like to offer a few pointers to try to maximize the chance that your MediaWiki programming project will be successful.

Let's start by giving a hypothetical case of a task that might require custom development. Your boss, freshly energized from attending an overpriced conference, and full of ideas about disrupting and pivoting, decides that what your internal wiki needs is "gamification"; and to that end, every 50th time someone makes an edit, the wiki should show an animated image of fireworks on that lucky user's screen after they hit the "Save" button.

So, you have a task at hand – and thankfully, unlike in many situations, it's at least well-defined. What should you do? The first step, and a very critical one, is to make sure that this functionality hasn't already been implemented in either core MediaWiki or in one of its extensions. There are a lot of interesting MediaWiki extensions out there, and a lot of functionality within core MediaWiki – this book covers only a subset of them. And it's almost always easier to reuse code (assuming it does what you need) than to create new code. Finding extensions was covered on page 98. If you search through there and can't find anything, another good step is to ask on the MediaWiki mailing list, IRC channel or users forum (page 4).

Let's say you tried those routes and it turned out that there was no such functionality in either MediaWiki or any of its extensions (and in this case, most likely there isn't). If you want this feature, your only option now is custom development, by either yourself or someone else. In theory, there are various approaches you could take: you could modify MediaWiki itself, putting the new code in one or more existing PHP files; you could modify the MediaWiki skin you're using (which is really just a subset of modifying MediaWiki); you could create a new skin, which holds the new functionality; you could modify an existing MediaWiki extension; or you could create a new extension.

In practice, though, only the last two of those options – modifying or creating an extension – are really appropriate solutions. Modifying MediaWiki itself should be avoided whenever possible. It may be tempting – just another 20 lines in some file, and you're done – but the problems come up as soon as you want to upgrade MediaWiki. If you get the MediaWiki code via download – i.e, not via Git – you need to document all of your changes to core, to make sure that your set of changes don't get lost when you upgrade the software. If you're getting MediaWiki from Git, it's easier, but you still need to deal with merge conflicts when you upgrade. In both cases, if the part of the code that you happen to have modified changes (and it often does), you need to figure out how to re-modify the code accordingly.

Lest you think this is a minor issue, there are many cases of MediaWiki-based wikis that are stuck for years at a time on a certain version, because, as the patches have piled up, upgrading MediaWiki becomes too costly to do on a regular basis. This happens for large wikis as well as small ones: Wikia and wikiHow are both major wikis that have been significantly behind in their MediaWiki versions at various times as a result of their many code customizations.

What about creating a new skin, containing the new functionality? That's not desirable either, for two reasons. First, it means that your users are forced to use one skin, which is inconvenient, and it's also confusing if any of your users do switch to a different skin. Second, maintaining a skin can be as much work as maintaining Media-Wiki patches, since the required structure for skins still changes quite a bit between MediaWiki version – which is part of why, sadly, there are so few working MediaWiki skins available for download, outside the ones that come bundled with MediaWiki. (Hopefully, in the future, skins will become more standardized and will change less from version to version.)

So that leaves working with extensions. If you're modifying an existing extension, it's good to talk to that extension's author(s), via email or talk page – hopefully they will be willing to accept your changes or additions in some form, since otherwise, you'll have to deal with the same issues of maintaining a patched set of code, that you would with changes to MediaWiki itself.

Finally, you can create a new extension – and for our hypothetical case, that's probably what you'd have to do. There is an extension, called "PostEdit", that displays a pop-up message after the user saves the page – and since version 1.22 of MediaWiki, its code has been merged into core MediaWiki – but there doesn't seem to be an extension that displays messages only some of the time.

So let's say you decide to create an extension. An important thing to note, when planning out extensions, is that most extensions are based around hooks. Hooks are lines in the core MediaWiki code (or in other extensions) where the code makes a call to allow other pieces of code to perform their own actions at that moment, or to modify some or all of the local variables. It's a fairly simple concept, once you understand the basic idea, but a powerful one, since it lets you modify a lot of MediaWiki's behavior without the need to touch any of the original code.

MediaWiki has hundreds of hooks scattered throughout its code, and there are many, probably hundreds, of hooks in various MediaWiki extensions as well. Ideally, any extension you create can accomplish what it needs to without the need to modify MediaWiki, or any other extension, possibly through the use of hooks.

You can find MediaWiki hooks via this very helpful page:

https://www.mediawiki.org/wiki/Manual:Hooks

In our hypothetical case, it seems like the hook "ArticleSaveComplete" would do the trick: it's called after the user hits the "Save" button and the article has finished saving. Each hook has its own documentation page, linked from the "Manual:Hooks" page, detailing its usage. Sometimes finding the right hook can be a matter of trial-and-error – and sometimes there's actually more than one hook that can be used, and it's a matter of finding the best fit.

What if there's no hook that fits, though? Then it becomes acceptable to modify the MediaWiki code – but ideally, only to insert a line that calls the new, needed hook. And even more ideally, once you create this new hook and get your extension working with it, you can send this small set of code as a patch to the MediaWiki developers, so that they can add it to the main code base. (You can, of course, send a patch of any size to the MediaWiki developers, but a single-line hook seems the most likely to get accepted and integrated, especially if you're just starting out as a MediaWiki developer, or if the feature you want to add is quite specific, like a celebratory animation.)

Now it's time to create the extension. Actual PHP development won't be covered in this book. We'll just say that it's good to copy from an existing MediaWiki extension that seems to do something relatively similar, rather than starting from scratch. Beyond that, there's useful documentation for developers on mediawiki.org, including at the "How to become a MediaWiki hacker" page; and, as you might imagine, it's good to have familiarity with PHP, JavaScript and the other relevant technologies.

Skip ahead a few days, or weeks or months, and now you've successfully created your extension, and learned something about MediaWiki development along the way. What's more editing of your company's wiki has gone up 70% due to the users' delight at occasionally seeing an image of fireworks when they make an edit. Your boss is already working on his triumphant presentation for the next conference. Are you done? Hopefully not, because there's still one important step that you should ideally take: releasing the extension as open-source software.

There can be obstacles to releasing software as open-source. Inertia is a big one: after all the time spent creating this software and getting it to work, why bother putting any more time and effort into it? Tied in with that is a low view of the importance of releasing the software: why would anyone else want to use my silly little extension? In some organizations releasing software as open-source may also run counter to the organization's principles: after we paid to develop this software, why should others get to use it for free? The organization may even have rules against doing such a thing. And finally, if the wiki is itself part of (or all of) the business (in which case most likely it's a public wiki), there's the practical argument: why should we release software that could then easily be used by any competitors, present or future?

Despite all of these objections, we still think releasing one's MediaWiki extension as open source is almost always the right thing to do. There are a variety of good reasons to release one's software:

- **It leads to better code.** Having many people, including experienced developers, look at, and use, the code means that bugs will be found (including security leaks), fixes will be suggested, and new features will potentially be added.

- **The code will be easier to maintain.** MediaWiki changes often, and chances are good that, left unattended, your extension's code will become incompatible with MediaWiki within a year or two, for any number of reasons. Having the extension be open source lets outside developers suggest, or directly add, fixes as new MediaWiki versions come out. If the code remains proprietary, you're left with two choices: be forced to debug your code any time there's a MediaWiki update on your wiki and an incompatibility arises; or keep your wiki on an old MediaWiki version forever for fear of breaking anything.

- **Instant translations to hundreds of languages.** If the extension's code is added to the MediaWiki Git repository, its translatable messages (the ones found in the extension's "i18n" file) will very quickly start getting translated into dozens or even hundreds of languages by MediaWiki's superb team of volunteer translators around the world. This is probably not a big deal if your extension is being used on just your local, single-language wiki – but if your wiki has users who speak even one other language, then the translation is worth it (for an examination of dealing with multiple languages on a wiki, see page 155).

- **Giving back.** This is the most intangible of the reasons, and depending on your (or your organization's) philosophy, it may be more or less compelling than the others. There definitely is a philanthropic argument, though. Unless you're a sociopath, you would probably agree that, all things being equal, it's nice to help others. And if you're using MediaWiki, you're already benefiting from the altruism of hundreds of people – not to mention the tens of thousands of developers of PHP, and the database system and operating system you're using, if those too are open source. This is not to argue that using open source software brings with it any responsibility to contribute back, but there definitely is a nice symmetry to benefiting from others' programming work and then giving back in return, even in a small way.

What about the case where the wiki you run is your business, and you don't want to give code away to any potential competitors? This is not a book on business strategy, but my experience is that fear of competitors, at least in the wiki world, is generally overblown. Wikis gain prominence and usefulness as a result of their user community and their content, and that's not something that's easy to duplicate. Chances are that, by the time anybody figures that imitating your wiki is a good idea, it will already have a significant built-in user base, and a lot of content. If you have an open license for your content, someone could potentially "fork" your contents and try to recreate your entire wiki, but I've never heard of that being attempted. (Wikipedia is the one exception – a few attempts have been made to recreate all of some language of Wikipedia on a separate wiki – though those have been done due to some dissatisfaction with how Wikipedia is run, as opposed to a money-making attempt; and they have never worked. Anyway, Wikipedia is a special case.) Meanwhile, releasing the software as open source gives you all the benefits described earlier.

So let's say you've decided to create a new extension, and release it as open source. Now what? There are only two steps you need to do: putting up the code somewhere online, and creating a documentation page.

You can put the code anywhere public (including directly on the extension's wiki page – a popular solution for smaller extensions, though not necessarily a good one). The best place to put the code, though, is on the MediaWiki Git repository. For that you need developer access, which is pretty easy to get – see here for the details:

> https://www.mediawiki.org/wiki/Developer_access

Then, you just need to create the documentation page for your extension. It should be on mediawiki.org, in the "Extension:" namespace; so if your extension is called "Page Save Surprise", it would be at the page "Extension:Page Save Surprise". (One note about extension naming: you have a choice about whether to put spaces in the name. The more common approach is to leave them out, in "CamelCase" style, but I prefer to include them, because it looks nicer. Either way is fine.)

Feel free to create your extension's page by copying the text from the page for some other extension (and then modifying it, of course); that's what most people do. Just make sure to set the new extension's status to "experimental", since that's most likely what it is at this point.

Now you're done. You can announce your new extension to the relevant mailing lists if you want, such as mediawiki-l (see page 4). If the extension is useful, people may start to ask questions, report bugs and contribute fixes, on the extension's talk page, via email and on Bugzilla. And, if you find that the process appeals to you, you can start improving and maintaining other extensions as well – there certainly are parts of the code that could benefit from the help. You're not obligated to do any of these things, but they're all appreciated, in some cases by many people.

Afterword: On semantic wikis

I hope that you've enjoyed reading this book, and that it will serve as a useful guide for MediaWiki, which in my opinion is, all things considered, the best wiki software at the moment. I hope that the book adequately explains core MediaWiki, outside of any extensions. And I also hope that, for those of you who aren't using Semantic MediaWiki and its related extensions, this book made a strong case for their use.

There's an interesting property of semantic wikis, which is that, once you've used them a few times, systems that aren't semantic wikis start to get annoying. This has happened to me, and I've heard of the effect from others. The limitations of other systems start to become apparent: for regular data systems, the most important is the lack of a version history, while for non-semantic wikis, it's the lack of any way to summarize or aggregate all the data contained in the wiki's pages, or to impose a structure on pages.

Regular data systems' lack of a version history means, most importantly, that access has to be tightly controlled: either only a few people can edit any of the data, or each specific set of data is restricted to some small group, with the entire set of permissions settable through some monstrous administrative interface. But it also means that the provenance of data tends to be unknown: if you see a field on the screen, you usually don't know who put it there, or when it was set, which can cause problems.

Of course, there are workarounds that can be done: you can have a "Notes" field, where everyone who edits the data is meant to summarize their changes, and maybe put in the date; but this is a hack, and any such protocol might not be followed, and even if it, it's never quite as informative as actually seeing all the changes.

But there's also the issue of the flexibility of data structures. In a semantic wiki, if you want to add a new field to a page, or remove a field, it's just a matter of adding or removing a few lines from some wiki pages, and possibly creating a new semantic property. The total time spent could be as little as five minutes. In a non-wiki system, it depends on the setup: creating or removing a field can possibly be done easily, or it might take a significant amount of work, requiring a programmer to re-code some part of the program, a database administrator to apply the necessary changes in the database, and then some QA team to make sure that the changes didn't break anything. Or, if you're using an off-the-shelf system, such a change might not be possible at all.

Non-semantic wikis have all that flexibility as well, but again, they don't have the data reuse, and they don't have the forms.

It is my belief that, in the future, all data systems will function like semantic wikis, in their flexibility, editability (in most cases, everyone who can read the content will also be able to edit it), and version history. That is not to say that all systems will be semantic wikis, and certainly not that all of them will use Semantic MediaWiki – Google Docs is a good example of a system that has these attributes to a large extent, but is not a semantic wiki. Still, semantic wikis are the easiest way to get all these features, and Semantic MediaWiki is currently the best and most advanced semantic wiki software. And of course it's free software, in both senses of the word. So I think SMW is positioned to become an important part of the software ecosystem in the future.

This doesn't even get to the issue of reuse of data between systems – in the general sense, and in the specific sense of the Semantic Web. Semantic MediaWiki is sometimes grouped in as a Semantic Web technology, though in most cases its users make no use of the Semantic Web, in the sense of importing or exporting content in RDF or a comparable format. But it certainly can be used to do both, and with extensions like External Data, it can make use of data in more standard formats as well. The Semantic Web, as a technology and framework, is growing in importance, and it certainly has had no shortage of buzz. If and when it ever achieves mainstream use, semantic wikis, and SMW in particular, will be a natural choice for publishing Semantic Web content.

Within this context, it's worth mentioning Wikidata again. This project will, if successful, create a massive, queryable database comprising all of the structured information that one expects to find on Wikipedia. It will be something new in the history of the world: a source of structured information that can, in theory, be used by computers to answer nearly any general-knowledge question. The fact that Wikidata and Semantic MediaWiki will most likely use a joint code base for storing their data is mostly secondary: Wikidata, if successful, will significantly raise both usage and awareness of the Semantic Web, in its various meanings. And at that point, SMW will hopefully stand as an obvious answer when people, in greater numbers, start to ask, "how we do add our own data to this thing?"

In short, semantic wikis solve a lot of problems, some of which people don't even view as problems before they've used one. And in the case of MediaWiki, the benefits of a semantic wiki are available just by downloading and installing some more extensions. It seems like a no-lose proposition. So, happy adventures in the world of collaborative data.

Index

Colophon

This book was created with the LyX document processor, which in turn uses the combined LaTeX and TeX typesetting system. The e-book version was generated using the applications Elyxer (which converts LyX files to HTML) and Calibre (which converts HTML files into e-books), along with a custom script to take care of some formatting issues. All of the applications listed here are open source, and all are highly recommended.

For the printed book, the main text uses the Palatino typeface, while headers and PHP code are in Helvetica, and wikitext and other specialized syntax (XML, CSV etc.) are in Courier.

About the author

Yaron Koren grew up in Israel and the United States. He has been a professional programmer since 1998. He has been doing MediaWiki development since 2006, and MediaWiki consulting since 2007. He currently runs the MediaWiki consulting company WikiWorks, and the MediaWiki-based wiki farm Referata. He lives in New York City with his wife.

Made in the USA
Lexington, KY
22 March 2016